THE
VEGETARIAN
KITCHEN

THE
VEGETARIAN
KITCHEN

Consulting Editor

Linda Fraser

HERMES
HOUSE

This edition published in 2001 by Hermes House
© Anness Publishing Limited 2001

Published in the USA by Hermes House, Anness Publishing Inc.
27 West 20th Street, New York, NY 10011

Hermes House is an imprint of Anness Publishing Inc.

All rights reserved. No part of this publication may be reproduced, stored in
a retrieval system, or transmitted in any way or by any means, electronic,
mechanical, photocopying, recording or otherwise, without the prior written
permission of the copyright holder.

Publisher: Joanna Lorenz
Senior Editor: Linda Fraser
Designer: Ian Sandom
Production Controller: Mark Fennell
Editorial Reader: Kate Henderson
Indexer: Diane Butcher
Photography: Edward Allwright, Karl Adamson, James Duncan, Michelle Garrett, Amanda
Heywood, David Jordan, Don Last, William Lingwood, Patrick McLeavey,
Thomas Odulate and Peter Reilly
Recipes: Catherine Atkinson, Maxine Clark, Matthew Drennan, Sarah Edmonds, Christine France,
Silvana Franco, Shirley Gill, Carole Handslip, Manisha Kanani, Lesley Mackley, Sue
Maggs, Annie Nichols, Anne Sheasby, Liz Trigg, Steven Wheeler and Jeni Wright

1 3 5 7 9 10 8 6 4 2

NOTES

Standard spoon and cup measures are level.

Large eggs are used unless otherwise stated.

CONTENTS

INTRODUCTION

Vegetarian food has finally become a major part of our cuisine. We no longer need to justify the inclusion of vegetarian dishes on restaurant menus, and a cookbook such as this is to be universally celebrated and not seen as catering to the few. With the plentiful supply of fresh vegetables, fruit, herbs, nuts, grains, beans and pasta that is available to us, the possibilities of creating really exciting and varied recipes have never been greater.

It is not only vegetarians who can enjoy vegetarian food. The fresh, light and innovative recipes that have come to the forefront of new-style vegetarian cooking provide a tempting departure from many of the heavier, non-vegetarian dishes. This book gathers together some of the best recipes in the world, all of them packed with fabulous tastes and textures.

We are constantly being urged to choose a diet rich in the complex carbohydrates found in cereals, grains, fruits and vegetables, all of which are abundant in vegetarian cooking. If you include dairy products in your diet, restrict your intake of fat by choosing skim or low-fat milk, yogurts and cheeses. By limiting the use of oils to unsaturated types, such as olive, sunflower, corn and peanut, you can reduce the level of fat in your diet considerably.

So whether you are a committed vegetarian, enjoy the occasional vegetarian meal, or just want something simple and satisfying, this book has a delicious recipe to suit every taste and occasion.

Fresh Vegetables

Thanks to the range of fresh produce, the choice for vegetarians has expanded enormously.

Beans
Cook lima beans or green beans until just tender-crisp.

Bell peppers
Green peppers have a fresh raw flavor, red, orange and yellow peppers are sweeter.

Broccoli
Quick to prepare, broccoli can be eaten raw or cooked.

Cabbage
There are many varieties of this nutritious vegetable – don't overcook.

Carrots
Sweet-flavored carrots are delicious raw or cooked.

Cauliflower
Can be eaten raw or cooked.

Celery root
Tastes very similar to celery.

Celery
Delicious raw in salads, or cooked in stews and soups.

Eggplant
This vegetable is delicious broiled, fried or stuffed.

Fennel
Aniseed-flavored fennel can be eaten raw or cooked.

Leeks
A versatile vegetable with a subtle oniony flavor.

Lettuce
Buy fresh whole heads or in bags of mixed greens.

Mushrooms
Use fresh or dried, cultivated and wild mushrooms.

Onions
Can be sautéed, roasted or even eaten raw in salads.

Parsnips
A sweet root vegetable with a distinct earthy flavor.

Potatoes
Rich in Vitamin C, potatoes can be cooked in many ways.

Spinach
This dark leaf can be eaten raw in salads or cooked.

Rutabagas and turnips
Sweet and nutty flavored – add to soups and casseroles.

Tomatoes
Use raw in salads, or add to soups, stews or stir-fries.

Dairy Products and Tofu

An important source of protein for vegetarians, these products are widely available.

Butter and margarine
Butter is a cow milk product – choose unsalted butter for shallow frying. Margarine is made from vegetable oils.

Buttermilk
Skim milk with an added bacterial culture, which gives it a natural tangy flavor.

Cheeses
Choose strong-flavored cheeses that melt well, such as Cheddar, Monteray Jack or Gruyère, for sauces and toppings, or for adding to homemade pastry. Parmesan is a full-flavored hard cheese, which is delicious finely shredded and added to pasta, or pared into fine slivers to scatter over salads. If a recipe calls for blue cheese, use Roquefort or Stilton if a strong flavor is required, and dolcelatte or cambozola for a milder result. Use crumbly white feta in salads – its piquant, salty taste is delicious with crisp leaves. Fresh goat cheese has an intense flavor. Mozzarella can be eaten raw, but melts well too and is perfect for topping pizzas and adding to baked pasta dishes.

Cream
Available in many forms, such as light, heavy, extra thick, whipping and sour cream, and crème fraîche.

Eggs
Rich in protein, eggs are used in sweet and savory dishes.

Farmer's cheese
This soft white cheese has a tangy flavor.

Milk
Cow milk comes in different forms: skim, low-fat and whole. Goat milk and sheep milk are also available.

Tofu
This is an unfermented bean curd made from soy beans that absorbs flavors readily. Various forms are available, from smooth tofu, which is useful for adding to sauces and is often used for desserts, to a firm type that can be cut into cubes and sautéed.

Yogurt
Available plain or flavored, yogurt may be made with cow, sheep or goat milk.

The Pantry

Your pantry should be the backbone of your kitchen. Stock it sensibly and you'll always have the wherewithal to make a tasty meal.

Canned beans and peas
Chickpeas, cannellini beans, green lentils, navy beans and red kidney beans survive the canning process well. Tip into a sieve, rinse under cold running water and drain well before use.

Canned vegetables
Although fresh vegetables are best for most cooking, some canned products are very useful. Artichoke hearts have a mild sweet flavor and are great for adding to stir-fries, salads, risottos or pizzas. Pimientos are canned whole red bell peppers, seeded and peeled. Use them for stews and soups. Canned tomatoes are an essential ingredient to have in the pantry. Additional useful items to include are ratatouille, water chestnuts and corn.

Mustard
Whole grain or Dijon mustards are used in both cooking and salad dressings.

Oils
Peanut or sunflower oils are bland and will not mask flavors. They are ideal for deep frying. Fiery chili oil will liven up vegetable stir-fries, while aromatic sesame oil will give them a rich nutty flavor. A good olive oil will suit most purposes (except deep frying – it is simply too expensive). Choose extra virgin olive oil, which has the best flavor, for making salad dressings, and adding to pasta dishes.

Olives
Green and black olives are available in brine or olive oil, as well as a variety of tasty marinades. Olive paste is useful for pasta sauces.

Strained tomatoes
This thick sauce, also called passata, is made from sieved and puréed tomatoes.

Pesto
This classic Italian sauce combines fresh basil, pine nuts, Parmesan cheese, garlic and olive oil, and is useful for flavoring pasta or broiled or roasted vegetables.

Soy sauce/shoyu
Soy sauce is a thin, salty, black liquid made from fermented soybeans. Shoyu, naturally brewed soy sauce, is fermented for much longer and so has fewer additives than soy sauce.

Stocks
There are three kinds of vegetable stocks or broths. Granules are ideal for light soups and risottos, bouillon cubes have a stronger flavor and are good for hearty soups, while vegetable extracts have a robust taste that is delicious in casseroles.

Sun-dried tomatoes
These deliciously sweet tomatoes, baked in the sun and dried, are sold in bags or in jars, steeped in olive oil.

Tahini paste
Made from ground sesame seeds, this paste is used in Middle Eastern cookery and, with chickpeas, is the basis for hummus.

Tomato Paste
This concentrated tomato paste is useful for adding flavour to sauces and is sold in cans, jars or tubes. A version made from sun-dried tomatoes is also avaailable.

Vinegars
White or red wine vinegars and sherry vinegar are ideal for salad dressings. Balsamic vinegar, with its distinctive sweet flavor, can be used to liven up roasted vegetables.

Spices and Dry Goods

Ground and whole spices, grains, cereals, dried fruit, flours, nuts, seeds, pasta and noodles are invaluable for vegetarian cooking.

Spices

Cardamom
This fragrant spice is used in sweet and savory dishes.

Chinese five-spice powder
This anise-flavored spice is made from a mixture of anise pepper, star anise, cassia, fennel seed and cloves.

Cinnamon
A sweet spice available whole, as sticks of bark or ground.

Cloves
This strongly scented spice is often used ground, mixed with other spices for sweet and savory dishes.

Coriander
This spice imparts a mildly hot, aromatic flavor.

Cumin
Sweet and pungent, with a distinctive taste, often used in Indian dishes.

Garam masala
An aromatic mixture of spices used widely in Indian dishes.

Saffron
The most expensive spice, saffron has a pungent scent and a bitter-sweet taste. The threads are steeped in a little liquid before use.

Turmeric
This ground spice has a strong, musty flavor and adds a deep-yellow color to food. It is sometimes used as a substitute for saffron.

Dry Goods

Barley
With its distinctive flavor and chewy texture, barley is often added to hearty soups and can be used as an alternative to rice in risottos.

Buckwheat
Nutty in texture and taste, this grain can be used as an alternative to rice in risottos and stir-fries, but is actually the seed from a type of grass.

Bulgur wheat
This whole wheat grain is steam-dried and cracked before sale, so only needs a brief soaking before use.

Couscous
Also made from wheat, this cracked grain is a staple in North Africa. It is usually steamed and served hot.

Dried fruit
Rich in dietary fiber, vitamins and minerals, dried fruits are delicious in a wide range of dishes including granola.

Flours
Instead of white refined flour, try experimenting with other flours, such as whole-wheat, buckwheat, soy or rye flours. Corn starch is often used as a thickening agent for sauces.

Millet
High in protein, millet is used extensively in South-East Asia and is cooked in the same way as rice.

Nuts and seeds
Almonds, brazil nuts, cashews, pecans and walnuts, and such seeds as sunflower, sesame and pumpkin, are all valuable sources of protein and calcium. Add to salads or rice dishes.

Pasta and noodles
While fresh pasta and noodles are usually preferred, both for flavor and for speed of cooking, the dried products are valuable pantry ingredients.

Rice
Types include long grain, basmati, short grain for desserts, and risotto rice, such as arborio. Black wild rice (actually the seeds of an aquatic grass) is also good.

Equipment

Stocking up on every item in your local cookware store will not make you a better cook, but some basic items are definitely worth investing in.

A few good pots and pans in various sizes and with tight-fitting lids are a must. Heavy-based and nonstick pans are best. A large nonstick frying pan or skillet is invaluable because the food cooks faster when spread over a wider surface area. For the same reason, a good wok is essential. Use a large pan or frying pan when the recipe calls for occasional stirring, and a wok for continuous movement, such as stir-frying.

Good-quality knives can halve your preparation time, but more importantly, a really sharp knife is safer than a blunt one. You can do yourself a lot of damage if your hand slips when you are pressing down hard with a blunt knife. For basic, day-to-day use, choose a good chopping knife, a small vegetable knife and a long serrated bread knife. If possible store knives safely in well-secured slotted racks. Drawer storage is not good for knives as the blades can easily become damaged when they are knocked around. If you do have to keep knives in a drawer, make sure they are stored with their handles towards the front for safe

lifting, and keep the blades protected in some way. Good sharp knives are essential and indispensable pieces of kitchen equipment, so it is worth taking care of them.

A few of the recipes in this book call for the use of a food processor, which does save time and effort but is not strictly necessary. Other essential pieces of kitchen equipment, which almost seem too obvious to mention, include chopping boards, a colander, a sieve, a grater, a whisk and some means of extracting citrus juice, be this a squeezer or a juicer.

For the vegetarian cook who likes to work speedily and efficiently, where you store your equipment is an important factor to consider. Use the stove as the pivot around which most of the action takes place. Hang pots, pans, whisks, spoons and strainers overhead within easy reach, keep a chopping board on an adjacent work surface and place ceramic pots filled with a variety of wooden spoons, spatulas, ladles, scissors, peelers and other kitchen utensils next to the stove, and all within easy reach.

wooden spatula

ladle

scissors

knives and peelers

vegetable knife

bread knife

whisks

slotted spoon

serving spoon

chopping board

grater

strainer

pots

wok

frying pan

Menus for Entertaining

When you have guests to feed, expand your vegetarian main course into an impressive meal. The menu suggestions below feature main course recipes from the book, accompanied by simple ideas for appetizers, accompaniments and desserts that can be rustled up in minutes.

Menu 1

Warm focaccia bread with Kosher salt and olives

Asparagus Rolls with Herb Butter Sauce

Lentil Stir-fry served with a green salad

Summer berries with Kirsch and vanilla sugar

Menu 2

Broiled cherry tomato and basil salad

Mushrooms with Leeks and Stilton

Potato, Broccoli and Red Bell Pepper Stir-fry

Baked banana and orange segments

Menu 3

Poached asparagus with crème fraîche and lemon

Crusty Rolls with Zucchini and Saffron

Red Fried Rice

Warm ginger cake with maple syrup

Menu 4

French bread slices with tapenade and mozzarella

Lemon and Parmesan Cappellini with Herb Bread

Fresh Spinach and Avocado Salad

Banana and amaretti with passionfruit cream

Menu 5

Fresh tomato and cilantro with poppadoms

Bengali-style Vegetables

Cumin-spiced Largé Zucchini and Spinach

Spiced potato and cauliflower
Fresh fruit

Menu 6

Crudités with mayonnaise dip

Potato, Spinach and Pine Nut Gratin

Vegetable Kebabs with Mustard and Honey

Broiled mascarpone plums

TECHNIQUES

Once mastered, the techniques described here will help you to prepare
vegetables speedily and with less waste, to produce better results with ease.

Peeling and Seeding Tomatoes

A simple and efficient way of preparing tomatoes.

1 Use a sharp knife to cut a small cross on the bottom of the tomato.

2 Turn the tomato over and cut out the core.

3 Immerse the tomato in boiling water for 10–15 seconds, then transfer to a bowl of cold water using a slotted spoon.

4 Lift out the tomato and peel (the skin should be easy to remove).

5 Cut the tomato in half crosswise and squeeze out the seeds.

6 Use a large knife to cut the peeled tomato into strips, then chop across the strips to make dice.

Chopping Onions

Uniform-sized dice make cooking easy. This method can't be beaten.

1 Peel the onion. Cut it in half with a large knife and set it cut-side down on a board. Make lengthwise vertical cuts along the onion, cutting almost but not quite through to the root.

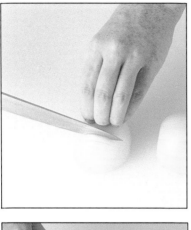

2 Make 2 horizontal cuts from the stalk and towards the root, but not through it.

3 Cut the onion crosswise to form small, even dice.

Slicing Onions

Use thin slices for sautéeing or to flavor oils for stir-frying, or use sweet onion slices in salads.

1 Peel the onion. Cut it in half with a large knife and set it cut-side down on a chopping board.

2 Cut out a triangular piece of the core from each half.

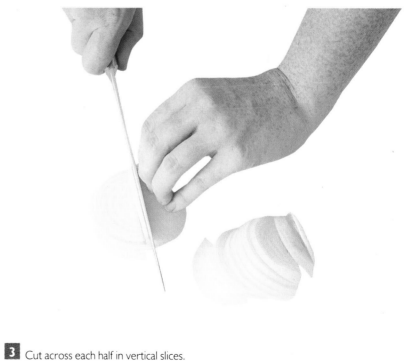

3 Cut across each half in vertical slices.

Shredding Cabbage

This method is useful for coleslaws, pickled cabbage or any cooked dish.

1 Use a large knife to cut the cabbage into quarters.

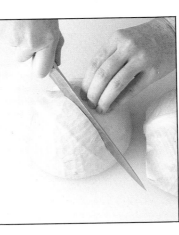

2 Cut out the core from each quarter.

3 Slice across each quarter to form fine, even shreds.

Cutting Carrot Julienne

Thin julienne strips of any vegetable make decorative accompaniments, or can be used in stir-fries.

1 Peel the carrot and use a large knife to cut it into 2 in lengths. Cut a thin sliver from one side of each piece so that it sits flat on the board.

2 Cut into thin lengthwise slices.

3 Stack the slices and cut through them to make fine strips.

Preparing Lemongrass

Use the whole stem and remove it before cooking, or chop the root.

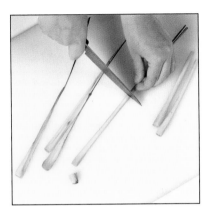

1 Cut off and discard the dry, leafy tops. Peel away any tough outer layers. Trim off the tops and end of the stem until you are left with about 4 inches.

2 Lay the lemongrass on a board. Set the flat side of a chef's knife on top and strike it firmly with your fist. Cut across the lemongrass to make thin slices.

Preparing Kaffir Lime Leaves

The distinctive lime-lemon aroma and flavor of kaffir lime leaves are a vital part of Thai cooking.

COOK'S TIP
Buy fresh lime leaves at Asian stores and freeze them for future use. Dried lime leaves are also now available.

1 You can tear, shred or cut kaffir lime leaves. Using a small, sharp knife, carefully remove the center vein. Cut the leaves crosswise into very fine strips.

Preparing Fresh Ginger

Fresh ginger root can be used in slices, strips or finely chopped (or grated).

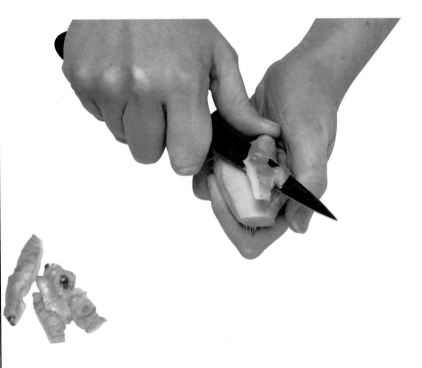

1 Using a small, sharp knife, peel the skin from the ginger root.

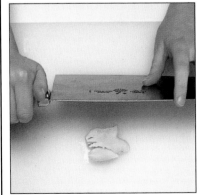

2 Place the ginger on a board, set the flat side of a cleaver or chef's knife on top and strike it firmly with your fist—this will soften the fiberous texture.

3 Chop the ginger as coarsely or finely as you wish, moving the blade backward and forward.

Preparing Bean Sprouts

Usually available at supermarkets, bean sprouts add a crisp texture to stir-fries.

1 Pick over the bean sprouts, discarding any pieces that are discolored, broken or wilted.

2 Rinse the bean sprouts under cold running water and drain well.

Preparing Scallions

Use scallions in stir-fries to flavor oil, as a vegetable in their own right or as a garnish.

1 Trim off the root and any discolored tops with a sharp knife. For an intense flavor in a stir-fry, cut the entire scallion into thin matchsticks.

2 Alternatively, slice the white and pale green part of the scallion diagonally and stir-fry with crushed garlic to flavor the cooking oil.

Chopping Cilantro

Chop cilantro just before you use it; the flavor will be much better.

1 Strip the leaves from the stalks and pile them on a chopping board.

2 Using a cleaver or chef's knife, cut the cilantro into small pieces, moving the blade back and forth until it is as coarsely or finely chopped as you wish.

Preparing Chilies

The flavor of chili is wonderful in cooking, but fresh chilies must be handled with care.

1 Wearing rubber gloves, remove the stalks from the chilies.

2 Cut in half lengthwise. Scrape out the seeds and fleshy, white ribs from each half, using a sharp knife. Chop or thinly slice according to the recipe.

Segmenting Oranges

Orange segments without any skin are useful for adding to salsas or serving alongside sweet dips.

1 Slice the bottom off the orange so it will stand upright on a cutting board. Using a sharp knife, remove the peel by slicing from the top to the bottom of the orange.

2 Hold the orange in one hand over a bowl. Slice toward the middle of the fruit, to one side of the segment, and then gently twist the knife to ease the segment away from the membrane and out of the orange. Repeat to remove all of the segments. Squeeze any juice from the remaining membrane into the bowl.

Preparing Avocados

Removing the flesh from avocados is easy to do.

1 Cut around the avocado, twist to separate the halves, remove the pit, and scoop out the flesh into a bowl.

2 Mash the flesh well with a fork or a potato masher, or transfer to a board and chop finely using a large knife.

Making Mayonnaise

Homemade mayonnaise tastes wonderful and is very quick and easy to prepare.

1 Place the egg yolks and lemon juice in a food processor or blender and process them briefly until lightly blended.

2 Pour the oil into a pitcher then, with the machine running, pour in the oil in a slow, steady stream.

3 Once half the oil has been added, add the remaining oil more quickly. Continue processing until the mayonnaise is thick and creamy, add a little lemon juice and season with salt and pepper to taste.

French Dressing

French vinaigrette is the most widely used salad dressing and is appreciated for its simplicity and style. For the best flavor, use the finest extra-virgin olive oil and go easy on the vinegar.

Makes about ¹/₂ cup

INGREDIENTS
¹/₃ cup extra-virgin olive oil, French or
    Italian
1 tbsp white-wine vinegar
1 tsp French mustard
pinch of superfine sugar

2 Add the mustard and sugar.

1 Place the olive oil and vinegar in a screw-top jar.

3 Replace the lid and shake well.

COOK'S TIP

Liquid dressings that contain extra-virgin olive oil should be stored at room temperature. Refrigeration can cause them to solidify.

French Herb Dressing

The delicate scents of fresh herbs combine especially well in a French dressing. Toss with a simple green salad and serve with good cheese and wine.

Makes about ¹/₂ cup

INGREDIENTS
4 tbsp extra-virgin olive oil, French or
    Italian
2 tbsp peanut or sunflower oil
1 tbsp lemon juice
4 tbsp finely chopped fresh herbs:
    parsley, chives, tarragon, and
    marjoram
pinch of superfine sugar

2 Add the lemon juice, herbs, and sugar.

1 Place the olive and peanut oil in a screw-top jar.

3 Replace the lid and shake well.

Relishes

These relishes are very quick and easy to prepare and will liven up vegetable burgers and pies.

QUICK BARBECUE RELISH

Making use of pantry ingredients, this quick relish is ideal for an impromptu barbecue. It has a tangy flavor.

3 tbsp sweet pickle
1 tbsp soy sauce
2 tbsp tomato ketchup
2 tsp mustard
1 tbsp cider vinegar
2 tbsp barbeque sauce

1 Mix together the pickle, soy sauce, tomato ketchup and mustard.

2 Add the vinegar and barbeque sauce and mix well. Cover and chill and use when required.

TOMATO RELISH

This cooked relish has a rich, concentrated tomato flavor. Serve it hot or cold with barbecued foods, or use to pep up a cheese sandwich.

1 tbsp olive oil
1 onion, finely chopped
1 garlic clove, crushed
2 tbsp flour
2 tbsp ketchup
1¼ cups crushed tomatoes
1 tsp sugar
1 tbsp fresh parsley, chopped

1 Heat the oil in a pan. Add the onion and garlic clove and sauté for 5 minutes. Add the flour and cook for 1 minute.

2 Stir in the ketchup, crushed tomatoes, sugar and fresh parsley. Bring to a boil and cook for 10 minutes. Cover and chill and use when required.

COOK'S TIP

Barbecue and Tomato relishes should be used as quickly as possible, but will keep for a few days in the refrigerator.

VARIATION

For a hot and spicy version of this relish, add 2 tsp chili sauce and 1 green chili, finely chopped at step two.

CUCUMBER RELISH

A cool, refreshing relish, it may also be used as a dip with crudités as a starter.

½ cucumber
2 celery stalks, chopped
1 green bell pepper, seeded and chopped
1 garlic clove, crushed
½ pint plain yogurt
1 tbsp chopped fresh cilantro
freshly ground black pepper

1 Dice the cucumber and place in a large bowl. Add the celery, green pepper and crushed garlic.

2 Stir in the yogurt and fresh cilantro. Season with the pepper. Cover and chill. Use the same day.

Melon and Basil Soup

A deliciously refreshing, chilled fruit soup, just right for a hot summer's day.

Serves 4–6

INGREDIENTS
2 cantaloupe or honeydew melons
⅓ cup superfine sugar
¾ cup water
finely grated zest and juice of 1 lime
3 tbsp shredded fresh basil
fresh basil leaves, to garnish

basil

sugar

lime

melon

1 Cut the melons in half across the middle. Scrape out the seeds and discard. Using a melon baller, scoop out 20–24 balls and set aside for the garnish. Scoop out the remaining flesh and place in a blender or food processor.

2 Place the sugar, water and lime zest in a small pan over a low heat. Stir until dissolved, bring to a boil and simmer for 2–3 minutes. Remove from the heat and leave to cool slightly. Pour half the mixture into the blender or food processor with the melon flesh. Blend until smooth, adding the remaining syrup and lime juice to taste.

3 Pour the mixture into a bowl, stir in the basil and chill. Serve garnished with basil leaves and melon balls.

COOK'S TIP
Add the syrup in two stages, as the amount of sugar needed will depend on the sweetness of the melon.

Chilled Fresh Tomato Soup

This effortless uncooked soup can be made in minutes.

Serves 4–6

INGREDIENTS

3–3½ lb ripe tomatoes, peeled and
    roughly chopped
4 garlic cloves, crushed
2 tbsp extra-virgin olive oil (optional)
2 tbsp balsamic vinegar
freshly ground black pepper
4 slices whole-wheat bread
low-fat ricotta cheese, to garnish

whole-wheat bread

garlic

ricotta cheese

peppercorns

tomato

COOK'S TIP

For the best flavor, it is important to use only fully ripened, succulent tomatoes in this soup.

1 Place the tomatoes in a blender with the garlic and olive oil if using. Blend until smooth.

2 Pass the mixture through a sieve to remove the seeds. Stir in the balsamic vinegar and season to taste with pepper. Leave in the fridge to chill.

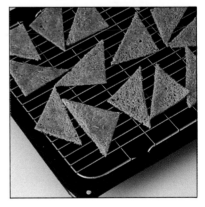

3 Toast the bread lightly on both sides. While still hot, cut off the crusts and slice in half horizontally. Place the toast on a board with the uncooked sides facing down and, using a circular motion, rub to remove any doughy pieces of bread.

4 Cut each slice into 4 triangles. Place on a griddle and toast the uncooked sides until lightly golden. Garnish each bowl of soup with a spoonful of ricotta cheese and serve with the melba toast.

Leek, Parsnip and Ginger Soup

A flavorful winter warmer, with the added spiciness of fresh ginger.

Serves 4–6

INGREDIENTS
2 tbsp olive oil
8 oz leeks, sliced
2 tbsp finely chopped fresh ginger root
1½ lb parsnips, roughly chopped
1¼ cups dry white wine, such as Sauvignon blanc
5 cups vegetable stock or water
salt and freshly ground black pepper
low-fat ricotta cheese, to garnish
paprika, to garnish

ginger

parsnip

vegetable stock

leeks

1 Heat the oil in a large pan and add the leeks and ginger. Cook gently for 2–3 minutes, until the leeks start to soften.

2 Add the parsnips and cook for a further 7–8 minutes.

3 Pour in the wine and stock or water and bring to a boil. Reduce the heat and simmer for 20–30 minutes or until the parsnips are tender.

4 Purée in a blender until smooth. Season to taste. Reheat and garnish with a swirl of ricotta cheese and a light dusting of paprika.

Broccoli and Almond Soup

The creaminess of the toasted almonds combines perfectly with the slight bitterness of the taste of broccoli.

Serves 4–6

INGREDIENTS
⅔ cup ground almonds
1 ½ lb broccoli
3¾ cups fresh vegetable stock or
    water
1¼ cups skim or low-fat milk
salt and freshly ground black pepper

ground almonds

skim milk

broccoli

1 Preheat the oven to 350°F. Spread the ground almonds evenly on a cookie sheet and toast in the oven for about 10 minutes, or until just golden. Reserve ¼ of the almonds and set aside for the garnish.

2 Cut the broccoli into small florets and steam for 6–7 minutes or until tender.

3 Place the remaining toasted almonds, broccoli, stock or water and milk in a blender and blend until smooth. Season to taste.

4 Reheat the soup and serve sprinkled with the reserved toasted almonds.

Red Onion and Beet Soup

This beautiful vivid ruby-red soup will look stunning at any dinner party.

Serves 4–6

INGREDIENTS
1 tbsp olive oil
12 oz red onions, sliced
2 garlic cloves, crushed
10 oz cooked beets, cut into
   thin sticks
5 cups fresh vegetable stock or water
1 cup cooked soup pasta
2 tbsp raspberry vinegar
salt and freshly ground black pepper
low-fat yogurt or ricotta cheese, to
   garnish
snipped chives, to garnish

garlic

red onion

beets

pasta

chives

COOK'S TIP
Try substituting cooked barley for the pasta to give extra nuttiness.

1 Heat the olive oil and add the onions and garlic.

2 Cook gently for about 20 minutes or until soft and tender.

3 Add the beets, stock or water, cooked pasta shapes and vinegar and heat through. Season to taste.

4 Ladle into bowls. Top each one with a spoonful of yogurt or ricotta cheese and sprinkle with chives.

Zucchini Soup with Small Pasta Shells

A pretty, fresh-tasting soup which could be made using cucumber instead of zucchini.

Serves 4–6

INGREDIENTS
4 tbsp olive or sunflower oil
2 onions, finely chopped
6¼ cups vegetable stock
2 lb zucchini
1 cup small soup pasta
fresh lemon juice
2 tbsp chopped fresh chervil
salt and ground black pepper
sour cream, to serve

zucchini

onion

soup pasta

chervil

1 Heat the oil in a large saucepan and add the onions. Cover and cook gently for about 20 minutes until very soft but not colored, stirring occasionally.

2 Add the stock and bring to a boil.

3 Meanwhile grate the zucchini and stir into the boiling stock with the pasta. Turn down the heat and simmer for 15 minutes until the pasta is tender. Season to taste with lemon juice, salt, and pepper.

4 Stir in the chervil and add a swirl of sour cream before serving.

COOK'S TIP
If no fresh stock is available, instead of using a bouillon cube, use canned chicken or beef consommé.

Fresh Tomato and Bean Soup

A rich, chunky tomato soup, with beans and cilantro.
Serve with olive ciabatta.

Serves 4

INGREDIENTS
2 lb ripe plum tomtoes
2 tbsp olive oil
2–3 onions, roughly chopped
2 garlic cloves, crushed
3¾ cups vegetable stock
2 tbsp sun-dried tomato paste
2 tsp paprika
1 tbsp cornstarch
15 oz can cannellini beans
2 tbsp chopped fresh cilantro
salt and ground black pepper
olive ciabatta, to serve

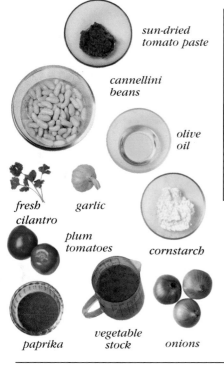

sun-dried tomato paste

cannellini beans

olive oil

fresh cilantro

garlic

plum tomatoes

cornstarch

paprika

vegetable stock

onions

1 First, peel the tomatoes. Using a sharp knife, make a small cross in each one and place in a bowl. Pour boiling water over them to cover and let stand for 30–60 seconds.

2 Drain the tomatoes and peel off the skins. Quarter them and then cut each piece in half again.

3 Heat the oil in a large saucepan and cook the onions and garlic for 3 minutes or until just beginning to soften.

4 Add the tomatoes to the onions, with the stock, sun-dried tomato paste and paprika. Season with a little salt and pepper. Bring to a boil and simmer for 10 minutes.

5 Mix the cornstarch to a paste with 2 tbsp water. Stir the beans into the soup with the cornstarch paste. Cook for a further 5 minutes.

6 Adjust the seasoning and stir in the chopped cilantro just before you serve with the olive ciabatta.

Succotash Soup Plate

Succotash is a traditional North American Indian dish of corn and beans. This version is enriched with milk (you could use cream for an ever-richer flavor) and it makes an appetizing and filling main course soup.

Serves 4

INGREDIENTS

4 tbsp butter
1 large onion, chopped
2 large carrots, peeled and cut into short sticks
3¾ cups milk
1 vegetable bouillon cube
2 medium-sized waxy potatoes, peeled and diced
1 thyme sprig
2 cups frozen corn
3 cups frozen lima beans or fava beans
2 tbsp chopped fresh parsley, to garnish

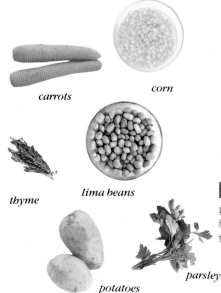

carrots

corn

thyme

lima beans

potatoes

parsley

1 Heat the butter in a large saucepan. Add the onion and carrots and cook over a gentle heat for 3–4 minutes, to soften without coloring.

2 Add the milk, bouillon cube, potatoes, thyme, corn and lima beans or fava beans. Simmer for 10 minutes until the potatoes are cooked through.

COOK'S TIP

Frozen corn and lima beans are best for flavor and convenience in this soup, although the canned variety may also be used.

3 Season to taste, ladle into soup plates and garnish with chopped fresh parsley.

Cauliflower, Bean and Fennel Seed Soup

The sweet, anise-licorice flavor of the fennel seeds gives a delicious edge to this hearty soup.

Serves 4–6

INGREDIENTS

1 tbsp olive oil
1 garlic clove, crushed
1 onion, chopped
2 tsp fennel seeds
1 cauliflower, cut into small florets
2 × 14 oz cans flageolet or cannellini
    beans, drained and rinsed
5 cups fresh vegetable stock or water
salt and freshly ground black pepper
chopped fresh parsley, to garnish
toasted slices of French bread, to
    serve

flageolet beans

French bread

onion

garlic

cauliflower

fennel seeds

parsley

1 Heat the olive oil. Add the garlic, onion and fennel seeds and cook gently for 5 minutes or until softened.

2 Add the cauliflower, half of the beans and the stock or water.

3 Bring to a boil. Reduce the heat and simmer for 10 minutes or until the cauliflower is tender.

4 Pour the soup into a blender and blend until smooth. Stir in the remaining beans and season to taste. Reheat and pour into bowls. Sprinkle with chopped parsley and serve with toasted slices of French bread.

Creamy Parmesan and Cauliflower Soup with Pasta Bows

A silky smooth, mildly cheesy soup that isn't overpowered by the cauliflower. It is an elegant dinner party soup served with the crisp melba toast.

Serves 6

INGREDIENTS
1 large cauliflower
5 cups vegetable stock
1½ cups pasta bows
 (farfalle)
⅔ cup light cream
freshly grated nutmeg
pinch of cayenne pepper
4 tbsp freshly grated
 Parmesan cheese
salt and pepper

FOR THE MELBA TOAST
3–4 slices day-old white bread
freshly grated Parmesan cheese
 for sprinkling
¼ tsp paprika

cauliflower

pasta bows

Parmesan cheese

nutmeg

1 Cut the leaves and central stalk away from the cauliflower and discard. Divide the cauliflower into florets.

2 Bring the stock to a boil and add the cauliflower. Simmer for about 10 minutes or until very soft. Remove the cauliflower with a slotted spoon and place in a food processor.

3 Add the pasta to the stock and simmer for 10 minutes until tender. Drain the pasta, reserving the liquid, and set aside. Pour the liquid over the cauliflower in the food processor. Add the cream or milk, nutmeg and cayenne to the cauliflower. Blend until smooth, then press through a sieve. Stir in the cooked pasta. Reheat the soup and stir in the Parmesan. Taste and adjust the seasoning.

4 Meanwhile make the melba toast. Preheat the oven to 350°F. Toast the bread lightly on both sides. Quickly cut off the crusts and split each slice in half horizontally. Scrape off any doughy bits and sprinkle with Parmesan and paprika. Place on a baking sheet and bake in the oven for 10–15 minutes or until uniformly golden. Serve with the soup.

Garlic, Chick-pea and Spinach Soup

This delicious, thick and creamy soup is richly flavored and perfect for vegetarians.

Serves 4

INGREDIENTS

2 tbsp olive oil
4 garlic cloves, crushed
1 onion, roughly chopped
2 tsp ground cumin
2 tsp ground coriander
5 cups vegetable stock
2 large potatoes, peeled
    and chopped
15 oz can chick-peas, drained
1 tbsp cornstarch
⅔ cup heavy cream
2 tbsp light tahini (sesame
    seed paste)
½ lb spinach
cayenne pepper
salt and ground black pepper

tahini   *cornstarch*

chick-peas *cayenne pepper* *ground coriander*

heavy cream   *garlic*   *potatoes*

onions   *spinach*   *vegetable stock*   *ground cumin*   *olive oil*

1 Heat the oil in a large saucepan and cook the garlic and onions for 5 minutes or until they are softened and golden brown.

2 Stir in the cumin and coriander and cook for another minute.

3 Pour in the stock and add the potatoes. Bring to a boil and simmer for 10 minutes. Add the drained chick-peas and simmer for a further 5 minutes, or until the potatoes are just tender.

4 Blend together the cornstarch, cream and tahini with plenty of seasoning. Stir into the soup with the spinach. Bring to a boil, stirring, and simmer for a further 2 minutes. Adjust the seasoning to taste, then serve immediately, sprinkled with a little cayenne pepper.

Tomato and Fresh Basil Soup

A soup for late summer, when fresh tomatoes are at their most flavorful.

Serves 4–6

INGREDIENTS
1 tbsp olive oil
2 tbsp butter
1 onion, finely chopped
2 lb ripe plum tomatoes, roughly chopped
1 garlic clove, roughly chopped
about 3 cups vegetable stock
½ cup dry white wine
2 tbsp sun-dried tomato paste
2 tbsp shredded fresh basil, plus a few whole leaves, to garnish
⅔ cup heavy cream
salt and ground black pepper

olive oil   garlic   vegetable stock

butter

heavy cream   onion

white wine   basil

plum tomatoes   sun-dried tomato paste

VARIATION
The soup can also be served chilled. Pour it into a container after sieving and chill for at least 4 hours. Serve in chilled bowls.

1 Heat the oil and butter in a large saucepan over medium heat until foaming. Add the onion and cook gently for about 5 minutes, stirring frequently, until it is softened but not brown.

2 Stir in the chopped tomatoes and garlic, then add the stock, white wine and sun-dried tomato paste, with salt and pepper to taste. Bring to a boil, then lower the heat, half-cover the saucepan and simmer gently for 20 minutes, stirring occasionally to prevent the tomatoes from sticking to the bottom of the pan.

3 Purée the soup with the shredded basil in a blender or food processor, then press through a sieve into a clean pan.

4 Add the heavy cream and heat through, stirring. Do not allow the soup to approach boiling point. Check the consistency and add more broth if necessary, then adjust the seasoning. Pour into heated bowls and garnish with whole basil sprigs. Serve immediately.

Vegetable Minestrone with Anellini

Serves 6–8

INGREDIENTS
large pinch of saffron threads
1 onion, chopped
1 leek, sliced
1 celery stalk, sliced
2 carrots, diced
2–3 garlic cloves, crushed
2½ cups vegetable stock
2 x 14 oz cans chopped
    tomatoes
½ cup frozen peas
½ cup anellini soup pasta
1 tsp sugar
1 tbsp chopped fresh parsley
1 tbsp chopped fresh basil
salt and ground black pepper

anellini *frozen peas* *onion*

saffron threads *basil* *stock*

parsley *chopped tomatoes*

carrot *celery*

garlic *leek*

1 Soak the pinch of saffron threads in 1 tablespoon of boiling water. Let stand for 10 minutes.

2 Meanwhile, put the prepared onion, leek, celery, carrots and garlic into a pan. Add the stock, bring to a boil, cover and simmer for 10 minutes.

3 Add the canned tomatoes, the saffron with its liquid, and the peas. Bring back to a boil and add the anellini. Simmer for 10 minutes until tender.

4 Season with salt, pepper and sugar to taste. Stir in the chopped herbs just before serving.

Stuffed Garlic Mushrooms with a Parsley Crust

These garlic mushrooms are perfect for dinner parties, or you could serve them in larger portions as a light supper dish with a green salad. Try them stuffed with a healthy dose of freshly chopped parsley.

Serves 4

INGREDIENTS
12 oz large portabello mushrooms, stems removed
3 garlic cloves, crushed
¾ cup butter, softened
3 cups finely crumbled fresh white breadcrumbs
1 cup fresh parsley, chopped
1 egg, beaten
salt and cayenne pepper
8 cherry tomatoes, to garnish

parsley

butter *egg*

garlic

mushrooms

breadcrumbs

1 Preheat the oven to 375°F. Arrange the mushrooms cup side uppermost on a baking tray. Mix together the crushed garlic and butter in a small bowl and divide ½ cup of the butter between the mushrooms.

2 Heat the remaining butter in a frying pan and lightly fry the breadcrumbs until golden brown. Place the chopped parsley in a bowl, add the breadcrumbs, season to taste and mix well.

3 Stir in the egg and use the mixture to fill the mushroom caps. Bake for 10–15 minutes until the topping has browned and the mushrooms have softened. Garnish with quartered tomatoes.

COOK'S TIP
If you are planning ahead, stuffed mushrooms can be prepared up to 12 hours in advance and kept in the refrigerator before baking.

Brie Parcels with Almonds

A sophisticated appetizer or light main course, served with crusty bread.

Serves 4

4 large vine leaves, preserved in
  brine
7 oz piece Brie cheese
2 tbsp chopped fresh chives
2 tbsp ground almonds
1 tsp crushed black
  peppercorns
1 tbsp olive oil
slivered almonds

vine leaves

Brie cheese

black peppercorns

chives

slivered almonds

olive oil

ground almonds

1 Rinse the vine leaves thoroughly in cold water and dry them well. Spread the leaves out on a board.

2 Cut the Brie into four chunks and place each chunk on a vine leaf.

3 Mix together the chives, ground almonds, peppercorns and oil; then place a spoonful on top of each piece of cheese. Sprinkle with slivered almonds.

4 Fold the vine leaves over, to enclose the cheese completely. Brush with oil and cook on a hot barbecue for 3–4 minutes, until the cheese is hot and melting. Serve immediately.

Roasted Garlic Toasts

A delicious appetizer or accompaniment to vegetable dishes.

Serves 4

2 whole garlic heads
extra-virgin olive oil
fresh rosemary sprigs
ciabatta loaf or thick baguette
chopped fresh rosemary
salt and freshly ground black
    pepper

ciabatta loaf

garlic

rosemary

extra-virgin olive oil

1 Slice the tops from the heads of garlic, with a sharp knife.

2 Brush with oil, and then wrap in foil, with a few sprigs of rosemary. Cook on a medium–hot barbecue for 25–30 minutes, turning occasionally, until soft.

3 Slice the bread and brush generously with oil. Toast on the barbecue until golden, turning once.

4 Squeeze the garlic cloves from their skins onto the toasts; then sprinkle the toasts with chopped fresh rosemary and a little extra olive oil, with salt and pepper to taste.

COOK'S TIP

Roast a few eggplant, pepper or onion slices, to spread over the toasts, for variety.

Eggplant, Tomato and Feta Rolls

Grilled eggplant wrapped around tangy feta cheese, flavored with basil and sun-dried tomatoes, make a wonderful combination of sunshine flavors.

Serves 4

2 large eggplant
olive oil
10–12 sun-dried tomatoes in oil, drained
handful of large, fresh basil leaves
5 oz feta cheese
salt and freshly ground black pepper

olive oil

eggplant

feta cheese

basil

sun-dried tomatoes in oil

COOK'S TIP

Vegetarians or vegans could use tofu in place of the feta cheese. For extra flavor, sprinkle the tofu with a little soy sauce before wrapping.

1 Slice the eggplant lengthwise into ¼-in thick slices. Sprinkle with salt and layer in a colander. Allow to drain for about 30 minutes.

2 Rinse the eggplant in cold water and dry well. Brush with oil on both sides and grill on a hot barbecue for 2–3 minutes, turning once, until golden brown and softened.

3 Arrange the sun-dried tomatoes over one end of each eggplant slice and top with the basil leaves. Cut the feta into short sticks and place on top. Season with salt and pepper.

4 Roll the eggplant slices around to enclose the filling. Cook on the barbecue for 2–3 minutes more, until hot. Serve with a thick French loaf.

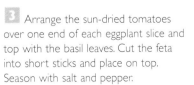

Eggplant, Roast Garlic and Red Pepper Pâté

This is a simple pâté of smoky baked eggplant, sweet pink peppercorns and red bell peppers, with more than a hint of garlic!

Serves 4

INGREDIENTS
3 medium eggplant
2 red bell peppers
5 whole garlic cloves
1½ tsp pink peppercorns in brine, drained and crushed
2 tbsp chopped fresh cilantro

eggplant

garlic

cilantro

pink peppercorns

red bell pepper

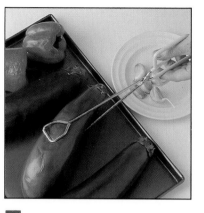

1 Preheat the oven to 400°F. Arrange the whole eggplant, peppers and garlic cloves on a cookie sheet and place in the oven. After 10 minutes remove the garlic cloves and turn over the eggplant and peppers.

2 Peel the garlic cloves and place in the bowl of a blender.

3 After a further 20 minutes remove the blistered and charred peppers from the oven and place in a paper bag. Leave to cool.

4 After a further 10 minutes remove the eggplant from the oven. Split in half and scoop the flesh into a sieve placed over a bowl. Press the flesh with a spoon to remove the bitter juices.

5 Add the mixture to the garlic in the blender and blend until smooth. Place in a large mixing bowl.

6 Peel and chop the red peppers and stir into the eggplant mixture. Mix in the peppercorns and fresh cilantro and serve at once.

Broiled Mixed Peppers with Feta and Green Salsa

Soft, smoky broiled bell peppers make a lovely combination with the slightly tart salsa.

Serves 4

INGREDIENTS

4 medium bell peppers in
   different colors
3 tbsp chopped fresh flat-leaf parsley
3 tbsp chopped fresh mint
½ small red onion, finely chopped
1 tbsp capers, coarsely chopped
¼ cup Greek olives, pitted and sliced
1 fresh green chili, seeded and finely
   chopped
4 tbsp pistachios, chopped
5 tbsp extra-virgin olive oil
3 tbsp fresh lime juice
½ cup medium-fat feta cheese,
   crumbled
1 oz gherkins, finely chopped

olives
feta cheese
green chili
mint
pistachios
bell peppers
gherkins
red onion

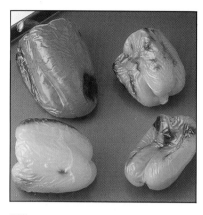

1 Preheat the broiler. Place the whole peppers on a tray and broil until charred and blistered.

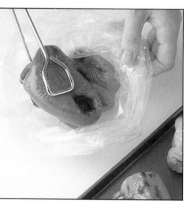

2 Place the peppers in a plastic bag and leave to cool.

COOK'S TIP
Feta cheese is quite salty so if preferred, soak in cold water and drain well before using.

3 Peel, seed and cut the peppers into even strips.

4 Mix all the remaining ingredients together, and stir in the pepper strips.

Artichokes with Garlic and Herb Butter

It is fun eating artichokes and even more fun to share one between two people. You can always have a second one to follow so that you get your fair share!

Serves 4

INGREDIENTS
2 large or 4 medium globe
    artichokes
salt

FOR THE GARLIC AND HERB BUTTER
6 tablespoons butter
1 garlic clove, very finely chopped
1 tablespoon chopped fresh
    mixed herbs

butter *garlic*

mixed herbs

globe artichokes

1 Wash the artichokes well in cold water. Using a sharp knife, cut off the stalks level with the bases. Cut off the top ½ inch of leaves. Snip off the pointed ends of the remaining leaves with kitchen scissors and discard.

2 Put the prepared artichokes in a large saucepan of lightly salted water. Bring to a boil, cover and cook for 40–45 minutes or until one of the lower leaves comes away easily from the artichoke when gently pulled.

3 Drain upside down while making the garlic and herb butter. Melt the butter in a small saucepan over low heat, add the garlic and cook for 30 seconds. Remove from the heat, stir in the herbs and pour into one or two small serving bowls.

4 Place the artichokes on serving plates and serve immediately with the garlic and herb butter.

COOK'S TIP

To eat an artichoke, pull off each leaf and dip into the garlic and herb butter. Scrape off the soft, fleshy base with your teeth. When the center is reached, pull out the hairy choke and discard it, as it is inedible. The heart can be cut up and eaten with the remaining garlic butter.

Stuffed Grape Leaves

Based on the Greek dolmades, but with a vegetarian brown rice stuffing, this makes an excellent appetizer, snack or buffet dish.

Makes about 40

INGREDIENTS
1 tablespoon sunflower oil
1 teaspoon sesame oil
1 onion, finely chopped
1¼ cups brown rice
2½ cups vegetable stock
1 small yellow bell pepper, seeded and finely chopped
½ cup dried apricots, finely chopped
2 lemons
⅔ cup pine nuts
3 tablespoons chopped fresh parsley
2 tablespoons chopped fresh mint
½ teaspoon apple pie spice
8-ounce package grape leaves preserved in brine, drained
2 tablespoons olive oil
freshly ground black pepper
lemon wedges, to garnish

To SERVE
1¼ cups low-fat plain yogurt
2 tablespoons chopped mixed fresh herbs
cayenne pepper

yogurt   cayenne pepper

mint   mixed herbs

pine nuts

onion

sunflower oil   sesame oil   yellow bell pepper   parsley   olive oil

grape leaves

apple pie spice

brown rice   vegetable stock   dried apricots   lemons

1 Heat the sunflower and sesame oils together in a large saucepan. Add the onion and cook gently for 5 minutes to soften. Add the rice, stirring to coat the grains in oil. Pour in the stock, bring to a boil, then lower the heat, cover the pan and simmer for 30 minutes, or until the rice is tender but al dente.

2 Stir in the chopped pepper and apricots, with a little more stock if necessary. Replace the lid and cook for another 5 minutes. Grate the zest from one of the lemons, then squeeze both.

4 Bring a saucepan of water to a boil and blanch the grape leaves for 5 minutes. Drain the leaves well, then lay them shiny side down on a board. Cut out any coarse stalks. Place a heap of the rice mixture in the center of each grape leaf. Fold the stem end over, then the sides and pointed end, to make neat parcels.

3 Drain off any stock that has not been absorbed by the rice. Stir in the pine nuts, herbs, spice, grated lemon zest and half the juice. Season with pepper and set aside.

5 Pack the parcels closely together in a shallow serving dish. Mix the remaining lemon juice with the olive oil. Pour the mixture over the grape leaves, cover and chill before serving. Garnish with lemon wedges. Spoon the yogurt into a bowl, stir in the chopped herbs and sprinkle with a little cayenne. Serve with the stuffed grape leaves.

COOK'S TIP
If grape leaves are not available, the leaves of Swiss chard, young spinach or cabbage can be used instead.

Breaded Eggplant with Hot Vinaigrette

Crisp on the outside, beautifully tender within, these eggplant slices taste wonderful with a spicy dressing flavored with chili and capers.

COOK'S TIP
When serving a salad with a warm dressing, use robust leaves that will stand up to the heat.

Serves 2

INGREDIENTS
1 large eggplant
1/2 cup all-purpose flour
2 eggs, beaten
2 cups fresh white bread crumbs
vegetable oil for frying
1 head radicchio
salt and freshly ground black pepper

FOR THE DRESSING
2 tbsp olive oil
1 garlic clove, crushed
1 tbsp capers, drained
1 tbsp white wine vinegar
1 tbsp chili oil

1 Remove the ends from the eggplant. Cut it into 1/4 in slices. Set aside.

2 Season the flour with a generous amount of salt and black pepper. Spread out in a shallow dish. Pour the beaten eggs into a second dish. Spread out the bread crumbs in a third.

3 Dip the eggplant slices in the flour, then in the beaten egg and finally in the bread crumbs, patting them on to make an even coating.

eggplant

bread crumbs

eggs

all-purpose flour

radicchio

capers

white wine vinegar

garlic clove

4 Pour vegetable oil into a large frying pan to a depth of about 1/4 in. Heat the oil, then fry the eggplant slices for 3–4 minutes, turning once. Drain well on paper towels.

5 Heat the olive oil in a small pan. Add the garlic and the capers, and cook over gentle heat for 1 minute. Increase the heat, add the vinegar, and cook for 30 seconds. Stir in the chili oil, and remove the pan from the heat.

6 Arrange the radicchio leaves on two plates. Top with the hot eggplant slices. Drizzle over the vinaigrette, and serve.

Vegetable Tempura

These deep-fried fritters are based on Kaki-age, a Japanese dish that often incorporates fish and shrimp as well as vegetables.

Makes 8

INGREDIENTS
2 medium zucchini
½ medium eggplant
1 large carrot
½ small Spanish onion
1 egg
½ cup ice water
1 cup all-purpose flour
salt and ground black pepper
vegetable oil,
   for deep-frying
sea salt flakes, lemon slices and
   Japanese soy sauce (*shoyu*),
   to serve

zucchini

carrot   *eggplant*

Spanish onion

all-purpose flour

egg   *vegetable oil*

COOK'S TIP
Paring strips of peel from the zucchini and eggplant will avoid too much tough skin in the finished dish.

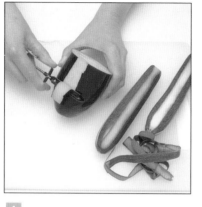
1 Using a potato peeler, pare strips of peel from the zucchini and eggplant to give a striped effect.

2 Cut the zucchini, eggplant and carrot into strips about 3–4 in long and ⅛ in wide.

3 Put the zucchini, eggplant and carrot in a colander and sprinkle liberally with salt. Let stand for about 30 minutes, then rinse thoroughly under cold running water. Drain well.

4 Thinly slice the onion from top to base, discarding the plump pieces in the middle. Separate the layers so that there are lots of fine long strips. Mix all the vegetables together and season with salt and pepper.

5 Make the batter immediately before frying: mix the egg and iced water in a bowl, then sift in the flour. Mix very briefly using a fork or chopsticks. Do not overmix – the batter should remain lumpy. Add the vegetables to the batter and mix to combine.

6 Meanwhile, half-fill a wok with oil and heat to 350°F. Scoop up one heaped tablespoon of the mixture at a time and carefully lower into the oil. Deep-fry in batches for about 3 minutes, until golden brown and crisp. Drain on paper towels. Serve each diner with salt, lemon slices and a tiny bowl of Japanese soy sauce for dipping.

Cheese-stuffed Pears

These pears, with their scrumptious creamy topping, make a sublime dish when served with a simple salad.

Serves 4

INGREDIENTS

¼ cup ricotta cheese
¼ cup Saga blue cheese
1 tbsp honey
½ celery stalk, finely sliced
8 green olives, pitted and roughly
   chopped
4 dates, pitted and cut into thin strips
pinch of paprika
4 ripe pears
⅔ cup apple juice

honey

pear

apple juice

dates

Saga blue

celery

olives

1 Preheat the oven to 400°F. Place the ricotta in a bowl and crumble in the Saga blue cheese. Add the rest of the ingredients except for the pears and apple juice and mix well.

2 Halve the pears lengthwise and use a melon baller to remove the cores. Place in a ovenproof dish and divide the filling equally between them.

3 Pour in the apple juice and cover the dish with foil. Bake for 20 minutes or until the pears are tender.

4 Remove the foil and place the dish under a hot broiler for 3 minutes. Serve immediately.

COOK'S TIP

Choose ripe pears in season such as Bartlett or Comice.

Nutty Cheese Balls

An extremely quick and simple recipe. Try making a smaller version to serve as canapés at a drinks party.

Serves 4

INGREDIENTS
1 cup low-fat ricotta cheese
¼ cup Saga blue cheese
1 tbsp finely chopped onion
1 tbsp finely chopped celery stalk
1 tbsp finely chopped parsley
1 tbsp finely chopped gherkin
1 tsp brandy or port (optional)
pinch of paprika
½ cup walnuts or pecans, roughly
    chopped
6 tbsp snipped chives
salt and freshly ground black pepper

celery

Saga blue cheese

gherkins   ricotta cheese

onion   walnuts

chives

parsley

paprika

1 Beat the ricotta cheese and Saga blue together using a spoon.

2 Mix in all the remaining ingredients except the snipped chives.

3 Divide the mixture into 12 pieces and roll into balls.

4 Roll each ball gently in the snipped chives. Leave in the refrigerator to chill for about an hour before serving.

Rice Cakes with Cream and Mixed Mushrooms

Serve with rich meat dishes, such as beef stroganoff or goulash, or as part of a vegetarian supper menu.

Serves 4

INGREDIENTS

¾ cup long-grain rice
1 egg
1 tablespoon all-purpose flour
4 tablespoons freshly grated
    Parmesan, Fontina or Pecorino
    cheese
4 tablespoons unsalted butter, plus
    extra for frying rice cakes
1 small onion, chopped
1½-2 cups assorted wild and
    cultivated mushrooms, trimmed
    and sliced
1 fresh thyme sprig
2 tablespoons Madeira or sherry
⅔ cup sour cream or crème fraîche
salt and freshly ground black pepper
paprika for dusting (optional)

Parmesan cheese   *flour*   *egg*

onion   *butter*   *long-grain rice*

mushrooms   *thyme*

sherry   *sour cream*   *paprika*

1 Bring a saucepan of water to a boil. Add the rice and cook for about 12 minutes. Rinse, drain and cool.

2 Beat the egg, flour and cheese together with a fork, then stir in the cooled cooked rice. Mix well and set aside. Melt half the butter and cook the onion until soft but not browned. Add the mushrooms and thyme and cook until the juices run. Add the Madeira or sherry. Increase the heat to reduce the juices and concentrate the flavor. Season to taste, transfer to a bowl, cover and keep hot.

3 Using a tablespoon, shape the rice mixture into cakes. Melt a pat of butter in a frying pan and fry the rice cakes in batches for 1 minute on each side. Add more butter as needed. Keep the cooked rice cakes hot.

4 When all the rice cakes are cooked, arrange on four warmed plates, top with sour cream or crème fraîche and add a spoonful of mushrooms. Dust with paprika, if using. Serve with a selection of cooked vegetables, if you like.

COOK'S TIP

Although the recipe specifies Parmesan, Fontina or Pecorino, you could use aged Cheddar cheese or even a hard goat cheese.

Oatmeal Tartlets with Minted Hummus

Serve these wholesome little tartlets with a crisp salad of Boston lettuce.

Serves 6

INGREDIENTS

1½ cups medium oatmeal
½ tsp baking soda
1 tsp salt
2 tbsp butter
1 egg yolk
2 tbsp skim milk
1 × 14 oz can chick-peas, rinsed and drained
juice of 1–2 lemons
1½ cups ricotta cheese
4 tbsp tahini
freshly ground black pepper
3 tbsp chopped fresh mint
2 tbsp pumpkin seeds
paprika, for dusting

tahini

pumpkin seeds

ricotta cheese

chick-peas

oatmeal

mint

lemon

1 Preheat the oven to 325°F. Mix together the oatmeal, baking soda and salt in a large bowl. Rub in the butter until the mixture resembles fine breadcrumbs. Stir in the egg yolk and add the milk if the mixture seems too dry.

2 Press into 3½ in tartlet pans. Bake for 25–30 minutes. Allow to cool.

3 Purée the chick-peas, the juice of 1 lemon, ricotta cheese and tahini in a food processor until smooth. Spoon into a bowl and season with black pepper and more lemon juice to taste. Stir in the chopped mint. Divide between the tartlet moulds, sprinkle with pumpkin seeds and dust with paprika.

Parsnip and Pecan Cheese Puffs with Watercress and Arugula Sauce

These scrumptious nutty puffs conceal a surprisingly sweet parsnip center.

Makes 18

INGREDIENTS
½ cup butter
1¼ cups water
¾ cup all-purpose flour
½ cup whole-wheat flour
3 eggs, beaten
1 oz Cheddar cheese, grated
pinch of cayenne pepper or paprika
⅓ cup pecans, chopped
1 medium parsnip, cut into
  ¾ in pieces
1 tbsp skim milk
2 tsp sesame seeds

FOR THE SAUCE
5 oz watercress, trimmed
5 oz arugula, trimmed
¾ cup low-fat yogurt
salt, grated nutmeg and freshly ground
  black pepper
watercress sprigs, to garnish

1 Preheat the oven to 400°F. Place the butter and water in a pot. Bring to a boil and add all the flour at once. Beat vigorously until the mixture leaves the sides of the pan and forms a ball. Remove from heat and allow the mixture to cool slightly. Beat in the eggs a little at a time until the mixture is shiny and soft enough to fall gently from a spoon.

2 Beat in the Cheddar, cayenne pepper or paprika and the chopped pecans.

3 Lightly grease a cookie sheet and drop onto it 18 heaped tablespoons of the mixture. Place a piece of parsnip on each and top with another heaped tablespoon of the mixture.

4 Brush the puffs with a little milk and sprinkle with sesame seeds. Bake in the oven for 25–30 minutes until golden.

pecans

parsnips

Cheddar

arugula

whole-wheat flour

all-purpose flour

yogurt

watercress

5 Meanwhile make the sauce. Bring a pan of water to a boil and blanch the watercress and arugula for 2–3 minutes. Drain and immediately refresh in cold water. Drain well and chop.

6 Purée the watercress and arugula in a blender or food processor with the yogurt until smooth. Season to taste with salt, nutmeg and freshly ground black pepper. To reheat, place the sauce in a bowl over a gently simmering pot of hot water and heat gently, taking care not to let the sauce curdle. Garnish with watercress.

Asparagus Rolls with Herb Butter Sauce

For a taste sensation, try tender asparagus spears wrapped in crisp filo pastry. The buttery herb sauce makes the perfect accompaniment.

Serves 2

INGREDIENTS
4 sheets of filo pastry
¼ cup butter, melted
16 young asparagus spears, trimmed

FOR THE SAUCE
2 shallots, finely chopped
1 bay leaf
⅔ cup dry white wine
6 oz butter, softened
1 tbsp chopped fresh herbs
salt and freshly ground black pepper
chopped chives, to garnish

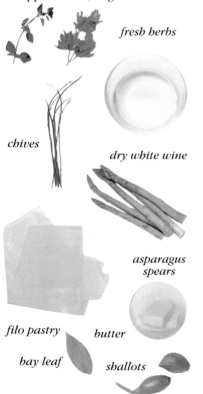

fresh herbs

chives

dry white wine

asparagus spears

filo pastry　*butter*

bay leaf　*shallots*

1 Preheat the oven to 400°F. Cut the filo sheets in half. Brush a half sheet with melted butter. Fold one corner of the sheet down to the bottom edge to give a wedge shape.

2 Lay 4 asparagus spears on top at the longest edge, and roll up toward the shortest edge. Using the remaining filo and asparagus spears, make three more rolls in the same way.

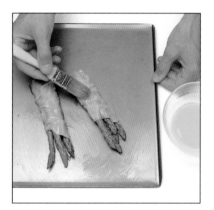

3 Lay the rolls on a greased baking sheet. Brush with the remaining melted butter. Bake in the oven for 8 minutes until golden.

4 Meanwhile, put the shallots, bay leaf and wine into a pan. Cover, and cook over a high heat until the wine is reduced to 3–4 tbsp.

5 Strain the wine mixture into a bowl. Whisk in the butter, a little at a time, until the sauce is smooth and glossy.

6 Stir in the herbs, and add salt and pepper to taste. Return to the pan, and keep the sauce warm. Serve the rolls on individual plates with a salad garnish, if desired. Serve the sauce separately, sprinkled with a few chopped chives.

Red Pepper and Watercress Filo Parcels

Peppery watercress combines well with sweet red bell pepper in these crisp little parcels.

Makes 8

INGREDIENTS
3 red bell peppers
6 oz watercress
1 cup ricotta cheese
¼ cup blanched almonds, toasted and chopped
salt and freshly ground black pepper
8 sheets of filo pastry
2 tbsp olive oil

ricotta

red bell pepper

watercress

almonds

filo pastry

1 Preheat the oven to 375°F. Place the peppers under a hot broiler until blistered and charred. Place in a paper bag. When cool enough to handle peel, seed and pat dry on kitchen paper.

2 Place the peppers and watercress in a food processor and pulse until coarsely chopped. Spoon into a bowl.

3 Mix in the ricotta and almonds, and season to taste.

4 Working with 1 sheet of filo pastry at a time, cut out 2 × 7 in and 2 × 2 in squares from each sheet. Brush 1 large square with a little olive oil and place a second large square at an angle of 90 degrees to form a star shape.

5 Place 1 of the small squares in the center of the star shape, brush lightly with oil and top with a second small square.

6 Top with ⅛ of the red pepper mixture. Bring the edges together to form a purse shape and twist to seal. Place on a lightly greased cookie sheet and cook for 25–30 minutes until golden.

Crusty Rolls with Zucchini and Saffron

Split, crusty rolls are filled with zucchini in a creamy tomato sauce flavored with saffron. Use a mixture of green zucchini and yellow summer squash, if possible.

Serves 4

INGREDIENTS
1½ lb small zucchini
1 tbsp olive oil
2 shallots, finely chopped
4 crusty rolls
7 oz can chopped tomatoes
pinch of sugar
a few saffron threads
¼ cup light cream
salt and freshly ground black pepper

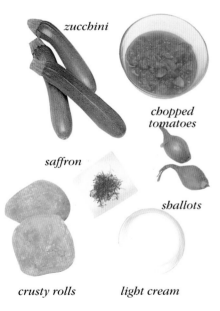

zucchini

chopped tomatoes

saffron

shallots

crusty rolls *light cream*

COOK'S TIP
To avoid heating your oven, heat the rolls in a microwave. Put them on a plate, cover with paper towels, and heat on HIGH for 30–45 seconds.

1 Preheat the oven to 350°F. Remove the ends from the zucchini, then, using a sharp knife, cut the zucchini into 1½ in lengths. Cut each piece into quarters lengthwise.

2 Heat the oil in a large frying pan. Add the shallots, and fry over moderate heat for 1–2 minutes. Put the rolls into the oven to warm through.

3 Add the zucchini to the shallots. Mix well, and cook for 6 minutes, stirring frequently, until just beginning to soften.

4 Stir in the tomatoes and sugar. Steep the saffron threads in a little hot water for a few minutes, then add to the pan with the cream. Cook for 4 minutes, stirring occasionally. Season to taste. Split open the rolls, and fill with the zucchini and sauce.

Brioche with Mixed Mushrooms

Mushrooms in a rich sherry sauce, served on toasted brioche, make a delectable, light lunch, but would also serve 6 as an appetizer.

Serves 4

INGREDIENTS
6 tbsp butter
1 vegetable bouillon cube
1½ lb shiitake mushrooms, caps only, sliced
8 oz white mushrooms, sliced
3 tbsp dry sherry
1 cup sour cream
2 tsp lemon juice
4 thick slices of brioche
salt and freshly ground black pepper

shiitake and white mushrooms

brioche

butter

bouillon cube

sour cream

lemon

COOK'S TIP
If shiitake mushrooms are too expensive or not available, substitute more white or crimini mushrooms. Always wipe the mushrooms with paper towels before use.

1 Melt the butter in a large pan. Crumble in the bouillon cube, and stir for about 30 seconds.

2 Add the shiitake and white mushrooms to the pan, and cook for 5 minutes over a moderate to high heat, stirring occasionally.

3 Stir in the sherry. Cook for 1 minute, then add the sour cream. Cook, stirring, over a gentle heat for 5 minutes. Stir in the lemon juice, and add salt and pepper to taste. Preheat the broiler.

4 Toast the brioche slices under the broiler until just golden on both sides. Spoon the mushrooms on top, heat briefly under the broiler, and serve. Fresh thyme may be used to garnish, if desired.

Ciabatta Rolls with Goat Cheese

The Tomato Relish gives a piquant bite that nicely complements the goat cheese. If you can't find the rolls, use a ciabatta loaf or country bread instead.

Makes 4

INGREDIENTS
2 ciabatta rolls
4 tbsp Tomato Relish
2 tbsp chopped fresh basil
6 oz goat cheese, thinly sliced
6 black olives, halved and pitted
1 sprig fresh basil, to garnish

ciabatta rolls

Tomato Relish

goat cheese

basil

olives

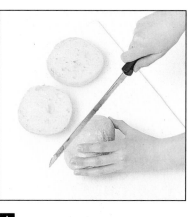

1 Cut the rolls in half and toast on one side only.

2 Spread a little relish over each half and sprinkle with the chopped basil.

3 Arrange the goat cheese slices on top, then scatter over a few olives. Place under a hot broiler until the goat cheese begins to melt, then serve garnished with a sprig of basil.

TOMATO RELISH

Makes scant 2 cups

3 tbsp olive oil
1 onion, chopped
1 red bell pepper, seeded and chopped
2 garlic cloves
¼ tsp chili powder
14 oz can chopped tomatoes
1 tbsp clear honey
2 tsp black olive paste
2 tbsp red wine vinegar
salt and pepper

Heat the oil and fry the onion and red bell pepper until softened. Add the garlic and the remaining ingredients, and season to taste. Simmer for 15 minutes until thickened.

Ciabatta with Mozzarella and Broiled Onion

Ciabatta is readily available in most supermarkets. It's even more delicious when made with spinach, sun-dried tomatoes, or olives, and you'll probably find these in your local grocery store.

Makes 4

INGREDIENTS
1 ciabatta loaf
4 tbsp red pesto
2 small onions
oil for brushing
½ lb mozzarella cheese
8 black olives

ciabatta loaf

tomato

onion

mozzarella cheese

olives

red pesto

1 Cut the bread in half horizontally and toast lightly. Spread with the red pesto.

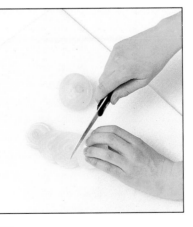

2 Peel the onions and cut horizontally into thick slices. Brush with oil and broil for 3 minutes until lightly browned.

3 Slice the cheese and arrange over the bread. Lay the onion slices on top and scatter some olives over. Cut in half diagonally. Place under a hot broiler for 2–3 minutes until the cheese melts and the onion chars.

Welsh Rarebit

This recipe is traditionally made with English brown ale or red wine, which gives it a delicious flavor. You can use other cheeses too, such as Stilton or Red Leicester. If you put a poached or fried egg on top, the dish becomes a Buck Rarebit.

Makes 4

INGREDIENTS
1 cup grated strong Cheddar cheese
2 tbsp brown ale or beer
1 tsp English mustard
cayenne pepper
4 slices bread

bread

brown ale

mustard

Cheddar cheese

cayenne pepper

1 Put the cheese in a saucepan with the brown ale, mustard, and cayenne pepper, and mix together thoroughly.

2 Heat gently, stirring constantly, until the cheese is just beginning to melt.

3 Meanwhile, toast the bread. Spread the cheese mixture over the toast.

4 Broil lightly until tinged brown here and there.

Fried Mozzarella Sandwich

This sandwich is very popular in southern Italy, where it is known as *Mozzarella in Carrozza*. Be sure to use mozzarella packed in brine for the best flavor. This is also excellent made with Cheddar or Swiss cheese.

Makes 2

INGREDIENTS
¼ lb mozzarella cheese, thickly sliced
4 thick slices white bread, crusts
    removed
salt and pepper
1 egg
2 tbsp milk
oil for shallow-frying

white bread

mozzarella cheese

egg

1 Lay the mozzarella slices on 2 slices of bread, sprinkle with salt and pepper, then top with the remaining bread slices to make 2 cheese sandwiches.

2 Mix the egg and milk together, season, and place in a large shallow dish.

3 Lay the sandwiches in the egg mixture, turn over so that they are saturated and leave there for a few minutes. Pour enough oil into a skillet to give ½ in depth. Heat the oil and fry the sandwiches for 3–4 minutes, turning them once, until golden brown and crisp. Drain well on paper towels.

VARIATION
Add 2 chopped sun-dried tomatoes or some black olive paste to the sandwich before soaking in egg.

Tostadas with Refried Beans

A tostada is a crisp, fried tortilla used as a base on which to pile the topping of your choice – a variation on a sandwich and a very tasty snack popular in Mexico and South America.

Makes 6

INGREDIENTS
2 tbsp vegetable oil
1 onion, chopped
2 garlic cloves, chopped
½ tsp chili powder
15 oz can borlotti or pinto
    beans, drained
⅔ cup vegetable stock
1 tbsp tomato paste
2 tbsp chopped fresh cilantro
6 wheat or corn tortillas
3 tbsp tomato salsa (see right)
2 tbsp sour cream
½ cup grated Cheddar cheese
salt and ground black pepper
cilantro leaves, to garnish

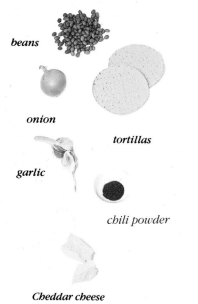

beans

onion

tortillas

garlic

chili powder

Cheddar cheese

1 Heat the oil in a pan and fry the onion until softened.

2 Add the garlic and chili powder and fry for 1 minute, stirring.

3 Mix in the beans and mash very roughly with a potato masher.

4 Add the vegetable stock, tomato paste, chopped cilantro and seasoning to taste. Mix thoroughly and cook for a few minutes.

5 Fry the tortillas in hot oil for about 1 minute until crisp, turning them once, then drain on paper towels.

TOMATO SALSA

Makes about 1¼ cups

1 small onion, chopped
1 garlic clove, crushed
2 fresh green chilies, seeded and
    finely chopped, or 1 tsp bottled
    chopped chilies
1 lb tomatoes, skinned and chopped
salt
2 tbsp chopped fresh cilantro

Stir all the ingredients together until
well mixed.

6 Put a spoonful of refried beans on
each tostada. Spoon over some Tomato
Salsa, then some sour cream, sprinkle
with grated Cheddar cheese, and garnish
with cilantro.

Zucchini, Carrots and Pecans in Pita Bread

Chunks of fried zucchini served with a tangy salad in pita pockets.

Serves 2

INGREDIENTS
2 carrots
$\frac{1}{4}$ cup pecan nuts
4 scallions, sliced
$\frac{1}{4}$ cup strained, plain yogurt
7 tsp olive oil
1 tsp lemon juice
1 tbsp chopped fresh mint
2 zucchini
$\frac{1}{4}$ cup all-purpose flour
2 pita breads
salt and freshly ground black pepper
shredded lettuce, to serve

zucchini

scallions

pecan nuts *lemon*

mint

strained, plain yogurt

carrots

1 Remove the ends from the carrots. Grate them coarsely into a bowl.

2 Stir in the pecans and scallions, and toss well together.

3 In a clean bowl, whisk the yogurt with 1½ tsp of the olive oil, the lemon juice and the fresh mint. Stir the dressing into the carrot mixture, and mix well. Cover, and chill until required.

4 Remove the ends from the zucchini. Cut them diagonally into slices. Season the flour with salt and pepper. Spread it on a plate, and coat the zucchini slices.

COOK'S TIP
Do not fill the pita breads too soon or the carrot mixture will make the bread soggy.

5 Heat the remaining oil in a large frying pan. Add the coated zucchini slices, and cook for 3–4 minutes, turning once, until browned. Drain the zucchini on paper towels.

6 Make a slit in each pita bread to form a pocket. Fill the pitas with the carrot mixture and the zucchini slices. Serve on a bed of shredded lettuce.

Rice Balls Filled with Manchego Cheese

For a really impressive Spanish tapa-style snack, serve these delicious rice balls.

Serves 6

INGREDIENTS
1 globe artichoke
¼ cup butter
1 small onion, finely chopped
1 garlic clove, crushed
⅔ cup risotto rice
scant 2 cups hot
    vegetable stock
⅔ cup freshly grated Parmesan
    cheese
5 oz Manchego cheese, very finely
    diced
3–4 tbsp polenta
olive oil, for frying
salt and ground black pepper
flat-leaf parsley, to garnish

onion *butter*

artichoke

polenta

risotto rice

garlic

stock *Parmesan cheese*

olive oil *Manchego cheese* *flat leaf parsley*

1 Remove the stalk, leaves and choke to leave just the heart of the artichoke. Chop the heart finely.

2 Melt the butter in a saucepan and gently fry the chopped artichoke heart, onion and garlic for 5 minutes until softened. Stir in the rice and cook for about 1 minute.

COOK'S TIP
Manchego cheese is made with sheep's milk from La Mancha in Spain. It is ideal for grating or broiling.

3 Keeping the heat fairly high, gradually add the stock, stirring constantly until all the liquid has been absorbed and the rice is cooked – this should take about 20 minutes. Season well, then stir in the Parmesan. Transfer to a bowl. Leave to cool, then cover and chill for at least 2 hours.

4 Spoon about 15 ml/1 tbsp of the mixture into one hand, flatten slightly, and place a few pieces of diced Manchego cheese in the centre. Shape to make a small ball. Flatten, then lightly roll in the polenta. Make about 12 cakes in total. Shallow fry in hot olive oil for about 4–5 minutes until the rice cakes are crisp and golden brown. Drain on kitchen paper and serve hot, garnished with parsley.

Chick-pea Falafel with Cilantro Dip

Little balls of spicy chick-pea purée, deep-fried until crisp, are served together with a cilantro-flavored mayonnaise.

Serves 4

INGREDIENTS
14 oz can chick-peas, drained
6 scallions, finely sliced
1 egg
$^1\!/_2$ tsp ground turmeric
1 garlic clove, crushed
1 tsp ground cumin
4 tbsp chopped fresh cilantro
oil for deep-frying
1 small red chili, seeded and
    finely chopped
3 tbsp mayonnaise
salt and freshly ground black pepper
cilantro sprig, to garnish

cilantro

scallions

chick-peas

ground
turmeric

ground
cumin

egg

garlic
clove   red
        chili

mayonnaise

COOK'S TIP
If you have time, chill the chick-pea purée before making it into balls. It will be easier to shape.

1 Turn the chick-peas into a food processor or blender. Add the scallions, and process to a smooth purée. Add the egg, ground turmeric, garlic, cumin and about 1 tbsp of the chopped cilantro. Process briefly to mix, then add salt and pepper to taste.

2 Working with clean, wet hands, shape the chick-pea mixture into about sixteen small balls.

3 Heat the oil for deep-frying to 350°F or until a cube of bread, when added to the oil, browns in 30–45 seconds. Deep-fry the falafel in batches for 2–3 minutes or until golden. Drain on paper towels. Then place in a serving bowl.

4 Stir the remaining cilantro and the chili into the mayonnaise. Garnish with the cilantro sprig, and serve alongside the falafel.

Deep-fried Florets with Tangy Thyme Mayonnaise

Cauliflower and broccoli make a sensational snack when coated in a beer batter and deep-fried. Serve with a tangy mayonnaise.

Serves 2–3

INGREDIENTS
6 oz cauliflower
6 oz broccoli
2 eggs, separated
2 tbsp olive oil
1 cup beer
1¼ cups all-purpose flour
pinch of salt
2 tbsp shredded fresh basil
vegetable oil for deep-frying
⅔ cup good quality mayonnaise
2 tsp chopped fresh thyme
2 tsp grated lemon rind
2 tsp lemon juice
sea salt, for sprinkling

eggs *basil* *all-purpose flour*
mayonnaise *broccoli*
cauliflower *beer*
thyme *lemon*

1 Break the cauliflower and broccoli into small florets, cutting large florets into smaller pieces. Set aside.

2 Beat the egg yolks, olive oil, beer, flour and salt in a bowl. Strain the batter, if necessary, to remove any lumps.

3 Whisk the egg whites until stiff. Fold into the batter with the basil.

4 Heat the oil for deep-frying to 350°F or until a cube of bread, when added to the oil, browns in about 30–45 seconds. Dip the florets in the batter, and deep-fry in batches for 2–3 minutes until the coating is golden and crisp. Drain on paper towels.

5 Mix the mayonnaise, thyme, lemon rind and juice in a small bowl.

6 Sprinkle the florets with sea salt and then serve with the thyme mayonnaise.

Cannellini Bean Dip

This soft bean dip or pâté is good spread on wheat crackers or toasted English muffins. Alternatively, it can be served with wedges of tomato and a crisp green salad.

Serves 4

INGREDIENTS
1 can (14 oz) cannellini beans
grated rind and juice of 1 lemon
2 tbsp olive oil
1 garlic clove, finely chopped
2 tbsp chopped fresh parsley
red Tabasco sauce, to taste
cayenne pepper
salt and black pepper

cannellini
beans

olive oil

lemon juice
and rind

garlic

parsley

red Tabasco
sauce

cayenne
pepper

1 Drain the beans in a strainer and rinse them well under cold water. Transfer to a shallow bowl.

2 Use a potato masher to roughly mash the beans, then stir in the lemon and olive oil.

3 Stir in the chopped garlic and parsley. Add Tabasco sauce and salt and black pepper to taste.

4 Spoon the mixture into a small bowl and dust lightly with cayenne pepper. Chill until ready to serve.

VARIATION
Other beans can be used for this dip – for example, pinto beans or kidney beans.

Hummus

This nutritious dip can be served with vegetable crudités or packed into a salad-filled pita, but it is best spread thickly on hot buttered toast.

Serves 4

INGREDIENTS
1 can (14 oz) chick-peas,
   drained
2 garlic cloves
2 tbsp tahini or smooth
   peanut butter
¼ cup olive oil
juice of 1 lemon
½ tsp cayenne pepper
1 tbsp sesame seeds
sea salt

garlic

chick-peas

sea salt

tahini

olive oil

lemon juice

cayenne pepper

sesame seeds

COOK'S TIP
Tahini is a thick and oily paste made from sesame seeds. It is available at health-food stores and supermarkets. Tahini is a classic ingredient in this Middle-Eastern dip; peanut butter would not be used in a traditional recipe but it is a convenient substitute.

1 Rinse the chick-peas well and place them in a blender or food processor with the garlic and a good pinch of sea salt. Process until very finely chopped.

2 Add the tahini or peanut butter and process until fairly smooth. With the motor still running, slowly pour in the oil and lemon juice.

3 Stir in the cayenne pepper and add more salt, to taste. If the mixture is too thick, stir in a little cold water. Transfer the purée to a serving bowl.

4 Heat a small non-stick pan and add the sesame seeds. Cook for 2–3 minutes, shaking the pan, until the seeds are golden. Let cool, then sprinkle over the purée.

Creamy Eggplant Dip

Spread this velvet-textured dip thickly onto toasted rounds of bread, then top them with slivers of sun-dried tomato to make wonderful, Italian-style crostini.

Serves 4

INGREDIENTS
1 large eggplant
1 small onion
2 garlic cloves
2 tbsp olive oil
¼ cup chopped fresh parsley
5 tbsp crème fraîche
red Tabasco sauce, to taste
juice of 1 lemon, to taste
salt and pepper

eggplant

garlic

onion

olive oil

parsley

crème fraîche

red Tabasco sauce

lemon juice

1 Preheat the broiler. Place the whole eggplant on a baking sheet and broil it for 20–30 minutes, turning occasionally, until the skin is blackened and wrinkled, and the eggplant feels soft when squeezed.

2 Cover the eggplant with a clean dish towel and let cool for about 5 minutes.

3 Finely chop the onion and garlic. Heat the oil in a frying pan and cook the onion and garlic for 5 minutes, until softened but not browned.

4 Peel the skin from the eggplant. Mash the flesh with a large fork or potato masher to make a pulpy purée.

5 Stir in the onion and garlic, parsley and crème fraîche. Add Tabasco, lemon juice and salt and pepper to taste.

6 Transfer the dip to a serving bowl and serve warm, or let cool and serve at room temperature.

COOK'S TIP
The eggplant can be roasted in the oven at 400°F for about 20 minutes, if preferred.

Blue Cheese Dip

This dip can be mixed up in next-to-no-time and is delicious served with pears. Add more yogurt to make a great dressing.

Serves 4

INGREDIENTS
5 oz blue cheese, such as
    Stilton or Danish Blue
⅔ cup cream cheese
5 tbsp plain yogurt
salt and pepper

blue cheese

cream cheese

plain yogurt

1 Crumble the blue cheese into a bowl. Using a wooden spoon, beat the cheese to soften it.

2 Add the cream cheese and beat well to blend the two cheeses together.

3 Gradually beat in the plain yogurt, adding enough to give you the consistency you prefer.

4 Season with lots of black pepper and a little salt. Chill until ready to serve.

COOK'S TIP
This is a very thick dip to which you can add a little more plain yogurt, or stir in a little milk, for a softer consistency.

Red Onion Raita

Raita is a traditional Indian accompaniment for hot curries. It is also delicious served with poppadums as a dip.

Serves 4

INGREDIENTS
1 tsp cumin seeds
1 small garlic clove
1 small green chili, seeded
1 large red onion
⅔ cup plain yogurt
2 tbsp chopped fresh
   cilantro, plus extra, to garnish
½ tsp sugar
salt

cumin seeds

garlic

green chili

red onion

cilantro

yogurt

sugar

1 Heat a small pan and dry-fry the cumin seeds for 1–2 minutes, until they release their aroma and begin to pop.

2 Lightly crush the seeds in a mortar and pestle or flatten them with the heel of a heavy-bladed knife.

3 Finely chop the garlic, chili and red onion. Stir into the yogurt with the crushed cumin seeds and cilantro.

4 Add sugar and salt to taste. Spoon the raita into a small bowl and chill until ready to serve. Garnish with extra cilantro before serving.

COOK'S TIP

For an extra tangy raita, stir in 1 tbsp lemon juice. To make a pretty garnish, reserve a few thin wedges of onion before chopping the rest.

Mellow Garlic Dip

Two whole heads of garlic may seem like a lot but, once cooked, it becomes sweet and mellow. Serve with crunchy bread sticks and chips.

Serves 4

INGREDIENTS
2 whole garlic heads
1 tbsp olive oil
¼ cup mayonnaise
5 tbsp plain yogurt
1 tsp whole-grain mustard
salt and pepper

garlic

olive oil

mayonnaise

plain yogurt

whole-grain mustard

1 Preheat the oven to 400°F. Separate the garlic cloves and place them in a small roasting pan.

3 Trim off the root end of each roasted garlic clove. Peel the cloves and discard the skins.

2 Pour the olive oil over the garlic cloves and turn them with a spoon to coat them evenly. Roast for 20–30 minutes, until the garlic is tender and softened. Let cool for 5 minutes.

4 Place the roasted garlic on a cutting board and sprinkle with salt. Mash with a fork until puréed.

5 Place the garlic in a small bowl and stir in the mayonnaise, yogurt and whole-grain mustard.

COOK'S TIP

If you are already cooking on a barbecue, leave the garlic heads whole and cook them on the hot grill until tender, then peel and mash.

VARIATION

For a low-fat version of this dip, use reduced-fat mayonnaise and low-fat plain yogurt.

6 Check and adjust the seasoning, then spoon the dip into a bowl. Cover and chill until ready to serve.

Tsatziki

Serve this classic Greek dip with strips of toasted pita bread.

Serves 4

INGREDIENTS
1 small cucumber
4 scallions
1 garlic clove
scant 1 cup plain
    yogurt
3 tbsp chopped fresh mint
fresh mint sprig, to garnish (optional)
salt and pepper

small cucumber

garlic

scallions

plain yogurt

mint

1 Trim the ends from the cucumber, then cut it into ¼-in dice.

2 Trim the scallions and garlic, then chop both very finely.

3 Beat the yogurt until smooth, if necessary, then gently stir in the cucumber, onions, garlic and mint.

4 Transfer the mixture to a serving bowl and add salt and plenty of freshly ground black pepper to taste. Chill until ready to serve and then garnish with a small mint sprig, if desired.

COOK'S TIP

Choose a good quality yogurt for this dip – a thick, rich yogurt will give the dip a deliciously rich, creamy texture.

Guacamole

Nachos or tortilla chips are the perfect accompaniment for this classic Mexican dip.

Serves 4

INGREDIENTS
2 ripe avocados
2 red chilies, seeded
1 garlic clove
1 shallot
2 tbsp olive oil, plus extra
   to serve
juice of 1 lemon
salt
chopped cilantro, to garnish

avocados

red chilies

shallot

olive oil

garlic

cilantro

lemon juice

1 Halve the avocados, remove their pits and, using a spoon, scoop out their flesh into a bowl.

2 Mash the flesh well with a potato masher or a large fork.

3 Finely chop the chilies, garlic and shallot, then stir into the mashed avocado with the olive oil and lemon juice. Add salt to taste.

4 Spoon the mixture into a small serving bowl. Drizzle on a little olive oil and scatter with chopped cilantro. Serve immediately.

VARIATION

Make a completely smooth guacamole by mixing the ingredients in a blender or food processor. For a chunkier version, add a diced tomato or red bell pepper.

Ratatouille Crêpes

These crêpes are made slightly thicker than usual to hold the juicy vegetable filling.

Serves 4

INGREDIENTS
¾ cup flour
¼ cup oatmeal
1 egg
1¼ cups skim milk
mixed salad, to serve

FOR THE FILLING
1 large eggplant, cut into 1 in
   cubes
1 garlic clove, crushed
2 medium zucchini, sliced
1 green bell pepper, seeded and sliced
1 red bell pepper, seeded and sliced
5 tbsp vegetable stock
7 oz can chopped tomatoes
1 tsp cornstarch
salt and freshly ground black pepper

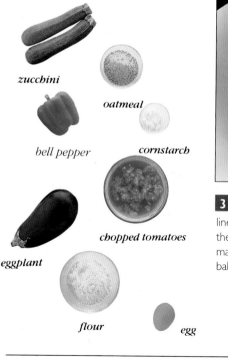

zucchini

oatmeal

bell pepper

cornstarch

chopped tomatoes

eggplant

flour

egg

1 Sift the flour and a pinch of salt into a bowl. Stir in the oatmeal. Make a well in the center, add the egg and half the milk and mix to a smooth batter. Gradually beat in the remaining milk. Cover the bowl and leave to stand for 30 minutes.

2 Spray a 7 in crêpe pan or heavy frying pan with non-stick cooking spray. Heat the pan, then pour in just enough batter to cover the base of the pan thinly. Cook for 2–3 minutes, until the underside is golden brown. Flip over and cook for a further 1–2 minutes.

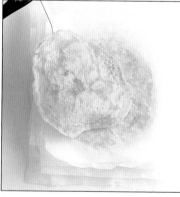

3 Slide the crêpe out onto a plate lined with non-stick baking paper. Stack the other crêpes on top as they are made, interleaving each with non-stick baking paper. Keep warm.

4 For the filling, put the eggplant in a colander and sprinkle well with salt. Leave to stand on a plate for 30 minutes. Rinse thoroughly and drain well.

5 Put the garlic clove, zucchini, peppers, stock and tomatoes into a large saucepan. Simmer uncovered and stir occasionally for 10 minutes. Add the eggplant and cook for a further 15 minutes. Blend the cornstarch with 2 tsp water and add to the saucepan. Simmer for 2 minutes. Season to taste.

6 Spoon the ratatouille mixture into the middle of each crêpe. Fold each one in half, then in half again to make a cone shape. Serve hot with a mixed salad.

Cucumber and Alfalfa Tortillas

Wheat tortillas are extremely simple to prepare at home. Served with a crisp, fresh salsa, they make a marvelous light lunch or supper dish.

Serves 4

INGREDIENTS
2 cups flour, sifted
pinch of salt
3 tbsp olive oil
½–⅔ cup warm water
lime wedges, to garnish

FOR THE SALSA
1 red onion, finely chopped
1 fresh red chili, seeded and finely chopped
2 tbsp chopped fresh dill or cilantro
½ cucumber, peeled and chopped
6 oz alfalfa sprouts

FOR THE SAUCE
1 large ripe avocado, peeled and pitted
juice of 1 lime
2 tbsp soft goat cheese
pinch of paprika

COOK'S TIP
When peeling the avocado be sure to scrape off the bright green flesh from immediately under the skin as this gives the sauce its vivid green color.

avocado

goat cheese

red chili

cucumber

dill

alfalfa sprouts

1 Mix all the salsa ingredients together in a bowl and set aside.

2 To make the sauce, place the avocado, lime juice and goat cheese in a food processor or blender and blend until smooth. Place in a bowl and cover with plastic wrap. Dust with paprika just before serving.

3 To make the tortillas, place the flour and salt in a food processor, add the oil and blend. Gradually add the water (the amount will vary depending on the type of flour). Stop adding water when a stiff dough has formed. Turn out onto a floured board and knead until smooth. Cover with a damp cloth.

4 Divide the mixture into 8 pieces. Knead each piece for a couple of minutes and form into a ball. Flatten and roll out each ball to a 9 in circle.

5 Heat an ungreased cast-iron pan. Cook 1 tortilla at a time for about 30 seconds on each side. Place the cooked tortillas in a clean dish-towel and repeat until you have 8 tortillas.

6 To serve, spread each tortilla with a spoonful of avocado sauce, top with salsa and roll up. Garnish with lime wedges.

Baked Herb Crêpes

These mouth-watering, light herb crêpes make a striking appetizer at a dinner party, but are equally splendid served with a crisp salad for lunch.

Serves 4

INGREDIENTS
2 tbsp chopped fresh herbs
  (e.g. parsley, thyme, and chervil)
1 tbsp sunflower oil, plus extra for
  frying
½ cup skim milk
3 eggs
¼ cup flour
pinch of salt
1 tbsp olive oil

FOR THE SAUCE
2 tbsp olive oil
1 small onion, chopped
2 garlic cloves, crushed
1 tbsp grated fresh ginger root
1 × 14 oz can chopped tomatoes

FOR THE FILLING
1 lb fresh spinach
¾ cup ricotta cheese
2 tbsp pine nuts, toasted
5 halves sun-dried tomatoes in olive
  oil, drained and chopped
2 tbsp shredded fresh basil
salt, nutmeg and freshly ground black
  pepper
4 egg whites

2 Heat a small non-stick crêpe or frying pan and add a very small amount of oil. Pour out any excess oil and pour in a ladleful of the batter. Swirl around to cover the base. Cook for 1–2 minutes, turn over and cook the other side. Repeat with the remaining batter to make 8 crêpes.

3 To make the sauce, heat the oil in a small pan. Add the onion, garlic and ginger and cook gently for 5 minutes until softened. Add the tomatoes and cook for a further 10–15 minutes until the mixture thickens. Purée in a blender, strain and set aside.

1 To make the crêpes, place the herbs and oil in a blender and blend until smooth, pushing down any whole pieces with a spatula. Add the milk, eggs, flour and salt and process again until smooth and pale green. Leave to rest for 30 minutes.

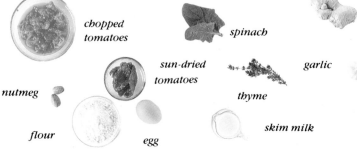

onion

parsley

ginger root

chopped tomatoes

spinach

sun-dried tomatoes

garlic

nutmeg

thyme

flour

egg

skim milk

4 To make the filling, wash the spinach, removing any large stalks, and place in a large pan with only the water that clings to the leaves. Cover and cook, stirring once, until the spinach has just wilted. Remove from the heat and refresh in cold water. Place in a sieve or colander, squeeze out the excess water and chop finely. Mix the spinach with the ricotta, pine nuts, sun-dried tomatoes and basil. Season with salt, nutmeg and freshly ground black pepper.

5 Preheat the oven to 375°F. Whisk the 4 egg whites until they form stiff peaks but are not dry. Fold ⅓ into the spinach and ricotta to lighten the mixture, then gently fold in the rest.

6 Taking one crêpe at a time, place on a lightly oiled cookie sheet. Place a large spoonful of filling on each one and fold into quarters. Repeat until all the filling and crêpes are used up. Bake in the oven for 10–15 minutes or until set. Reheat the tomato sauce to serve with the crêpes.

COOK'S TIP
If preferred, use plain sun-dried tomatoes without any oil, and soak them in warm water for 20 minutes before using.

Buckwheat Blinis

These delectable light pancakes originated in Russia. For a special occasion, serve with a small glass of chilled vodka.

Serves 4

INGREDIENTS
1 tsp easy-blend dry yeast
1 cup skim or low-fat milk, warmed
⅓ cup buckwheat flour
⅓ cup flour
2 tsp sugar
pinch of salt
1 egg, separated
oil, for frying

FOR THE AVOCADO CREAM
1 large avocado
⅓ cup low-fat ricotta cheese
juice of 1 lime

FOR THE PICKLED BEETS
8 oz beets
3 tbsp lime juice
snipped chives, to garnish
cracked black peppercorns, to garnish

beets

egg   *avocado*

buckwheat flour

lime   *chives*

ricotta cheese

skim milk

1 Mix the dry yeast with the milk, then mix with the next 4 ingredients and the egg yolk. Cover with a cloth and leave to prove for about 40 minutes. Whisk the egg white until stiff but not dry and fold into the blini mixture.

2 Heat a little oil in a non-stick pan and add a ladleful of batter to make a 4 in pancake. Cook for 2–3 minutes on each side. Repeat with the remaining batter mixture to make 8 blinis.

3 Cut the avocado in half and remove the pit. Peel and place the flesh in a blender with the ricotta cheese and lime juice. Blend until smooth.

4 Peel the beets and shred finely. Mix with the lime juice. To serve, top each blini with a spoonful of avocado cream. Serve with the pickled beets and garnish with snipped chives and cracked black peppercorns.

Vegetable Fajita

A colorful medley of mushrooms and bell peppers in a spicy sauce, wrapped in tortillas and served with creamy guacamole.

Serves 2

INGREDIENTS
1 onion
1 red bell pepper
1 green bell pepper
1 yellow bell pepper
1 garlic clove, crushed
8 oz mushrooms
6 tbsp vegetable oil
2 tbsp medium chili powder
salt and freshly ground black pepper

FOR THE GUACAMOLE
1 ripe avocado
1 shallot, coarsely chopped
1 green chili, seeded and
  coarsely chopped
juice of 1 lime

TO SERVE
4–6 flour tortillas, warmed
1 lime, cut into wedges
cilantro sprigs

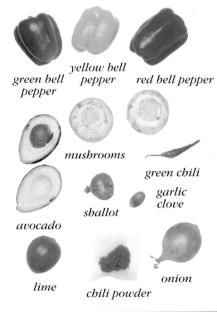

green bell pepper

yellow bell pepper

red bell pepper

mushrooms

green chili

garlic clove

shallot

avocado

lime

chili powder

onion

1 Slice the onion. Cut the bell peppers in half, remove the seeds, and cut the flesh into strips. Combine the onion and peppers in a bowl. Add the crushed garlic, and mix lightly.

2 Remove the mushroom stalks. Save for making stock, or discard. Slice the mushroom caps, and add to the pepper mixture in the bowl. Mix the oil and chili powder in a cup, pour over the vegetable mixture, and stir well. Set aside.

3 Make the guacamole. Cut the avocado in half, and remove the pit and the peel. Put the flesh into a food processor or blender with the shallot, green chili and lime juice. Process for 1 minute until smooth. Scrape into a small bowl, cover tightly, and put in the refrigerator to chill until required.

4 Heat a frying pan or wok until very hot. Add the marinated vegetables, and stir-fry over a high heat for 5–6 minutes until the mushrooms and pepper are just tender. Season well. Spoon a little of the filling on to each tortilla, and roll up. Garnish with fresh cilantro, and serve with the guacamole and lime wedges.

Egg and Lentil Curry

A few Indian spices can transform eggs and lentils into a tasty, economical curry.

Serves 4

INGREDIENTS

⅓ cup green lentils
3 cups vegetable broth
6 eggs
2 tablespoons oil
3 cloves
¼ teaspoon black peppercorns
1 onion, finely chopped
2 green chilies, finely chopped
2 garlic cloves, crushed
1-inch piece ginger root,
    finely chopped
2 tablespoons curry paste
14-ounce can chopped tomatoes
½ teaspoon sugar
½ teaspoon garam masala

vegetable broth

chopped tomatoes

green lentils

onion

green chili

oil

curry paste

ginger

garlic

garam masala

eggs

cloves

sugar

black peppercorns

1 Wash the lentils under cold running water, checking for small stones. Put in a large heavy-bottomed saucepan with the broth. Cover and simmer gently for about 15 minutes or until the lentils are soft. Drain and set aside.

2 Cook the eggs in boiling water for 10 minutes. When cool enough to handle, peel and cut in half lengthwise.

3 Heat the oil in a large saucepan and fry the cloves and peppercorns for about 2 minutes. Add the onion, chilies, garlic and ginger and fry the mixture for another 5-6 minutes.

4 Stir in the curry paste and fry for 2 minutes.

5 Stir in the tomatoes and sugar with ³/₄ cup water.

6 Simmer for 5 minutes until the sauce thickens. Add the eggs, drained lentils and garam masala. Cover and simmer for about 10 minutes, then serve.

Sweet Potato Roulade

Sweet potato works particularly well as the base for this roulade. Serve in thin slices for a truly impressive dinner party dish.

Serves 6

INGREDIENTS

1 cup low-fat ricotta cheese
5 tbsp low-fat yogurt
6–8 scallions, finely sliced
2 tbsp chopped brazil nuts, roasted
1 lb sweet potatoes, peeled and
   coarsely cubed
12 allspice berries, crushed
4 eggs, separated
¼ cup Edam or Gouda cheese, finely
   grated
salt and freshly ground black pepper
1 tbsp sesame seeds

yogurt

sesame seeds

sweet potato

ricotta cheese

Edam

brazil nuts

scallions

peppercorns

egg

1 Preheat the oven to 400°F. Grease and line a 13 × 10 in jelly roll pan with parchment paper, snipping the corners with scissors to fit neatly into the pan.

2 In a small bowl, mix together the ricotta, yogurt, scallions and brazil nuts. Set aside.

3 Boil or steam the sweet potato until tender. Drain well. Place in a food processor with the allspice and blend until smooth. Spoon into a bowl and stir in the egg yolks and Edam. Season to taste.

4 Whisk the egg whites until stiff but not dry. Fold ⅓ of the egg whites into the sweet potatoes to lighten the mixture before gently folding in the rest.

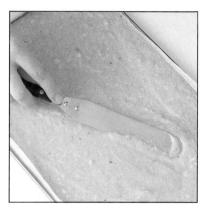

5 Pour into the prepared pan, tipping it to get the mixture right into the corners. Smooth gently with a spatula and cook in the oven for 10–15 minutes.

COOK'S TIP
Choose the orange-fleshed variety of sweet potato for the most striking color.

6 Meanwhile, lay a large sheet of waxed paper on a clean dish-towel and sprinkle with the sesame seeds. When the roulade is cooked, tip it onto the paper, trim the edges and roll it up. Leave to cool. When cool carefully unroll, spread with the filling and roll up again. Cut into slices to serve.

Spanish Omelet

Spanish omelet belongs in every cook's repertoire and can vary according to what you have in store. This version includes white beans and is finished with a layer of toasted sesame seeds.

VARIATION

You can also use sliced cooked potatoes, any seasonal vegetables, baby artichoke hearts and chick-peas in a Spanish omelet.

Serves 4

INGREDIENTS
2 tbsp olive oil
1 tsp sesame oil
1 Spanish onion, chopped
1 small red bell pepper, deseeded and diced
2 celery stalks, chopped
1 × 14 oz can soft white beans, drained
8 eggs
3 tbsp sesame seeds
salt and freshly ground black pepper
4 oz green salad, to serve

celery

red bell pepper

white beans

sesame oil

sesame seeds

eggs

1 Heat the olive and sesame oils in a 12 in paella or frying pan. Add the onion, pepper and celery and cook to soften without coloring.

2 Add the beans and continue to cook for several minutes to heat through.

3 In a small bowl beat the eggs with a fork, season well and pour over the ingredients in the pan.

4 Stir the egg mixture with a flat wooden spoon until it begins to stiffen, then allow to firm over a low heat for about 6–8 minutes.

5 Preheat a moderate broiler. Sprinkle the omelette with sesame seeds and brown evenly under the broiler.

6 Cut the omelet into thick wedges and serve warm with a green salad.

Omelet aux Fines Herbs

Eggs respond well to fast cooking and combine beautifully with a handful of fresh herbs. Serve with French fries and a green salad.

Serves 1

INGREDIENTS
3 eggs
2 tbsp chopped fresh parsley
2 tbsp chopped fresh chervil
2 tbsp chopped fresh tarragon
1 tbsp chopped fresh chives
1 tbsp butter
salt and freshly ground black pepper
12 oz frozen French fries,
   to serve
4 oz green salad, to serve
1 tomato, to serve

eggs

tarragon

chives

chervil

butter

parsley

1 Break the eggs into a bowl, season to taste and beat with a fork, then add the chopped herbs.

2 Heat an omelet or frying pan over a high heat, add the butter and cook until it foams and browns. Quickly pour in the beaten egg and stir briskly with the back of the fork. When the egg is two-thirds scrambled, let the omelet finish cooking for 10–15 seconds more.

3 Tap the handle of the omelet or frying pan sharply with your fist to make the omelet jump up the sides of the pan, fold and turn onto a plate. Serve with French fries, green salad and a halved tomato.

COOK'S TIP

From start to finish, an omelet should be cooked and on the table in less than a minute. For best results use free-range eggs at room temperature.

Soufflé Omelet

This delectable soufflé omelet is light and delicate enough to melt in your mouth.

Serves 1

INGREDIENTS
2 eggs, separated
2 tbsp cold water
1 tbsp chopped fresh cilantro
salt and freshly ground black pepper
½ tbsp olive oil
2 tbsp mango chutney
¼ cup Jarlsberg or Swiss cheese, grated

Jarlsberg

mango chutney

eggs

cilantro

COOK'S TIP

A light hand is essential to the success of this dish. Do not overmix the egg whites into the yolks or the mixture will be heavy.

1 Beat the egg yolks together with the cold water, cilantro and seasoning.

2 Whisk the egg whites until stiff but not dry and gently fold into the egg yolk mixture.

3 Heat the oil in a frying pan, pour in the egg mixture and reduce the heat. Do not stir. Cook until the omelet becomes puffy and golden brown on the underside (carefully lift one edge with a spatula to check).

4 Spoon on the chutney and sprinkle on the Jarlsberg. Fold over and slide onto a warm plate. Eat immediately. (If preferred, before adding the chutney and cheese, place the pan under a hot broiler to set the top.)

Tomato Omelet Envelopes

Delicious chive omelet, folded and filled with a tasty tomato mixture and lots of melting Camembert cheese.

Serves 2

INGREDIENTS
1 small onion
4 tomatoes
2 tbsp vegetable oil
4 eggs
2 tbsp chopped fresh chives
4 oz Camembert cheese, rind
  removed and diced
salt and freshly ground black pepper

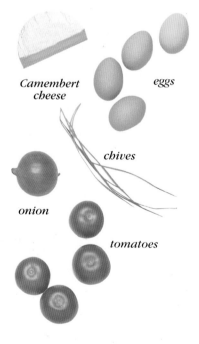

Camembert cheese

eggs

chives

onion

tomatoes

1 Cut the onion in half. Cut each half into thin wedges. Cut the tomatoes into wedges of similar size.

2 Heat 1 tbsp of the oil in a frying pan. Cook the onion for 2 minutes over a moderate heat. Then raise the heat, and add the tomato wedges. Cook for 2 minutes more. Then remove the pan from the heat.

3 Beat the eggs with the chives in a bowl. Add salt and pepper to taste. Heat the remaining oil in an omelet pan. Add half the egg mixture, and tilt the pan to spread thinly. Cook for 1 minute.

4 Flip the omelet over, and cook for 1 minute more. Remove from the pan, and keep hot. Make a second omelet with the remaining egg mixture.

5 Return the tomato mixture to a high heat. Add the cheese, and toss the mixture over the heat for 1 minute.

6 Divide the mixture between the omelets, and fold them over. Serve at once. Add crisp lettuce leaves and chunks of whole-wheat bread, if desired.

COOK'S TIP
You may need to wipe the pan clean between the omelets, and reheat a little more oil.

Stir-fried Vegetables with Cilantro Omelet

This is a great supper dish for vegetarians. The glaze is added here only to make the mixture shine, it is not intended as a sauce.

Serves 3–4

INGREDIENTS
FOR THE OMELET
2 eggs
2 tbsp water
3 tbsp chopped cilantro
salt and ground black pepper
1 tbsp peanut oil

FOR THE GLAZED VEGETABLES
1 tbsp cornstarch
2 tbsp dry sherry
1 tbsp sweet chili sauce
½ cup vegetable stock, or
    vegetable bouillon cube
    and water
2 tbsp peanut oil
1 tsp fresh ginger,
    finely grated
6-8 scallions, sliced
4 oz snow peas
1 yellow bell pepper,
    seeded and sliced
4 oz fresh shiitake or
    white mushrooms
3 oz (drained weight)
    canned water chestnuts, rinsed
4 oz beansprouts
½ small Chinese cabbage,
    coarsely shredded

egg

cilantro

snow peas

peanut oil

scallion

mushrooms

yellow pepper

stock

sweet chili sauce

Chinese cabbage

beansprouts

1 Make the omelet: whisk the eggs, water, cilantro and seasoning in a small bowl. Heat the oil in a wok. Pour in the eggs, then tilt the wok so that the mixture spreads to an even layer. Cook over high heat until the edges are slightly crisp.

2 With a wok or spatula, flip the omelet over and cook the other side for about 30 seconds, until lightly browned. Turn the omelet onto a board and allow to cool. When cold, roll up loosely and cut into thin slices. Wipe the wok clean.

3 In a bowl, blend together the cornstarch, soy sauce, chili sauce and stock. Set aside.

4 Heat the wok until hot, add the oil and swirl it around, add the ginger and scallions and stir-fry for a few seconds to flavor the oil. Add the snow peas, pepper, mushrooms and water chestnuts and stir-fry for 3 minutes.

VARIATION
Vary the combination of
vegetables used according to
availability and taste.

5 Add the beansprouts and Chinese
cabbage and stir-fry for 2 minutes.

6 Pour in the glaze ingredients and
cook, stirring, for about 1 minute until
the glaze thickens and coats the
vegetables. Turn the vegetables onto a
warmed serving plate and top with the
omelet shreds. Serve at once.

Pumpkin and Pistachio Risotto

This elegant combination of creamy golden rice and orange pumpkin can be as pale or bright as you like by adding different quantities of saffron.

Serves 4

INGREDIENTS
5 cups fresh vegetable stock or water
generous pinch of saffron threads
2 tbsp olive oil
1 medium onion, chopped
2 garlic cloves, crushed
1 lb arborio rice
2 lb pumpkin, peeled, seeded and cut
    into ¾ in cubes
¾ cup dry white wine
½ oz Parmesan cheese, finely grated
½ cup pistachios
3 tbsp chopped fresh marjoram or
    oregano, plus extra leaves, to
    garnish
salt, freshly grated nutmeg and ground
    black pepper

1 Bring the stock or water to a boil and reduce to a low simmer. Ladle a little stock into a small bowl. Add the saffron threads and leave to infuse.

4 Gradually add the stock or water, a ladleful at a time, allowing the rice to absorb the liquid before adding more and stirring all the time. After 20–30 minutes the rice should be golden yellow and creamy, and *al dente* when tested.

2 Heat the oil in a large saucepan. Add the onion and garlic and cook gently for about 5 minutes until softened. Add the rice and pumpkin and cook for a few more minutes until the rice looks transparent.

3 Pour in the wine and allow it to boil hard. When it is absorbed add ¼ of the stock and the infused saffron and liquid. Stir constantly until all the liquid is absorbed.

saffron

pumpkin

white wine

garlic

onion

marjoram

Parmesan

arborio rice

pistachios

5 Stir in the Parmesan cheese, cover the pan and leave to stand for 5 minutes.

6 To finish, stir in the pistachios and marjoram or oregano. Season to taste with a little salt, nutmeg and pepper, and scatter over a few extra marjoram or oregano leaves.

COOK'S TIP
Italian arborio rice must be used to make an authentic risotto. Choose unpolished white arborio as it contains more starch.

Wild Rice Rösti with Carrot and Orange Purée

Rösti is a traditional dish from Switzerland. This variation has the extra nuttiness of wild rice and a bright simple sauce as a fresh accompaniment.

COOK'S TIP
Make individual rösti and serve topped with a mixed julienne of vegetables for an unusual appetizer

Serves 6

INGREDIENTS
½ cup wild rice
2 lb large potatoes
3 tbsp walnut oil
1 tsp yellow mustard seeds
1 onion, coarsely grated and drained
   in a sieve
2 tbsp fresh thyme leaves
salt and freshly ground black pepper

FOR THE PURÉE
12 oz carrots, peeled and roughly
   chopped
rind and juice of 1 large orange

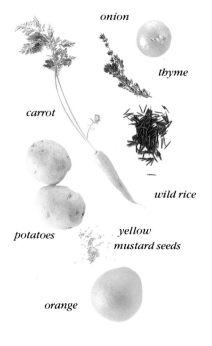

onion

thyme

carrot

wild rice

potatoes

yellow
mustard seeds

orange

1 For the purée, place the carrots in a pan, cover with cold water and add 2 pieces of orange rind. Bring to a boil and cook for 10 minutes or until tender. Drain well and discard the rind.

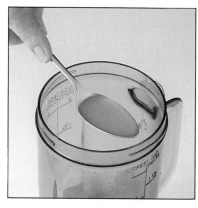

2 Purée the mixture in a blender with 4 tbsp of the orange juice. Return to the pan to reheat.

3 Place the wild rice in a clean pan and cover with water. Bring to a boil and cook for 30–40 minutes, until the rice is just starting to split, but still crunchy. Drain the rice.

4 Scrub the potatoes, place in a large pan and cover with cold water. Bring to a boil and cook for 10–15 minutes until just tender. Drain well and leave to cool slightly. When the potatoes are cool, peel and coarsely grate them into a large bowl. Add the cooked rice.

5 Heat 2 tbsp of the walnut oil in a non-stick frying pan and add the mustard seeds. When they start to pop, add the onion and cook gently for 5 minutes until softened. Add to the bowl of potato and rice, together with the thyme, and mix thoroughly. Season to taste with salt and pepper.

6 Heat the remaining oil in the frying pan and add the potato mixture. Press down well and cook for 10 minutes or until golden brown. Cover the pan with a plate and flip over, then slide the rösti back into the pan for another 10 minutes to cook the other side. Serve with the reheated carrot and orange purée.

Thai Fragrant Rice

A lovely, soft, fluffy rice dish, perfumed with fresh lemon grass.

Serves 4

INGREDIENTS
1 piece of lemon grass
2 limes
1 cup brown basmati rice
1 tbsp olive oil
1 onion, chopped
1 in piece of fresh ginger root, peeled and finely chopped
1½ tsp coriander seeds
1½ tsp cumin seeds
3 cups fresh vegetable stock or water
4 tbsp chopped fresh cilantro
lime wedges, to serve

onion

lime

ginger

lemon grass

coriander seeds

basmati rice

cumin seeds

cilantro

1 Finely chop the lemon grass.

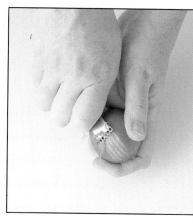

2 Remove the zest from the limes using a zester or fine grater.

3 Rinse the rice in plenty of cold water until the water runs clear. Drain through a sieve.

4 Heat the oil in a large pan and add the onion and spices, lemon grass and lime zest and cook gently for 2–3 minutes.

5 Add the rice and cook for another minute, then add the stock and bring to a boil. Reduce the heat to very low and cover the pan. Cook gently for 30 minutes then check the rice. If it is still crunchy, cover the pan again and leave for a further 3–5 minutes. Remove from the heat.

6 Stir in the fresh cilantro, fluff up the grains, cover and leave for 10 minutes. Serve with lime wedges.

COOK'S TIP

Other varieties of rice, such as white basmati or long grain, can be used for this dish but you will need to adjust the cooking times accordingly.

Red Fried Rice

This vibrant rice dish owes its appeal as much to the bright colors of red onion, red bell pepper and tomatoes as it does to their flavors.

Serves 2

INGREDIENTS
¾ cup basmati rice
2 tbsp peanut oil
1 small red onion, chopped
1 red bell pepper, seeded and chopped
8 oz cherry tomatoes, halved
2 eggs, beaten
salt and freshly ground black pepper

eggs

basmati rice

cherry tomatoes

red onion

red bell pepper

1 Wash the rice several times under cold running water. Drain well. Bring a large pan of water to a boil. Add the rice, and cook for 10–12 minutes.

2 Meanwhile, heat the oil in a wok until very hot. Add the onion and red pepper, and stir-fry for 2–3 minutes. Add the cherry tomatoes, and stir-fry for 2 minutes more.

3 Pour in the beaten eggs all at once. Cook for 30 seconds without stirring, then stir to break up the egg as it sets.

4 Drain the cooked rice thoroughly. Add to the wok, and toss it over the heat with the vegetable and egg mixture for 3 minutes. Season the fried rice with salt and pepper to taste.

Rice and Vegetable Stir-Fry

If you have some leftover cooked rice and a few vegetables to spare, then you've got the basis for this quick and tasty side dish.

Serves 4

INGREDIENTS

1/2 cucumber
1 small red or yellow bell pepper
2 carrots
3 tablespoons sunflower or peanut oil
2 scallions, sliced
1 garlic clove, crushed
1/4 small green cabbage, shredded
scant 1/2 cup cup long-grain rice, cooked
2 tablespoons light soy sauce
1 tablespoon sesame oil
fresh parsley or cilantro, chopped (optional)
1 cup unsalted cashew nuts, almonds or peanuts
salt and freshly ground black pepper

cucumber

scallions

carrots

garlic

bell pepper

green cabbage

soy sauce

long-grain rice

sunflower oil

parsley

sesame oil

cashew nuts

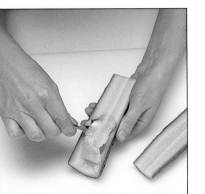

1 Halve the cucumber lengthwise and scoop out the seeds with a teaspoon. Slice the flesh diagonally. Set aside.

2 Cut the red or yellow pepper in half and remove the core and seeds. Slice the pepper thinly.

3 Peel the carrots and cut into thin slices. Heat the oil in a wok or large frying pan and stir-fry the sliced scallions, garlic, carrots and pepper for 3 minutes, until the vegetables are crisp but still tender.

4 Add the cabbage and cucumber and cook for another minute or two, until the leaves begin to wilt. Mix in the rice, soy sauce, sesame oil and seasoning. Reheat the mixture thoroughly, stirring and tossing all the time. Add the herbs, if using, and nuts. Check the seasoning and adjust if necessary. Serve piping hot.

Stuffed Vegetables

Vegetables such as bell peppers make wonderful containers for savory fillings. Instead of sticking to one type of vegetable, serve a selection. Thick, creamy plain yogurt is the ideal accompaniment.

Serves 3-6

INGREDIENTS
1 eggplant
1 large green bell pepper
2 large tomatoes
1 large onion, chopped
2 garlic cloves, crushed
3 tablespoons olive oil
1 cup brown rice
2½ cups vegetable stock
1 cup pine nuts
⅓ cup currants
3 tablespoons chopped fresh dill
3 tablespoons chopped fresh parsley
1 tablespoon chopped fresh mint
extra olive oil, to sprinkle
salt and freshly ground black pepper
strained plain yogurt and fresh dill
      sprigs, to serve

1 Halve the eggplant, scoop out the flesh with a sharp knife and chop finely. Salt the insides of the shells and let drain upside down for 20 minutes while you prepare the other ingredients. Halve the pepper, seed and core.

2 Cut the tops from the tomatoes, scoop out the insides and chop roughly along with the tomato tops. Set the tomato shells aside. Cook the onion, garlic and chopped eggplant in the oil for 10 minutes, then stir in the rice and cook for 2 minutes. Add the tomato flesh, stock, pine nuts, currants and seasoning. Bring to a boil, cover and lower the heat. Simmer for 15 minutes, then stir in the herbs.

eggplant

garlic

tomatoes

yogurt

green bell pepper

onion

olive oil

brown rice

pine nuts

vegetable stock

dill

parsley

mint

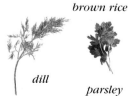
currants

3 Preheat the oven to 375°F. Blanch the eggplant and pepper halves in boiling water for about 3 minutes, then drain them upside down on paper towels.

4 Spoon the rice filling into all six vegetable containers and place on a lightly greased shallow baking dish. Drizzle some olive oil over the stuffed vegetables and bake for 25–30 minutes. Serve hot, topped with spoonfuls of yogurt and the dill sprigs.

Pigeon Peas Cook-up Rice

This African-style rice dish is made with the country's most commonly used peas. It is flavored with creamed coconut.

Serves 4-6

INGREDIENTS
2 tablespoons butter or margarine
1 onion, chopped
1 garlic clove, crushed
2 tablespoons chopped scallions
1 large carrot, diced
about 1 cup pigeon peas
1 fresh thyme sprig or 1 teaspoon
    dried thyme
1 cinnamon stick
2½ cups vegetable stock
4 tablespoons creamed coconut or
    coconut cream (unsweetened)
1 red chili, chopped
2¼ cups long-grain rice
salt and freshly ground black pepper

butter *onion* *scallion*
cinnamon

garlic *carrot* *chili*

vegetable stock

creamed coconut

long-grain rice

thyme

COOK'S TIP

Pigeon peas are also known as Congo peas. The fresh peas can be difficult to obtain, but you will find them in specialty shops. Drain the salted water from canned peas and rinse before using them in this recipe.

1 Melt the butter or margarine in a large, heavy saucepan, add the chopped onion and crushed garlic and sauté over medium heat for about 5 minutes, stirring occasionally.

2 Add the scallions, carrot, pigeon peas, thyme, cinnamon, stock, creamed coconut or coconut cream, chili and seasoning. Bring to a boil.

3 Reduce the heat and stir in the rice. Cover and simmer over low heat for 10–15 minutes, or until all the liquid has been absorbed and the rice is tender. Stir with a fork to fluff up the rice before serving.

Nut Pilaf with Omelet Rolls

A wonderful mixture of textures – soft, fluffy rice with crunchy nuts and omelet rolls.

Serves 2

INGREDIENTS
1 cup basmati rice
1 tbsp sunflower oil
1 small onion, chopped
1 red bell pepper, finely diced
1½ cups hot vegetable bouillon,
  made from a cube
2 eggs
¼ cup salted peanuts
1 tbsp soy sauce
salt and freshly ground black pepper
parsley sprigs, to garnish

salted peanuts *parsley* *onion*

bouillon cube *eggs*

basmati rice *red bell pepper*

soy sauce

1 Wash the rice several times under cold running water. Drain thoroughly. Heat half the oil in a large frying pan. Fry the onion and bell pepper for 2–3 minutes. Then stir in the rice and bouillon. Bring to a boil, and cook for 10 minutes until the rice is tender.

2 Meanwhile, beat the eggs lightly with salt and pepper to taste. Heat the remaining oil in a second large frying pan. Pour in the eggs, and tilt the pan to cover the base thinly. Cook the omelet for 1 minute. Then flip it over, and cook the other side for 1 minute.

3 Carefully slide the omelet on to a clean board, and roll it up tightly. Cut the omelet roll into eight slices.

4 Stir the peanuts and soy sauce into the pilaf, and add black pepper to taste. Turn the pilaf into a serving dish. Arrange the omelet rolls on top, and garnish with the parsley. Serve at once.

Kedgeree with Green Beans and Mushrooms

Crunchy green beans and mushrooms are the star ingredients in this vegetarian version of an old favorite.

Serves 2

INGREDIENTS

¾ cup basmati rice
1¼ cups cold water
3 eggs
6 oz green beans, trimmed
¼ cup butter
1 onion, finely chopped
8 oz crimini mushrooms, quartered
2 tbsp light cream
1 tbsp chopped fresh parsley
salt and freshly ground black pepper

light cream

crimini mushrooms

parsley

onion

butter

green beans

eggs

basmati rice

1 Wash the rice several times under cold running water. Drain thoroughly. Bring a pan of water to a boil. Add the rice, and cook for 10–12 minutes until tender. Drain thoroughly.

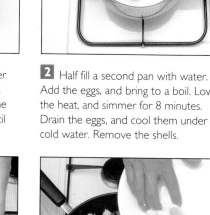

2 Half fill a second pan with water. Add the eggs, and bring to a boil. Lower the heat, and simmer for 8 minutes. Drain the eggs, and cool them under cold water. Remove the shells.

3 Bring another pan of water to a boil, and cook the green beans for 5 minutes. Drain, and refresh under cold running water. Then drain again.

4 Melt the butter in a large frying pan. Add the onions and mushrooms. Cook for 2–3 minutes over a moderate heat.

5 Add the green beans and rice to the onion mixture. Stir lightly to mix. Cook for 2 minutes. Cut the hard-boiled eggs in wedges, and add them to the pan.

6 Stir in the cream and parsley, taking care not to break up the eggs. Reheat the kedgeree, but do not allow it to boil. Serve at once.

Nutty Rice and Mushroom Stir-fry

This delicious and substantial supper dish can be eaten hot or cold with salads.

Serves 4–6

INGREDIENTS
12 oz long grain rice
3 tbsp sunflower oil
1 small onion, roughly chopped
8 oz portabello mushrooms, sliced
½ cup hazelnuts, roughly
 chopped
½ cup pecans, roughly
 chopped
½ cup almonds, roughly
 chopped
4 tbsp fresh parsley, chopped
salt and freshly ground black pepper

rice

almonds

portabello mushrooms

hazelnuts

pecans

1 Rinse the rice, then cook for about 10–12 minutes in 2½–3 cups water in a saucepan with a tight-fitting lid. When cooked, refresh under cold water. Heat the wok, then add half the oil. When the oil is hot, stir-fry the rice for 2–3 minutes. Remove and set aside.

2 Add the remaining oil and stir-fry the onion for 2 minutes until softened.

3 Mix in the portabello mushrooms and stir-fry for 2 minutes.

4 Add all the nuts and stir-fry for 1 minute. Return the rice to the wok and stir-fry for 3 minutes. Season with salt and pepper. Stir in the parsley and serve.

Pilau Rice Flavored with Whole Spices

This fragrant rice dish will make a perfect accompaniment to any Indian meal.

Serves 4-6

INGREDIENTS
generous pinch saffron threads
2½ cups hot vegetable stock
¼ cup butter
1 onion, chopped
1 garlic clove, crushed
½ cinnamon stick
6 green cardamoms
1 bay leaf
⅓ cup golden raisins
1⅓ cups basmati rice, rinsed
   and drained
1 tbsp vegetable oil
½ cup cashews

saffron

stock

cinnamon
stick

onion

bay leaf

butter

oil

garlic

golden
raisins

cardamoms

cashew nuts

basmati
rice

1 Add the saffron threads to the hot stock and set aside. Heat the butter in a large saucepan and fry the onion and garlic for 5 minutes. Stir in the cinnamon stick, cardamoms and bay leaf and cook for 2 minutes.

2 Add the rice and cook, stirring, for 2 minutes more. Pour in the stock and saffron mixture and add the raisins. Bring to a boil, stir, then lower the heat. Cover the pan and leave to cook gently for about 15 minutes or until the rice is tender and all the liquid has been absorbed.

3 Meanwhile, heat the oil in a wok or frying pan and fry the cashew nuts until browned. Drain on kitchen paper. Scatter over the rice and serve.

VARIATION
You can add a mixture of nuts to this recipe, if you like, such as almonds, peanuts or hazelnuts. Some nuts may be bought complete with their brown, papery skins, which should be removed before use. The flavor of all nuts is improved by toasting.

COOK'S TIP
Remember to keep all spices stored in separate airtight containers. This helps them to retain their flavor as well as preventing their aromas from spreading to other ingredients in your pantry.

Vegetable Biryani

Aromatic, spicy rice cooked with fresh vegetables makes a delicious vegetarian main course.

Serves 4–6

INGREDIENTS
1 cup long grain rice
2 whole cloves
seeds of 2 cardamom pods
scant 2 cups vegetable
  stock
2 garlic cloves
1 small onion, coarsely chopped
1 tsp cumin seeds
1 tsp ground coriander
½ tsp ground turmeric
½ tsp chili powder
1 large potato, peeled and cut into
  1 in cubes
2 carrots, sliced
½ cauliflower, broken into florets
2 oz green beans, cut into
  1 in lengths
2 tbsp chopped fresh cilantro
2 tbsp lime juice
salt and freshly ground black pepper
sprig of fresh cilantro, to garnish

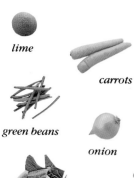

lime

carrots

green beans

onion

cilantro

cauliflower

1 Put the rice, cloves and cardamom seeds into a large, heavy saucepan. Pour over the stock and bring to a boil.

2 Reduce the heat, cover and simmer for 20 minutes, or until all the stock has been absorbed.

3 Meanwhile put the garlic cloves, onion, cumin seeds, coriander, turmeric, chili powder and seasoning into a blender or food processor together with 2 tbsp water. Blend to a paste.

4 Preheat the oven to 350°F. Spoon the spicy paste into a flameproof casserole and cook over a low heat for 2 minutes, stirring occasionally.

5 Add the potato, carrots, cauliflower, beans and 6 tbsp water. Cover and cook over a low heat for a further 12 minutes, stirring occasionally. Add the chopped cilantro.

6 Spoon the rice over the vegetables. Sprinkle over the lime juice. Cover and cook in the oven for 25 minutes, or until the vegetables are tender. Fluff up the rice with a fork before serving and garnish with a sprig of fresh cilantro.

Vegetable Pilaf

Cashews, corn kernels and peas flavor this delicious rice accompaniment.

Serves 4–6

INGREDIENTS
1 cup basmati rice
2 tbsp oil
½ tsp cumin seeds
2 bay leaves
4 cardamom pods
4 cloves
1 onion, finely chopped
1 carrot, finely diced
½ cup frozen peas, thawed
⅓ cup frozen corn
    kernels, thawed
1 oz cashew nuts, lightly fried
2 cups water
¼ tsp ground cumin
¼ tsp ground coriander
½ tsp salt

peas

basmati rice

ground coriander

cumin seeds

carrot

corn kernels

ground cumin

bay leaves

cashew nuts

oil

onion

cardamom pods

cloves

salt

1 Wash the basmati rice in several changes of cold water. Put into a bowl and cover with water. Set aside to soak for 30 minutes.

2 Heat the oil in a large frying pan and fry the cumin seeds for 2 minutes. Add the bay leaves, cardamom pods and cloves and fry for 2 minutes.

3 Add the onion and fry for 5 minutes, until lightly browned.

4 Stir in the carrot and cook for 3–4 minutes.

5 Drain the rice and add to the pan with the peas, corn and cashew nuts. Fry for 4–5 minutes.

6 Add the water, remaining spices and salt. Bring to a boil, cover, and simmer for 15 minutes over low heat, until all the water is absorbed. Allow to stand, covered, for 10 minutes before serving.

Mexican-style Rice

This side dish is the perfect accompaniment to spicy dishes, such as vegetable fajitas. It is garnished with a stunning but dangerous display of flowers made from red chilies.

Serves 6

INGREDIENTS

1¾ cups long grain rice
1 onion, chopped
2 garlic cloves, chopped
1 lb tomatoes, peeled, seeded and chopped
4 tbsp vegetable oil
3¾ cups vegetable stock
1½ cups peas, thawed if frozen
salt and freshly ground black pepper
fresh cilantro and 4–6 chili flowers, to garnish

long grain rice

garlic

onion

tomatoes

corn oil

stock

cilantro

red chilies

peas

1 Soak the rice in a bowl of hot water for 15 minutes. Drain, rinse well under cold running water, drain again and set aside. Combine the onion, garlic and tomatoes in a food processor and process to a purée.

2 Heat the oil in a large frying pan. Add the drained rice and sauté until it becomes golden brown. Using a slotted spoon, to leave behind as much oil as possible, transfer the rice to a saucepan.

COOK'S TIP

To make chili flowers, it is a good idea to wear rubber gloves and avoid touching your face or eyes, as the essential oils will cause a painful reaction. Slice the red chilies from tip to stem end into four or five sections. Place in a bowl of iced water until they curl back to form flowers, then drain. Wash hands or gloves thoroughly.

3 Reheat the oil remaining in the pan and cook the tomato, garlic and onion purée for 2–3 minutes. Tip it into the saucepan of rice and pour in the stock. Season to taste. Bring to a boil, reduce the heat to the lowest possible setting, cover the pan and cook for about 15–20 minutes until almost all the liquid has been absorbed.

4 Stir the peas into the rice mixture and cook, without a lid, until all the liquid has been absorbed and the rice is tender. Stir the mixture from time to time. Transfer the rice to a serving dish and garnish with the drained chili flowers and sprigs of cilantro. Warn the diners that the chili flowers are hot and should be approached with caution.

Leek, Mushroom and Lemon Risotto

A delicious risotto, packed full of flavor, makes a marvelous treat for friends and family.

Serves 4

INGREDIENTS

8 oz trimmed leeks
2–3 cups cremini mushrooms
2 tbsp olive oil
3 garlic cloves, crushed
6 tbsp butter
1 large onion, roughly chopped
1³/₄ cups risotto rice
5 cups simmering vegetable stock
grated zest of 1 lemon
3 tbsp lemon juice
²/₃ cup freshly grated Parmesan
    cheese
¹/₄ cup mixed chopped fresh chives
    and flat-leaf parsley
salt and freshly ground black pepper
lemon wedges, to serve

leeks

olive oil

mushrooms

lemon

butter

risotto rice

Parmesan cheese

onion

parsley

garlic

vegetable stock

chives

1 Wash the leeks well. Slice them in half lengthwise and chop them roughly. Wipe the mushrooms with paper towels and chop them roughly.

2 Heat the oil in a large saucepan and cook the garlic for 1 minute. Add the leeks, mushrooms and plenty of seasoning and cook over medium heat for about 10 minutes, or until softened and browned. Remove from the pan and set aside.

3 Add 2 tablespoons of the butter to the pan. As soon as it has melted, add the onion and cook over medium heat for 5 minutes, until softened and golden.

4 Stir in the rice and cook for about 1 minute, until the grains begin to look translucent and are coated in the fat. Add a ladleful of stock to the pan and cook gently, stirring occasionally, until the liquid has been absorbed.

5 Continue to add stock, a ladleful at a time, until all the stock has been absorbed. This should take 25–30 minutes. The risotto will turn thick and creamy and the rice should be tender but not sticky.

6 Just before serving, stir in the leeks, mushrooms, remaining butter, grated lemon zest and juice. Add half the grated Parmesan and herbs. Adjust the seasoning and sprinkle with the remaining Parmesan and herbs. Garnish with parsley, if you like, and serve with lemon wedges.

Risotto-stuffed Eggplant with Spicy Tomato Sauce

Eggplants are a challenge to the creative cook and allow for some unusual recipe ideas. Here, they are stuffed and baked with a cheese and pine nut topping.

COOK'S TIP

Don't be put off by the amount of oil eggplant absorb when cooking. Use olive oil and remember that good oils are low in saturated fat and are believed to fight against heart disease.

Serves 4

INGREDIENTS
4 small eggplant
7 tbsp olive oil
1 small onion, chopped
scant 1 cup arborio rice
3⅔ cups ready-made or fresh
   vegetable stock
1 tbsp white wine vinegar
8 fresh basil sprigs, to garnish

FOR THE TOPPING
¼ cup freshly grated Parmesan
   cheese
1 tbsp pine nuts

FOR THE TOMATO SAUCE
1¼ cups crushed tomatoes or
   puréed tomatoes
1 tsp mild curry paste
pinch of salt

onion

eggplant

pine nuts

Parmesan cheese

crushed tomatoes

rice

1 Preheat the oven to 400°F. Cut the eggplant in half lengthwise and take out their flesh with a small knife. Brush with 2 tbsp of the oil, place on a baking sheet and cook in the preheated oven for 6–8 minutes.

2 Chop the reserved eggplant flesh and heat the remainder of the olive oil in a medium saucepan. Add the eggplant flesh and the onion and cook over a gentle heat for 3–4 minutes until soft.

3 Add the rice, stir in the stock and simmer uncovered for a further 15 minutes. Stir in the vinegar.

4 Increase the oven temperature to 450°F. Spoon the rice into the eggplant skins, top with cheese and pine nuts, and return to the oven to brown for 5 minutes.

5 To make the sauce, combine the crushed tomatoes or puréed tomatoes with the curry paste, heat and add salt to taste.

6 Spoon the sauce onto four large serving plates and position two eggplant halves on each. Garnish with basil sprigs.

Sweet Vegetable Couscous

A wonderful combination of sweet vegetables and spices, this makes a substantial winter dish.

Serves 4–6

INGREDIENTS

1 generous pinch of saffron threads
3 tbsp boiling water
1 tbsp olive oil
1 red onion, sliced
2 garlic, cloves
1–2 fresh red chilies, seeded and
  finely chopped
½ tsp ground ginger
½ tsp ground cinnamon
1 × 14 oz can chopped
  tomatoes
1¼ cups fresh vegetable stock or
  water
4 medium carrots, peeled and cut into
  ¼ in slices
2 medium turnips, peeled and cut into
  ¾ in cubes
1 lb sweet potatoes, peeled and cut
  into ¾ in cubes
⅓ cup raisins
2 medium zucchini, cut into ¼ in
  slices
1 × 14 oz can chick-peas, drained and
  rinsed
3 tbsp chopped fresh parsley
3 tbsp chopped fresh cilantro
1 lb quick-cooking couscous

1 Leave the saffron to infuse in the boiling water.

2 Heat the oil in a large saucepan. Add the onion, garlic and chilies and cook gently for 5 minutes.

3 Add the ground ginger and cinnamon and cook for a further 1–2 minutes.

4 Add the tomatoes, stock or water, infused saffron and liquid, carrots, turnips, sweet potatoes and raisins, cover and simmer for 25 minutes.

red onion

zucchini

red chili

carrot

garlic

chick-peas

turnip

couscous

sweet potato

chopped tomatoes

raisins

5 Add the zucchini, chick-peas, parsley and cilantro and cook for another 10 minutes.

6 Meanwhile prepare the couscous following the package instructions and serve with the vegetables.

Eggplant Pilaf

This hearty dish is made with bulgur and eggplant, flavored with fresh mint.

Serves 2

INGREDIENTS
2 eggplant
4–6 tbsp sunflower oil
1 small onion, finely chopped
1 cup bulgur
scant 2 cups vegetable bouillon,
  made from a cube
2 tbsp pine nuts, toasted
1 tbsp chopped fresh mint
salt and freshly ground black pepper

FOR THE GARNISH
lime wedges
lemon wedges
torn mint leaves

mint

pine nuts

bouillon cube

onion

bulgur

eggplant

COOK'S TIP
To cut down on the cooking time, soak the bulgur in water to cover by 1 in for up to 8 hours. Drain, and then continue as described in the recipe below, reducing the cooking time to just 8 minutes.

1 Remove the ends from the eggplant. Using a sharp knife, cut them into neat sticks and then into ½ in dice.

2 Heat 4 tbsp of the oil in a large frying pan. Add the onion, and sauté for 1 minute.

3 Add the diced eggplant, Cook over a high heat, stirring frequently, for about 4 minutes until just tender. Add the remaining oil, if needed.

4 Stir in the bulgur, mixing well. Then pour in the vegetable bouillon. Bring to a boil. Then lower the heat, and simmer for 10 minutes or until all the liquid has evaporated. Season to taste.

5 Add the pine nuts, and stir gently with a wooden spoon. Stir in the mint.

6 Spoon the pilaf on to individual plates, and garnish each portion with lime and lemon wedges. Sprinkle with torn mint leaves for extra color.

Buckwheat Couscous with Goat Cheese and Celery

Couscous is made from cracked, partially cooked wheat, which is dried and then reconstituted in water or stock. It tastes of very little by itself, but carries the flavor of other ingredients very well.

Serves 4

INGREDIENTS
1 egg
2 tbsp olive oil
1 small bunch scallions, chopped
2 celery stalks, sliced
1 cup couscous
½ cup buckwheat
3 tbsp chopped fresh parsley
finely grated zest of ½ lemon
¼ cup chopped walnuts, toasted
5 oz strongly flavored goat
   cheese
salt and freshly ground black pepper
Romaine lettuce leaves, to serve

buckwheat

egg

celery

goat
cheese

parsley

walnuts

1 Boil the egg for 10 minutes, cool, peel and set aside. Heat the oil in a saucepan and add the scallions and celery. Cook for 2–3 minutes until soft.

2 Add the couscous and buckwheat and cover with 2½ cups of boiling salted water. Cover and return to a simmer. Remove from the heat and allow the couscous to soften and absorb the water for about 3 minutes. Transfer the mixture to a large bowl.

3 Grate the hard-cooked egg finely into a small bowl and add the chopped parsley, lemon zest and walnuts. Fold into the couscous, season, and crumble in the goat cheese. Mix well and then turn out into a shallow dish. Serve warm with a salad of Romaine lettuce.

VARIATION
Couscous is ideal as a filling for pita breads when accompanied with crisp salad leaves.

Lentil Stir-fry

Mushrooms, artichokes, sugar snap peas and lentils make a satisfying stir-fry supper.

Serves 2–3

INGREDIENTS

4 oz sugar snap peas
1 oz butter
1 small onion, chopped
4 oz cup or white mushrooms,
   sliced
14 oz can artichoke hearts,
   drained and halved
14 oz can green lentils, drained
4 tbsp light cream
1/4 cup shaved almonds, toasted
salt and freshly ground black pepper
French bread, to serve

light cream

green lentils

cup mushrooms

sugar snap peas

shaved almonds

artichoke hearts

onion

1 Bring a pan of salted water to a boil. Add the sugar snap peas, and cook for about 4 minutes until just tender. Drain, and refresh under cold running water. Then drain again. Pat dry the peas with paper towels, and set aside.

2 Melt the butter in a frying pan. Add the chopped onion and cook for 2–3 minutes, stirring occasionally.

3 Add the sliced mushrooms to the onion. Stir until combined. Then cook for 2–3 minutes until just tender. Add the artichokes, sugar snap peas and lentils to the pan. Stir-fry for 2 minutes.

4 Stir in the cream and almonds, and cook for 1 minute. Season to taste. Serve at once, with chunks of French bread.

COOK'S TIP
Use strained, plain yogurt instead of the cream, if you like.

Lentils and Rice

Lentils are cooked with whole and ground spices,
potatoes, rice and onions to produce an
authentic Indian-style risotto.

Serves 4

INGREDIENTS
³/₄ cup red split lentils
½ cup basmati rice
1 large potato
1 large onion
2 tbsp oil
4 whole cloves
¼ tsp cumin seeds
¼ tsp ground turmeric
2 tsp salt
1¼ cups water

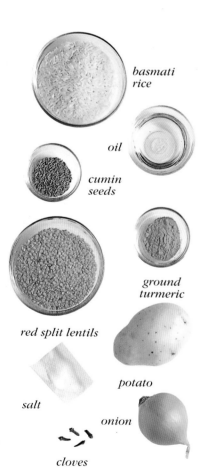

basmati rice

oil

cumin seeds

ground turmeric

red split lentils

potato

salt

onion

cloves

1 Wash the red split lentils and rice in several changes of cold water. Put into a bowl and cover with water. Let soak for 15 minutes then drain.

2 Peel then cut the potato into 1-inch chunks.

3 Thinly slice the onion.

4 Heat the oil in a large heavy-bottomed saucepan and fry the cloves and cumin seeds for 2 minutes, until the seeds are beginning to sputter.

5 Add the onion and potatoes and fry for 5 minutes. Add the lentils, rice, turmeric and salt and fry for 3 minutes.

6 Add the water. Bring to a boil, cover and simmer for 15–20 minutes, until all the water has been absorbed and the potatoes are tender. Let stand, covered, for about 10 minutes before serving.

Mung Beans with Potatoes

Mung beans are one of the quicker-cooking beans which do not require soaking and are therefore very easy to use. In this recipe they are cooked with potatoes and traditional Indian spices to give a tasty nutritious dish.

Serves 4

INGREDIENTS
1 cup mung beans
3 cups water
8 oz potatoes, cut into
    ¾-inch chunks
2 tbsp oil
½ tsp cumin seeds
1 green chili, finely chopped
1 garlic clove, crushed
1-inch piece ginger root,
    finely chopped
¼ tsp ground turmeric
½ tsp cayenne pepper
1 tsp salt
1 tsp sugar
4 curry leaves
5 tomatoes, peeled and
    finely chopped
1 tbsp tomato paste
curry leaves, to garnish
plain rice, to serve

potatoes

mung beans

tomatoes

oil

cayenne
pepper

tomato
paste

ginger

sugar

garlic

cumin
seeds

ground
turmeric

green
chili

curry
leaves

salt

1 Wash the beans. Bring to a boil in the water, cover and simmer until soft, about 30 minutes. Parboil the potatoes for 10 minutes in another saucepan, then drain well.

2 Heat the oil and fry the cumin seeds, until they sputter. Add the chili, garlic and ginger and fry for 3–4 minutes.

3 Add the turmeric, cayenne pepper, salt and sugar and cook for 2 minutes, stirring to prevent the mixture from sticking to the saucepan.

4 Add the curry leaves, tomatoes and tomato paste and simmer for 5 minutes, until the sauce thickens. Add the tomato sauce and potatoes to the mung beans and mix together. Serve with plain boiled rice, and garnish with curry leaves.

Spicy Bean and Lentil Loaf

An appetizing, meat-free and high-fiber savory loaf, ideal for picnics or a packed lunch.

Serves 12

INGREDIENTS

2 tsp olive oil
1 onion, finely chopped
1 garlic clove, crushed
2 stalks celery, finely chopped
1 can (14 oz) red kidney beans,
  rinsed and drained
1 can (14 oz) lentils, rinsed
  and drained
1 egg
1 carrot, coarsely grated
½ cup hazelnuts, finely chopped
½ cup reduced-fat aged Cheddar
  cheese, finely grated,
1 cup fresh whole-wheat
  bread crumbs
1 tbsp tomato paste
1 tbsp ketchup
1 tsp each ground cumin,
  ground coriander and
  chili powder
salt and ground black pepper

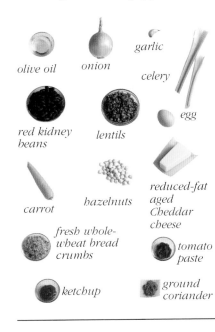

olive oil
onion
garlic
celery
red kidney beans
lentils
egg
carrot
hazelnuts
reduced-fat aged Cheddar cheese
fresh whole-wheat bread crumbs
tomato paste
ketchup
ground coriander
ground cumin
chili powder

1 Preheat the oven to 350°F. Lightly grease a 2-lb loaf pan. Heat the oil in a saucepan, add the onion, garlic and celery and cook gently for 5 minutes, stirring occasionally. Remove the pan from the heat and cool slightly.

2 Rinse and drain the beans and lentils. Put in a blender or food processor with the onion mixture and egg, and process until smooth.

3 Transfer the mixture to a bowl, add all the remaining ingredients and mix well. Season to taste.

4 Spoon the mixture into the prepared pan and level the surface. Bake for about 1 hour, then remove from the pan and serve hot or cold in slices.

Mixed Bean Chili

Serves 6

INGREDIENTS
1 onion, finely chopped
1–2 garlic cloves, crushed
1 large green chili, seeded
   and chopped
²/₃ cup vegetable stock
14 oz can chopped tomatoes
2 tbsp tomato paste
¹/₂ cup red wine
1 tsp dried oregano
7 oz green beans, sliced
14 oz can red kidney
   beans, drained
14 oz can cannellini
   beans, drained
14 oz can chickpeas, drained
1 lb spaghetti
salt and ground black pepper

spaghetti

onion

garlic

green chili

green beans

tomato paste

red kidney beans

cannellini beans

chopped tomatoes

red wine

vegetable stock

chickpeas

1 To make the sauce, put the chopped onion, garlic and chili into a non-stick pan with the stock. Bring to a boil and cook for 5 minutes until tender.

2 Add the tomatoes, tomato paste, wine, seasoning and oregano. Bring to a boil, cover and simmer the sauce for 20 minutes.

3 Cook the green beans in boiling, salted water for about 5–6 minutes until tender. Drain thoroughly.

4 Add all the beans to the sauce and simmer for 10 more minutes. Cook the spaghetti in a large pan of boiling, salted water until *al dente*. Drain thoroughly. Transfer to a serving dish and top with the chili beans.

Chili Bean Bake

The contrasting textures of spicy beans, vegetables and crunchy cornbread topping make this a memorable meal.

Serves 4

INGREDIENTS

1⅓ cups red kidney beans
1 bay leaf
1 large onion, finely chopped
1 garlic clove, crushed
2 celery stalks, sliced
1 tsp ground cumin
1 tsp chili powder
14 oz can chopped tomatoes
1 tbsp tomato paste
1 tsp dried mixed herbs
1 tbsp lemon juice
1 yellow bell pepper, seeded and
    diced
salt and freshly ground black pepper
mixed salad, to serve

FOR THE CORNBREAD TOPPING

1½ cups corn meal
1 tbsp whole-wheat flour
1 tsp baking powder
1 egg, beaten
¾ cup skim milk

kidney beans

celery

tomato paste

bell pepper

1 Soak the beans overnight in cold water. Drain and rinse well. Pour 4 cups of water into a large, heavy saucepan together with the beans and bay leaf and boil rapidly for 10 minutes. Lower the heat, cover and simmer for 35–40 minutes, or until the beans are tender.

2 Add the onion, garlic clove, celery, cumin, chili powder, chopped tomatoes, tomato paste and dried mixed herbs. Half-cover the pan with a lid and simmer for a further 10 minutes.

3 Stir in the lemon juice, yellow pepper and seasoning. Simmer for a further 8-10 minutes, stirring occasionally, until the vegetables are just tender. Discard the bay leaf and spoon the mixture into a large casserole.

4 Preheat the oven to 425°F. For the topping, put the corn meal, flour, baking powder and a pinch of salt into a bowl and mix together. Make a well in the center and add the egg and milk. Mix and pour over the bean mixture. Bake in the preheated oven for 20 minutes, or until brown.

Lemon and Ginger Spicy Beans

An extremely quick delicious meal, made with canned beans for speed. You probably won't need extra salt as canned beans tend to be already salted.

Serves 4

INGREDIENTS
2 tbsp roughly chopped fresh ginger root
3 garlic cloves, roughly chopped
1 cup cold water
1 tbsp sunflower oil
1 large onion, thinly sliced
1 fresh red chili, seeded and finely chopped
¼ tsp cayenne pepper
2 tsp ground cumin
1 tsp ground coriander
½ tsp ground turmeric
2 tbsp lemon juice
⅓ cup chopped fresh cilantro
1 × 14 oz can black-eyed peas, drained and rinsed
1 × 14 oz can adzuki beans, drained and rinsed
1 × 14 oz can navy beans, drained and rinsed
freshly ground black pepper

garlic

red chili

adzuki beans

ginger

ground coriander

black-eyed peas

ground turmeric

ground cumin

navy beans

onion

1 Place the ginger, garlic and 4 tbsp of the cold water in a blender and mix until smooth.

2 Heat the oil in a pan. Add the onion and chili and cook gently for 5 minutes until softened.

3 Add the cayenne pepper, cumin, ground coriander and turmeric and stir-fry for 1 minute.

4 Stir in the ginger and garlic paste from the blender and cook for another minute.

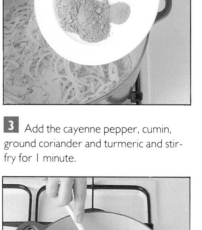

5 Add the remaining water, lemon juice and fresh cilantro, stir well and bring to a boil. Cover the pan tightly and cook for 5 minutes.

6 Add all the beans and cook for a further 5–10 minutes. Season with pepper to taste and serve.

Creamy Cannellini Beans with Asparagus

Cannellini beans in a creamy sauce contrast with tender asparagus in this tasty toast topper.

Serves 2

INGREDIENTS

2 tsp butter
1 small onion, finely chopped
1 small carrot, grated
1 tsp fresh thyme leaves
14 oz can cannellini beans, drained
$2/3$ cup light cream
4 oz young asparagus spears, trimmed
2 slices of fresh sliced whole-wheat bread
salt and freshly ground black pepper

whole-wheat bread   *carrot*   *thyme*

asparagus spears   *butter*

light cream

onion   *cannellini beans*

parsley

1 Melt the butter in a pan. Add the onion and carrot, and fry over a moderate heat for 4 minutes until soft. Add the thyme leaves.

2 Rinse the cannellini beans under cold running water. Drain thoroughly. Then add to the onion and carrot. Mix lightly.

3 Pour in the cream, and heat slowly to just below boiling point, stirring occasionally. Remove the pan from the heat, and add salt and pepper to taste. Preheat the broiler.

4 Place the asparagus spears in a saucepan. Pour over just enough boiling water to cover. Poach for 3–4 minutes until the spears are just tender.

5 Meanwhile, toast the bread under the broiler until both sides are golden.

6 Place the toast on individual plates. Drain the asparagus, and divide the spears between the slices of toast. Spoon the bean mixture over each portion, and serve.

Mixed Bean Curry

You can use any combination of beans that you have in the storecupboard for this recipe.

Serves 4

INGREDIENTS

⅓ cup red kidney beans
⅓ cup black-eyed peas
⅓ cup navy beans
⅓ cup small cannellini beans
2 tbsp oil
1 tsp cumin seeds
1 tsp black mustard seeds
1 onion, finely chopped
2 garlic cloves, crushed
1-inch piece ginger root, grated
2 green chilies, finely chopped
2 tbsp curry paste
½ tsp salt
14-oz can chopped tomatoes
2 tbsp tomato paste
1 cup water
2 tbsp chopped cilantro
chopped cilantro, to garnish

2 Drain the beans and put into a large heavy saucepan with double their volume of cold water. Boil rapidly for 10 minutes. Skim off any scum. Cover and simmer for 1½ hours or until the beans are soft.

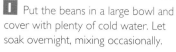

black mustard seeds

chopped tomatoes

curry paste

cumin seeds

red kidney beans

black-eyed peas

oil

onion

tomato paste

navy beans

small cannellini beans

ginger

green chilies

cilantro

garlic

1 Put the beans in a large bowl and cover with plenty of cold water. Let soak overnight, mixing occasionally.

3 Heat the oil in a large saucepan and fry the cumin seeds and mustard seeds for 2 minutes, until the seeds begin to sputter. Add the onion, garlic, ginger and chili and fry for 5 minutes.

4 Add the curry paste and fry for another 2–3 minutes, stirring, then add the salt.

5 Add the tomatoes, tomato paste and the water and simmer for 5 minutes.

6 Add the drained beans and the cilantro. Cover and simmer for about 30–40 minutes, until the sauce thickens and the beans are cooked. Garnish with chopped cilantro.

COOK'S TIP
Depending on the types of beans you use, you may need to adjust the cooking time.

Vegetarian Cassoulet

Every town in southwest France has its own version of this popular classic. Warm French bread is all that is needed to complete this hearty vegetable version.

Serves 4–6

INGREDIENTS
2 cups dried navy beans
1 bay leaf
2 onions
3 whole cloves
2 garlic cloves, crushed
1 tsp olive oil
2 leeks, thickly sliced
12 baby carrots
4 oz white mushrooms
14 oz can chopped tomatoes
1 tbsp tomato paste
1 tsp paprika
1 tbsp chopped fresh thyme
2 tbsp chopped fresh parsley
2 cups fresh white bread crumbs
salt and freshly ground black pepper
sprig of fresh thyme, to garnish

COOK'S TIP
If you're short of time use canned navy beans — you'll need two 14 oz cans. Drain, reserving the bean juices and make up to 1⅔ cups with vegetable stock.

1 Soak the beans overnight in plenty of cold water. Drain and rinse under cold running water. Put them in a saucepan together with 7½ cups of cold water and the bay leaf. Bring to a boil and cook rapidly for 10 minutes.

2 Peel one of the onions and spike with cloves. Add to the beans and reduce the heat. Cover and simmer gently for 1 hour, until the beans are almost tender. Drain, reserving the stock but discarding the bay leaf and onion.

3 Chop the remaining onion and put it into a large flameproof casserole together with the garlic cloves and olive oil. Cook gently for 5 minutes, or until softened.

chopped tomatoes *bay leaf*

leek

bread crumbs

carrots   *mushrooms*

4 Preheat the oven to 325°F. Add the leeks, carrots, mushrooms, chopped tomatoes, tomato paste, paprika, thyme and 1⅔ cups of the reserved stock to the casserole.

5 Bring to a boil, cover and simmer gently for 10 minutes. Stir in the cooked beans and parsley. Season to taste.

6 Sprinkle with the bread crumbs and bake uncovered in the preheated oven for 35 minutes, or until the topping is golden brown and crisp. Serve garnished with a sprig of fresh thyme.

Three Bean Salad with Yogurt Dressing

This tangy bean and pasta salad is great on its own or can be served as a side dish.

Serves 3–4

INGREDIENTS

3 oz penne or other dried
  pasta shapes
2 tomatoes
7 oz canned red kidney beans,
  drained
7 oz canned cannellini beans,
  drained
7 oz canned chick-peas, drained
1 green bell pepper, seeded and
  diced
3 tbsp plain yogurt
2 tbsp sunflower oil
grated rind of ½ lemon
2 tsp whole-grain mustard
1 tsp chopped fresh oregano
salt and freshly ground black pepper

penne

oregano

green bell pepper

red kidney beans

cannellini beans

plain yogurt

chick-peas

lemon

whole-grain mustard

tomatoes

1 Bring a large pan of salted water to a boil. Add the pasta, and cook for 10–12 minutes until just tender. Drain. Cool under cold water, and drain again.

2 Make a cross with the tip of a sharp knife in each of the tomatoes. Plunge them into a bowl of boiling water for 30 seconds. Remove with a slotted spoon or spatula, run under cold water, and peel away the skins. Cut the tomatoes into segments.

3 Drain the canned beans and chick-peas in a colander. Rinse them under cold water, and drain again. Turn into a bowl. Add the tomato segments, green bell pepper and pasta.

4 Whisk the yogurt until smooth. Gradually whisk in the oil, lemon rind and mustard. Stir in the oregano and salt and pepper to taste. Pour the dressing over the salad, and toss well.

Polenta and Baked Tomatoes

A staple of northern Italy, polenta is a nourishing, filling food, served here with a delicious fresh tomato and olive topping.

Serves 4–6

INGREDIENTS
9 cups water
1¼ lb quick-cooking polenta
12 large ripe plum tomatoes, sliced
4 garlic cloves, thinly sliced
2 tbsp chopped fresh oregano or
　marjoram
½ cup black olives, pitted
salt and freshly ground black pepper
2 tbsp olive oil

black olives

marjoram

plum
tomatoes

garlic

oregano

polenta

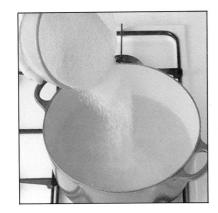

1 Place the water in a large saucepan and bring to a boil. Whisk in the polenta and simmer for 5 minutes.

2 Remove the pan from the heat and pour the thickened polenta into a 9 in × 13 in jelly roll pan. Smooth out the surface with a spatula until level, and leave to cool.

3 Preheat the oven to 350°F. With a 3 in round pastry cutter, stamp out 12 rounds of polenta. Lay them so that they slightly overlap in a lightly oiled ovenproof dish.

4 Layer the tomatoes, garlic, oregano or marjoram and olives on top of the polenta, seasoning the layers as you go. Sprinkle with the olive oil, and bake uncovered for 30–35 minutes. Serve immediately.

Red Bell Pepper Polenta with Sunflower Salsa

This recipe is inspired by Italian and Mexican cookery. Cornmeal polenta is a staple food in Italy, served with brightly colored vegetables. Mexican *Pipian* is a salsa made from sunflower seeds, chili and lime.

Serves 4

INGREDIENTS
3 young zucchinis
oil, for greasing
5 cups light vegetable
   stock
2 cups fine polenta or
   cornmeal
1 × 7 oz jar red peppers, drained
   and sliced
4 oz green salad, to serve

FOR THE SUNFLOWER SALSA
3 oz sunflower seeds, toasted
1 cup crustless white
   bread
scant 1 cup vegetable
   stock
1 garlic clove, crushed
½ red chili, deseeded and chopped
2 tbsp chopped fresh cilantro
1 tsp sugar
1 tbsp lime juice
pinch of salt

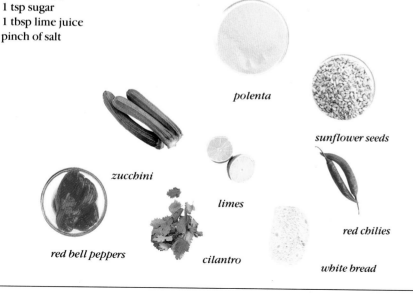

polenta

sunflower seeds

zucchini

limes

red chilies

red bell peppers

cilantro

white bread

1 Bring a saucepan of salted water to a boil. Add the zucchinis and simmer over a low heat for 2–3 minutes. Refresh under cold running water and drain. When they are cool, cut into strips.

2 Lightly oil a 9 in loaf pan and line with a single sheet of waxed paper.

3 Bring the vegetable stock to a simmer in a heavy saucepan. Add the polenta in a steady stream, stirring continuously for about 2–3 minutes until thickened.

4 Partly fill the lined pan with the polenta mixture. Layer the sliced zucchinis and peppers over the polenta. Fill the pan with the remaining polenta and leave to set for about 10–15 minutes. Polenta should be served warm or at room temperature.

COOK'S TIP

Sunflower salsa will keep for up to 10 days in the refrigerator. It is delicious poured over a simple dish of pasta.

5 To make the salsa, grind the sunflower seeds to a thick paste in a food processor. Add the remaining ingredients and combine thoroughly.

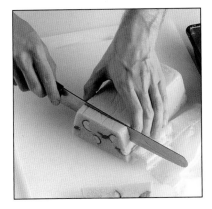

6 Turn the warm polenta out onto a board, remove the paper and cut into thick slices with a large wet knife. Serve with the salsa and a green salad.

PASTA AND NOODLES

Basic Pasta Dough

Serves 3–4

INGREDIENTS
1³/₄ cups all-purpose flour
pinch of salt
2 eggs
2 teaspoons of cold water

Making pasta on a work surface

1 Sift the flour and salt onto a clean work surface and make a well in the center with your hand.

2 Put the eggs and water in the well. Using a fork, beat the eggs gently together, then gradually draw in the flour from the sides to make a thick paste.

3 When the mixture becomes too stiff to use a fork, use your hands to mix until dough is firm. Knead the dough for about 5 minutes, until smooth. (This can be done in an electric food mixer fitted with a dough hook.) Cover with plastic wrap to prevent it drying out and leave to rest for 20–30 minutes.

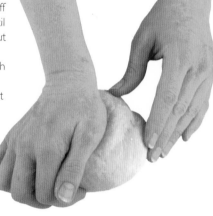

Making pasta in a bowl

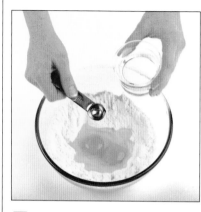

1 Sift the flour and salt into a glass bowl and make a well in the center. Add the eggs and water.

2 Using a fork, beat the eggs gently together, then gradually draw in the flour from the sides, to make a thick paste.

3 When the mixture becomes too stiff to use a fork, use your hands to mix until dough is firm. Knead the dough for 5 minutes until smooth. (This can be done in an electric food mixer fitted with a dough hook.) Cover with plastic wrap to prevent it drying out and leave to rest for 20–30 minutes.

VARIATIONS

TOMATO: add 4 teaspoons of concentrated tomato paste to the eggs before mixing.
SPINACH: add 4 ounces frozen spinach, thawed and squeezed of excess moisture. Moisten with the eggs, before adding to the flour.
HERB: add 3 tablespoons finely chopped fresh herbs to the eggs before mixing the dough.
WHOLE-WHEAT: use 5 ounces whole-wheat flour and 2 ounces all-purpose flour. Add an extra 2 teaspoons cold water (whole-wheat flour will absorb more liquid than white flour).
PAPRIKA: use 1 teaspoon ground paprika sifted with the flour.

Rolling out pasta dough by hand

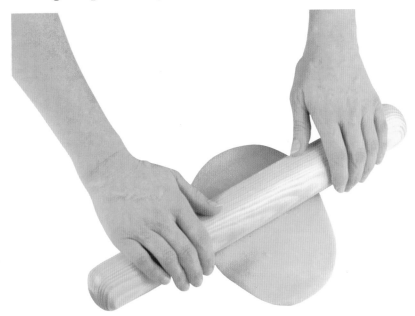

1 Cut the basic dough in quarters. Use one quarter at a time and cover the rest with plastic wrap, so it does not dry out. Flatten the dough and dust liberally with flour. Start rolling out the dough, making sure you roll it evenly.

2 As the dough becomes thinner, keep on rotating it on the work surface by gently lifting the edges with your fingers and supporting it over the rolling pin. Make sure you don't tear the dough.

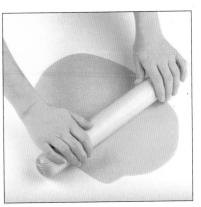

3 Continue rolling out the dough until it has reached the desired thickness, about ⅛-inch thick.

Rolling out dough using a pasta machine

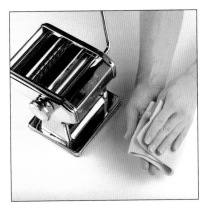

1 Cut the basic dough into quarters. Use one quarter at a time and cover the rest with plastic wrap, so it does not dry out. Flatten the dough and dust liberally with flour. Start with the machine set to roll at the thickest setting. Pass the dough through the rollers several times, dusting the dough from time to time with flour until it is smooth.

2 Fold the strip of dough into three, press the ends well together and pass through the machine again. Repeat the folding and rolling several times on each setting.

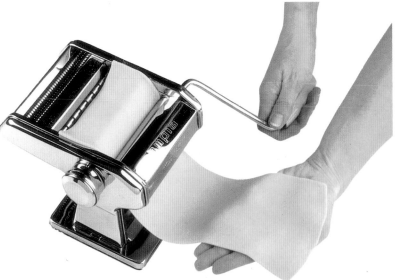

3 Guide the dough through the machine but don't pull or stretch it or the dough will tear. As the dough is worked through all the settings, it will become thinner and longer. Guide the dough over the back of your hand, as the dough is rolled out to a thin sheet. Pasta used for stuffing, such as ravioli or tortellini, should be used as soon as possible. Otherwise, lay the rolled sheets on a clean dish towel, lightly dusted with sifted flour, and leave to dry for 10 minutes before cutting. This makes it easier to cut and prevents the strands of pasta sticking together.

Cutting pasta shapes

Until you are confident at handling and shaping pasta dough, it is easier to work with small quantities. Always keep the dough well covered with plastic wrap to prevent it drying out, until you are ready to work with it.

Shaping ravioli

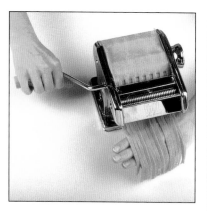

Cutting out spaghetti
To cut spaghetti, fit the appropriate attachment to the machine or move the handle to the appropriate slot. Cut the pasta sheets into 10-inch lengths and pass these through the machine. Guide the strands over the back of your hand as they appear out of the machine.

Cutting out tagliatelle
To cut tagliatelle, fit the appropriate attachment to the machine or move the handle to the appropriate slot. Cut the pasta sheets into 10-inch lengths and pass these through the machine as for spaghetti.

1 To make square ravioli, place spoonfuls of filling on a sheet of dough at intervals of 2–3 inches, leaving a 1-inch border. Brush the dough between the spoonfuls of filling with egg white.

Cutting out lasagne
Take a sheet of pasta dough and cut out neat rectangles about 7 x 3 inches to make sheets of lasagne. Lay on a clean dish towel to dry.

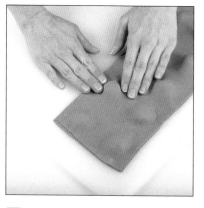

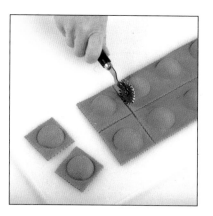

2 Lay a second sheet of pasta carefully over the top. Press around each mound of filling, removing any air pockets.

3 Using a fluted pastry wheel or a sharp knife, cut between the filling.

Making farfalle

Making tagliatelle

1 Roll the pasta dough through a pasta machine until the sheets are very thin. Then cut into long strips 1½-inches wide.

2 Cut the strips into small rectangles. Run a pastry wheel along the two shorter edges of the little rectangles – this will give the bows a decorative edge.

3 Moisten the center of the strips and using a finger and thumb, gently pinch each rectangle together in the middle to make little pasta bows.

1 Lightly flour some spinach-flavored pasta dough and roll it up into a strip 12 x 4 inches.

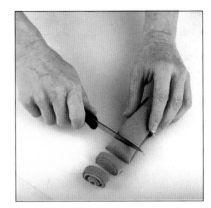

2 Using a sharp knife, cut straight across the roll.

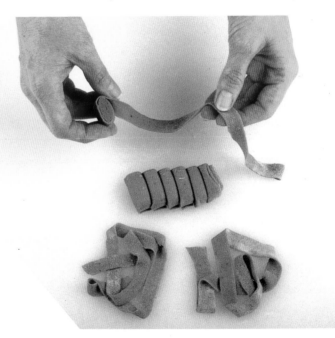

3 Carefully unravel each little roll as you cut it to make ribbons of fresh tagliatelle.

Penne with Eggplant and Mint Pesto

This splendid variation on the classic Italian pesto uses fresh mint rather than basil for a different flavor.

Serves 4

INGREDIENTS
2 large eggplant
salt
1 lb penne
2 oz walnut halves

FOR THE PESTO
1 oz fresh mint
½ oz flat-leaf parsley
1½ oz walnuts
1½ oz Parmesan cheese, finely grated
2 garlic cloves
6 tbsp olive oil
salt and freshly ground black pepper

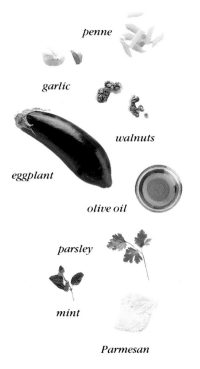

penne

garlic

walnuts

eggplant

olive oil

parsley

mint

Parmesan

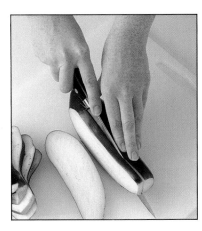

1 Cut the eggplant lengthwise into 1 cm/½ in slices.

2 Cut the slices again crosswise to give short strips.

3 Layer the strips in a colander with salt and leave to stand for 30 minutes over a plate to catch any juices. Rinse well in cool water and drain.

4 Place all the pesto ingredients except the oil in a blender or food processor, blend until smooth, then gradually add the oil in a thin stream until the mixture comes together. Season to taste.

5 Cook the penne following the instructions on the side of the package for about 8 minutes or until nearly cooked. Add the eggplant and cook for a further 3 minutes.

6 Drain well and mix in the mint pesto and walnut halves. Serve immediately.

Campanelle with Yellow Pepper Sauce

Roasted yellow bell peppers make a deliciously sweet and creamy sauce to serve with pasta.

Serves 4

INGREDIENTS
2 yellow bell peppers
¼ cup soft goat cheese
½ cup low-fat ricotta cheese
salt and freshly ground black pepper
1 lb short pasta such as campanelle or fusilli
¼ cup sliced almonds, toasted to serve

bell pepper

ricotta cheese

sliced almonds

goat cheese

campanelle

1 Place the whole yellow peppers under a preheated broiler until charred and blistered. Place in a paper bag to cool. Peel and remove the seeds.

2 Place the pepper flesh in a blender with the goat cheese and ricotta cheese. Blend until smooth. Season with salt and lots of black pepper.

3 Cook the pasta following the instructions on the side of the package until *al dente*. Drain well.

4 Toss with the sauce and serve sprinkled with the toasted sliced almonds.

Spaghetti with Black Olive and Mushroom Sauce

A rich pungent sauce topped with sweet cherry tomatoes.

Serves 4

INGREDIENTS

1 tbsp olive oil
1 garlic clove, chopped
8 oz mushrooms, chopped
Generous ½ cup black olives, pitted
2 tbsp chopped fresh parsley
1 fresh red chili, seeded and chopped
1 lb spaghetti
8 oz cherry tomatoes
slivers of Parmesan cheese, to serve
    (optional)

garlic

mushrooms

red chilies

cherry tomatoes

black olives

spaghetti

parsley

1 Heat the oil in a large pan. Add the garlic and cook for 1 minute. Add the mushrooms, cover, and cook over a medium heat for 5 minutes.

2 Place the mushrooms in a blender or food processor with the olives, parsley and red chili. Blend until smooth.

3 Cook the pasta following the instructions on the side of the package until *al dente*. Drain well and return to the pan. Add the olive mixture and toss together until the pasta is well coated. Cover and keep warm.

4 Heat an ungreased frying pan and shake the cherry tomatoes around until they start to split (about 2–3 minutes). Serve the pasta topped with the tomatoes and garnished with slivers of Parmesan, if desired.

Tagliatelle with Pea Sauce, Asparagus and Fava Beans

A creamy pea sauce makes a wonderful combination with the crunchy young vegetables.

Serves 4

INGREDIENTS
1 tbsp olive oil
1 garlic clove, crushed
6 scallions, sliced
1 cup baby peas, defrosted if frozen
12 oz fresh young asparagus
2 tbsp chopped fresh sage, plus
    extra leaves, to garnish
finely grated rind of 2 lemons
1¾ cups fresh vegetable stock or
    water
8 oz fava beans, defrosted if frozen
1 lb tagliatelle
4 tbsp low-fat yogurt

lemon

garlic

asparagus

beans

peas

yogurt *tagliatelle*

sage

scallions

1 Heat the oil in a pan. Add the garlic and scallions and cook gently for 2–3 minutes until softened.

2 Add the peas and ⅓ of the asparagus, together with the sage, lemon rind and stock or water. Bring to a boil, reduce the heat and simmer for 10 minutes until tender. Purée in a blender until smooth.

3 Meanwhile, remove the outer skins from the fava beans and discard.

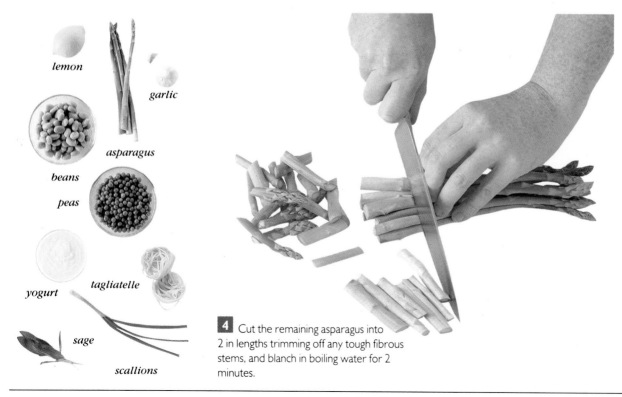

4 Cut the remaining asparagus into 2 in lengths trimming off any tough fibrous stems, and blanch in boiling water for 2 minutes.

5 Cook the tagliatelle following the instructions on the side of the package until *al dente*. Drain well.

166

COOK'S TIP

Frozen peas and beans have been suggested here to cut down the preparation time, but the dish tastes even better if you use fresh young vegetables when in season.

6 Add the cooked asparagus and shelled beans to the sauce and reheat. Stir in the yogurt and toss into the tagliatelle. Garnish with a few extra sage leaves and serve.

Capellini with Arugula, Snow Peas and Pine Nuts

A light but filling pasta dish with the added pepperiness of fresh arugula.

Serves 4

INGREDIENTS

9 oz capellini or angel-hair pasta
8 oz snow peas
6 oz arugula
¼ cup pine nuts, roasted
2 tbsp Parmesan cheese, finely grated (optional)
2 tbsp olive oil (optional)

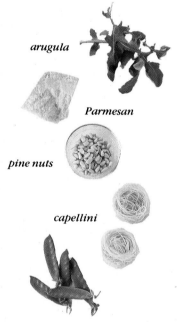

arugula

Parmesan

pine nuts

capellini

snow peas

1 Cook the capellini or angel-hair pasta following the instructions on the side of the package until *al dente*.

2 Meanwhile, carefully top and tail the snow peas.

3 As soon as the pasta is cooked, drop in the arugula and snow peas. Drain immediately.

4 Toss the pasta with the roasted pine nuts, and Parmesan and olive oil if using. Serve at once.

COOK'S TIP

Olive oil and Parmesan are optional as they obviously raise the fat content.

Pasta Bows with Fennel and Walnut Sauce

A scrumptious blend of walnuts and crisp steamed fennel.

Serves 4

INGREDIENTS
½ cup walnuts, shelled and roughly
  chopped
1 garlic clove
1 oz fresh flat-leaf parsley leaves,
  picked from the stems
½ cup ricotta cheese
1 lb pasta bows
1 lb fennel bulbs
chopped walnuts, to garnish

garlic

pasta bows

ricotta

fennel

parsley

walnut halves

chopped walnuts

1 Place the chopped walnuts, garlic and parsley in a food processor. Pulse until roughly chopped. Transfer to a bowl and stir in the ricotta.

2 Cook the pasta following the instructions on the side of the package until *al dente*. Drain well.

3 Slice the fennel thinly and steam for 4–5 minutes until just tender but still crisp.

4 Return the pasta to the pan and add the walnut mixture and the fennel. Toss well and sprinkle with the chopped walnuts. Serve immediately.

Pasta with Spring Vegetables

This delicious vegetarian dish is perfect for a light lunch or supper.

Serves 4

INGREDIENTS
4 oz broccoli flowerets
4 oz baby leeks
8 oz asparagus
1 small fennel bulb
4 oz fresh or frozen peas
3 tbsp butter
1 shallot, chopped
3 tbsp chopped fresh mixed herbs,
    such as parsley, thyme and sage
1¼ cups heavy cream
12 oz penne
salt and ground black pepper
freshly grated Parmesan cheese,
    to serve

broccoli

peas

butter

penne

heavy cream

Parmesan cheese

mixed herbs

shallot
baby leeks

asparagus

fennel

1 Divide the broccoli flowerets into tiny sprigs. Cut the leeks and asparagus diagonally into 2 in lengths. Trim the fennel bulb and remove any tough outer leaves. Cut into wedges, leaving the layers attached at the root ends so that the pieces stay intact.

2 Cook each prepared vegetable, including the peas, separately in boiling salted water until just tender – use the same water for each vegetable. Drain well and keep warm.

3 Melt the butter in a separate pan, add the chopped shallot and cook, stirring occasionally, until softened but not browned. Stir in the herbs and cream and cok for a few minutes until slightly thickened. Meanwhile, bring a large pan of salted water to the boil.

4 Add the pasta to the boiling water and cook according to the packet instructions until it is just *al dente*. Drain well and add to the sauce with the vegetables. Toss gently and season with plenty of pepper. Serve hot with a sprinkling of freshly grated Parmesan.

Tagliatelle with Mushrooms

The mushroom sauce is quick to make and the pasta cooks very quickly; both need to be cooked as near to serving as possible, so careful coordination is required.

Serves 4

INGREDIENTS
about 4 tbsp butter
8–12 oz chanterelles
1 tbsp all-purpose flour
⅔ cup milk
6 tbsp crème fraîche
1 tbsp chopped fresh parsley
10 oz fresh or dried tagliatelle
olive oil, for tossing
salt and ground black pepper

butter
flour
chanterelles
milk
crème fraîche
parsley
olive oil
tagliatelle

COOK'S TIP
Chanterelles are a little tricky to wash, as they are so delicate. However, since these are woodland mushrooms, it's important to clean them thoroughly. Hold each one by the stalk and let cold water run under the gills to dislodge hidden dirt. Shake gently to dry.

1 Melt 3 tablespoons of the butter in a frying pan and fry the mushrooms for 2–3 minutes over low heat until the juices begin to run, then increase the heat and cook until the liquid has almost evaporated. Transfer the cooked mushrooms to a bowl using a slotted spoon.

2 Stir the flour into the pan, adding a little more butter if necessary, and cook for about 1 minute, then gradually stir in the milk to make a smooth sauce.

3 Add the crème fraîche, mushrooms, parsley and seasoning and stir well. Cook very gently to heat through and then keep warm while cooking the pasta.

4 Bring a large pot of salted water to a boil. Add the pasta and cook according to the package instructions until it is just al dente. Drain well, toss with a little olive oil and then transfer to a warmed serving plate. Pour the mushroom sauce on top and serve immediately while it is hot.

VARIATION
If chanterelles are unavailable, use other wild mushrooms of your choice.

Double Tomato Tagliatelle

Sun-dried tomatoes add pungency to this dish, while the broiled fresh tomatoes add bite.

Serves 4

INGREDIENTS

3 tbsp olive oil
1 garlic clove, crushed
1 small onion, chopped
$\frac{1}{4}$ cup dry white wine
6 sun-dried tomatoes, chopped
2 tbsp chopped fresh parsley
$\frac{1}{2}$ cup pitted black olives, halved
1 lb fresh tagliatelle
4 tomatoes, halved
Parmesan cheese, to serve
salt and freshly ground black pepper

parsley

garlic clove

tomatoes

sun-dried tomatoes

tagliatelle

dry white wine

onion

black olives

Parmesan cheese

COOK'S TIP

It is essential to buy Parmesan in a piece for this dish. Find a good source – fresh Parmesan should not be unacceptably hard – and shave or grate it yourself. The flavor will be much more intense than that of the pre-grated product.

1 Heat 2 tbsp of the oil in a pan. Add the garlic and onion, and cook for 2–3 minutes, stirring occasionally. Add the wine, sun-dried tomatoes and the parsley. Cook for 2 minutes. Stir in the black olives.

2 Bring a large pan of salted water to a boil. Add the fresh tagliatelle, and cook for 2–3 minutes until just tender. Preheat the broiler.

3 Put the tomatoes on a baking sheet, and brush with the remaining oil. Broil for 3–4 minutes.

4 Drain the pasta, return it to the pan, and toss with the sauce. Serve with the broiled tomatoes, freshly ground black pepper and shavings of Parmesan.

Pasta with Cilantro and Broiled Eggplant

Pasta with a piquant sauce of cilantro and lime – a variation on the classic pesto – is superb served with broiled eggplant.

Serves 2

INGREDIENTS

½ oz cilantro leaves
2 tbsp pine nuts
2 tbsp freshly grated Parmesan cheese
3 garlic cloves
juice of ½ lime
7 tbsp olive oil
8 oz dried cellentani or other pasta shapes
1 large eggplant
salt and freshly ground black pepper

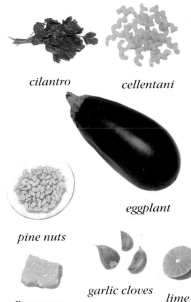

cilantro   *cellentani*

eggplant

pine nuts

garlic cloves   *lime*

Parmesan cheese

1 Process the cilantro leaves, pine nuts, Parmesan, garlic, lime juice and 4 tbsp of the olive oil in a food processor or blender for 30 seconds until almost smooth. Bring a large pan of salted water to a boil. Add the pasta, and cook for 10–12 minutes until cooked but still firm to the bite.

2 Meanwhile, cut the eggplant in half lengthwise. Then cut each half into ¼ in slices. Spread out on a baking sheet, brush with the remaining oil, and season well with salt and black pepper.

3 Broil the eggplant slices for about 4 minutes. Turn them over, and brush with the remaining oil. Season as before. Broil for 4 minutes more.

4 Drain the pasta, turn it into a bowl, and toss with the cilantro sauce. Serve with the broiled eggplant slices.

Pasta Primavera

Serves 4

INGREDIENTS

8 oz thin asparagus spears, cut
  in half
4 oz snow peas, trimmed
4 oz whole baby corn
8 oz whole baby carrots,
  trimmed
1 small red bell pepper, seeded
  and chopped
8 scallions, sliced
8 oz torchietti or rotini
²/₃ cup low-fat cottage cheese
²/₃ cup low-fat yogurt
1 tbsp lemon juice
1 tbsp chopped parsley
1 tbsp chopped chives
skim milk (optional)
salt and ground black pepper
sun-dried tomato bread, to serve

scallions

red bell pepper

baby corn   *parsley*

baby carrots   *lemon*

chives   *torchietti*

snow peas

asparagus spears

1 Cook the asparagus spears in a pan of boiling, salted water for 3–4 minutes. Add the snow peas halfway through the cooking time. Drain and rinse both under cold water.

2 Cook the baby corn, carrots, red pepper and spring onions in the same way until tender. Drain and rinse.

low-fat yogurt   *low-fat cottage cheese*

3 Cook the pasta in a large pan of boiling, salted water until *al dente*. Drain thoroughly.

4 Put the cottage cheese, yogurt, lemon juice, parsley, chives and seasoning into a food processor or blender and process until smooth. Thin the sauce with skim milk, if necessary. Put into a large pan with the pasta and vegetables, heat gently and toss carefully. Transfer to a serving plate and serve with sun-dried tomato bread.

Tagliatelle with Sun-dried Tomatoes

Sun-dried tomatoes give this sauce a deliciously intense flavor – use drained sun-dried tomatoes in oil if you prefer.

Serves 4

INGREDIENTS

1 garlic clove, crushed
1 celery stalk finely sliced
1 cup sun-dried tomatoes, finely
    chopped
scant ½ cup red wine
8 plum tomatoes
12 oz dried tagliatelle
salt and freshly ground black pepper

sun-dried tomatoes

celery   *tagliatelle*

plum tomatoes

1 Put the garlic, celery, sun-dried tomatoes and wine into a large saucepan. Gently cook for 15 minutes.

2 Plunge the plum tomatoes into a saucepan of boiling water for 1 minute, then into a saucepan of cold water. Slip off their skins. Halve, remove the seeds and cores and roughly chop the flesh.

3 Add the plum tomatoes to the saucepan and simmer for a further 5 minutes. Season to taste.

4 Meanwhile, cook the tagliatelle in plenty of lightly salted rapidly boiling water for 8-10 minutes, or until *al dente*. Drain well. Toss with half the sauce and serve on warmed plates, topped with the remaining sauce.

Tagliatelle with Spinach Gnocchi

Serves 4–6

INGREDIENTS
1 lb mixed flavored tagliatelle
flour, for dusting
shavings of Parmesan cheese,
   to garnish

FOR THE SPINACH GNOCCHI
1 lb frozen chopped spinach
1 small onion, finely chopped
1 garlic clove, crushed
¼ tsp ground nutmeg
14 oz low-fat cottage cheese
4 oz dried white bread crumbs
3 oz semolina or flour
2 oz grated Parmesan cheese
3 egg whites
salt and pepper

FOR THE TOMATO SAUCE
1 onion, finely chopped
1 stick celery, finely chopped
1 red bell pepper, seeded and diced
1 garlic clove, crushed
²⁄₃ cup vegetable stock
14 oz can tomatoes
1 tbsp tomato paste
2 tsp sugar
1 tsp dried oregano

1 To make the tomato sauce, put the chopped onion, celery, pepper and garlic into a non-stick pan. Add the stock, bring to a boil and cook for 5 minutes or until tender.

2 Add the tomatoes, tomato paste, sugar and oregano. Season to taste, bring to a boil and simmer for 30 minutes until thick, stirring occasionally.

3 Meanwhile, put the frozen spinach, onion and garlic into a saucepan, cover and cook until the spinach is defrosted. Remove the lid and increase the heat to remove excess water. Season with salt, pepper and nutmeg. Cool the spinach in a bowl, add the remaining ingredients and mix thoroughly.

celery

garlic

egg

nutmeg

onion

low-fat cottage cheese

flavored tagliatelle

red bell pepper

spinach

grated Parmesan cheese

dried white bread crumbs

vegetable stock

tomato paste

tomatoes

semolina

4 Shape the mixture into about 24 ovals with two dessertspoons and place them on a lightly floured tray. Place in the refrigerator for 30 minutes.

5 Have a large shallow pan of boiling, salted water ready. Cook the gnocchi in batches, for about 5 minutes. (The water should simmer gently and not boil.) As soon as the gnocchi rise to the surface, remove them with a slotted spoon and drain thoroughly.

6 Cook the tagliatelle in a large pan of boiling, salted water until *al dente*. Drain thoroughly. Transfer to warmed serving plates, top with gnocchi and spoon over the tomato sauce. Top with shavings of Parmesan cheese and serve at once.

Pasta Rapido with Parsley Pesto

Pasta suppers can often be dull. Here's a fresh, lively sauce that will stir the appetite.

Serves 4

INGREDIENTS
1 lb dried pasta
¾ cup whole almonds
½ cup slivered almonds, toasted
¼ cup freshly grated Parmesan
    cheese
pinch of salt

FOR THE SAUCE
1½ oz fresh parsley
2 garlic cloves, crushed
3 tbsp olive oil
3 tbsp lemon juice
1 tsp sugar
1 cup boiling water

1 Bring a large saucepan of salted water to a boil. Toss in the pasta and cook according to the instructions on the package. Toast the whole and slivered almonds separately under a moderate broiler until golden brown. Put the slivered almonds aside until required.

pasta

lemon

parsley

garlic

Parmesan cheese

slivered almonds

almonds

2 For the sauce, chop the parsley finely in a food processor. Add the whole almonds and grind to a fine consistency. Add the garlic, olive oil, lemon juice, sugar and water. Combine to make a sauce.

3 Drain the pasta and combine with half of the sauce. (The remainder of the sauce will keep in a screw-topped jar in the refrigerator for up to ten days.) Top with Parmesan and slivered almonds.

COOK'S TIP

To prevent pasta from sticking together during cooking, use plenty of water and stir well before the water returns to a boil.

Penne with Fennel, Tomato and Blue Cheese

The anise flavor of the fennel makes it the perfect partner for tomato, especially when topped with blue cheese.

Serves 2

INGREDIENTS
1 fennel bulb
8 oz penne or other dried
  pasta shapes
2 tbsp extra virgin olive oil
1 shallot, finely chopped
1¼ cups strained tomatoes
pinch of sugar
1 tsp chopped fresh oregano
4 oz blue cheese
salt and freshly ground black pepper

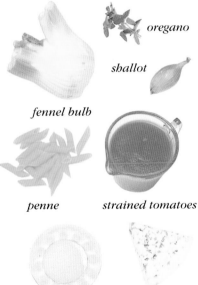

oregano

shallot

fennel bulb

penne

strained tomatoes

sugar

blue cheese

1 Cut the fennel bulb in half. Cut away the hard core and root. Slice the fennel thinly, then cut the slices into strips.

2 Bring a large pan of salted water to a boil. Add the pasta, and cook for 10–12 minutes until just tender.

3 Meanwhile, heat the oil in a small saucepan. Add the fennel and shallot, and cook for 2–3 minutes over a high heat, stirring occasionally.

4 Add the tomatoes, sugar and oregano. Cover the pan, and simmer gently for 10–12 minutes, until the fennel is tender. Add salt and pepper to taste. Drain the pasta, and return it to the pan. Toss with the sauce. Serve with blue cheese crumbled over the top.

Lemon and Parmesan Capellini with Herb Bread

Cream is thickened with Parmesan and flavored with lemon to make a superb sauce for pasta.

Serves 2

INGREDIENTS
½ whole-wheat stick
¼ cup butter, softened
1 garlic clove, crushed
2 tbsp chopped fresh herbs
8 oz dried or fresh capellini
1 cup light cream
3 oz Parmesan cheese, grated
finely grated rind of 1 lemon
salt and freshly ground black pepper

garlic clove

rosemary

Parmesan cheese

thyme

capellini

butter

lemon

light cream

whole-wheat stick

parsley

oregano

1 Preheat the oven to 400°F. Cut the whole-wheat stick into thick slices.

2 Put the butter in a bowl, and beat with the garlic and herbs. Spread thickly over each slice of bread.

3 Reassemble the stick. Wrap in foil. Support on a baking sheet, and bake for 10 minutes.

4 Meanwhile, bring a large pan of water to a boil, and cook the pasta until just tender. Dried pasta will take 10–12 minutes; fresh pasta will be ready in 2–3 minutes.

5 Pour the cream into another pan, and bring to a boil. Stir in the Parmesan and lemon rind. The sauce should thicken in about 30 seconds.

6 Drain the pasta, return it to the pan, and toss with the sauce. Season to taste, and sprinkle with a little chopped fresh parsley and grated lemon rind, if desired. Serve with the hot herb bread.

Mushroom Macaroni and Cheese

Macaroni cheese is an all-time classic from the mid-week menu. Here it is served in a light creamy sauce with mushrooms and topped with pine nuts.

Serves 4

INGREDIENTS

1 lb quick-cooking elbow macaroni
3 tbsp olive oil
8 oz portabello mushrooms, sliced
2 fresh thyme sprigs
4 tbsp all-purpose flour
1 vegetable bouillon cube
2½ cups milk
½ tsp celery salt
1 tsp Dijon mustard
1½ cups grated Cheddar cheese
¼ cup freshly grated Parmesan cheese
2 tbsp pine nuts
salt and freshly ground black pepper

macaroni

thyme

pine nuts

portabello mushrooms

Parmesan cheese

Dijon mustard

Cheddar cheese

1 Bring a pan of salted water to a boil. Add the macaroni and cook according to the package instructions.

2 Heat the oil in a heavy saucepan. Add the mushrooms and thyme, cover and cook over a gentle heat for 2–3 minutes. Stir in the flour and draw from the heat, add the bouillon cube and stir continuously until evenly blended. Add the milk a little at a time, stirring after each addition. Add the celery salt, mustard and Cheddar cheese and season. Stir and simmer briefly for 1–2 minutes.

3 Preheat a moderate broiler. Drain the macaroni well, toss into the sauce and turn out into four individual dishes or one large flameproof gratin dish. Scatter with grated Parmesan cheese and pine nuts, then broil until brown and bubbly.

COOK'S TIP

Tightly closed mushrooms are best for white cream sauces. Open mushrooms can darken a pale sauce to an unattractive sludgy grey.

Spicy Ratatouille and Penne

Serves 6

INGREDIENTS

1 small eggplant
2 zucchini, thickly sliced
7 oz firm tofu, cubed
3 tbsp dark soy sauce
1 garlic clove, crushed
2 tsp sesame seeds
1 small red bell pepper, seeded
  and sliced
1 onion, finely chopped
1–2 garlic cloves, crushed
²/₃ cup vegetable stock
3 firm ripe tomatoes, peeled, seeded
  and quartered
1 tbsp chopped mixed herbs
8 oz penne
salt and ground black pepper
crusty bread, to serve

tomatoes
zucchini
eggplant
red bell pepper
garlic
tofu
onion
penne
sesame seeds
vegetable stock
soy sauce

1 Wash and cut the eggplant into 1-inch cubes. Put into a colander with the zucchini, sprinkle with salt and leave to drain for 30 minutes.

2 Mix the tofu with the soy sauce, garlic and sesame seeds. Cover and marinate for 30 minutes.

3 Put the pepper, onion and garlic into a saucepan with the stock. Bring to a boil, cover and cook for 5 minutes until tender. Remove the lid and boil until all the stock has evaporated. Add the tomatoes and herbs and cook for 3 minutes more. Season to taste.

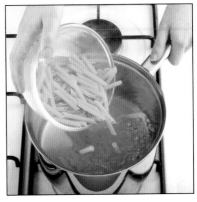

4 Meanwhile cook the pasta in a large pan of boiling, salted water until *al dente*. Drain thoroughly. Toss the pasta with the vegetables and tofu. Transfer to a shallow 10-inch square ovenproof dish and broil until lightly browned. Transfer to a serving dish and serve with fresh crusty bread.

Vegetarian Lasagne

Serves 6–8

INGREDIENTS
1 small eggplant
1 large onion, finely chopped
2 garlic cloves, crushed
²/₃ cup vegetable stock
8 oz mushrooms, sliced
14 oz can chopped tomatoes
2 tbsp tomato paste
²/₃ cup red wine
¼ tsp ground ginger
1 tsp mixed dried herbs
10–12 sheets lasagne
1 oz low-fat margarine
1 oz flour
1¼ cups skim milk
large pinch of grated nutmeg
7 oz low-fat cottage cheese
1 egg, beaten
½ oz grated Parmesan cheese
1 oz reduced-fat Cheddar
   cheese, grated
salt and ground black pepper

1 Wash the eggplant and cut it into 1-inch cubes. Put the onion and garlic into a saucepan with the stock, cover and cook for about 5 minutes or until tender.

2 Add the diced eggplant, sliced mushrooms, tomatoes, tomato paste, wine, ginger, seasoning and herbs. Bring to a boil, cover and cook for 15–20 minutes. Remove the lid and cook rapidly to reduce the liquid by half.

3 To make the sauce, put the margarine, flour, skim milk and nutmeg into a pan. Whisk together over the heat until thickened and smooth. Season to taste.

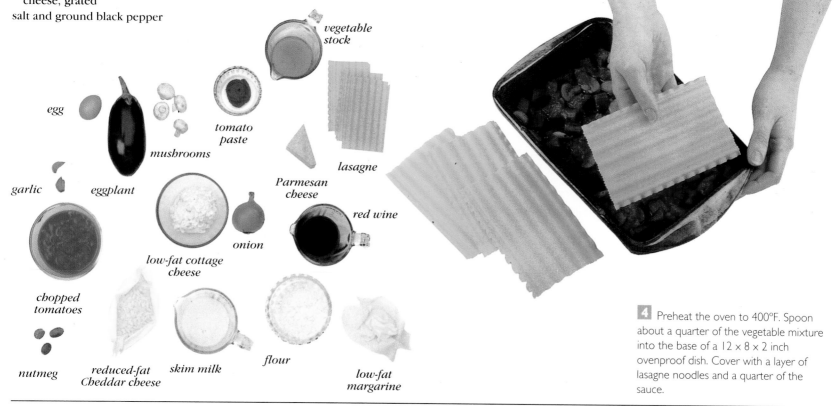

vegetable stock

egg

mushrooms

tomato paste

lasagne

garlic

eggplant

Parmesan cheese

red wine

onion

low-fat cottage cheese

chopped tomatoes

nutmeg

reduced-fat Cheddar cheese

skim milk

flour

low-fat margarine

4 Preheat the oven to 400°F. Spoon about a quarter of the vegetable mixture into the base of a 12 x 8 x 2 inch ovenproof dish. Cover with a layer of lasagne noodles and a quarter of the sauce.

5 Repeat with two more layers, then cover with the cottage cheese. Beat the egg into the remaining sauce and pour over the top. Sprinkle with the two grated cheeses.

6 Bake for 25–30 minutes or until the top is golden brown.

Vegetarian Cannelloni

Serves 4-6

INGREDIENTS

1 onion, finely chopped
2 garlic cloves, crushed
2 carrots, coarsely grated
2 stalks celery, finely chopped
⅔ cup vegetable stock
4 oz red or green lentils
14 oz can chopped tomatoes
2 tbsp tomato paste
½ tsp ground ginger
1 tsp fresh thyme
1 tsp chopped fresh rosemary
1½ oz low-fat margarine
1½ oz flour
2½ cups skim milk
1 bay leaf
large pinch grated nutmeg
16–18 cannelloni tubes
1 oz reduced-fat Cheddar
    cheese, grated
1 oz grated Parmesan cheese
1 oz fresh white bread crumbs
salt and ground black pepper
flat-leaf parsley, to garnish

flour

low-fat margarine

reduced-fat Cheddar cheese

onion   *garlic*   *celery*

rosemary

white bread crumbs

bay leaf   *thyme*

skim milk

red lentils   *Parmesan cheese*

carrots

cannelloni tubes

nutmeg

chopped tomatoes   *vegetable stock*   *tomato paste*

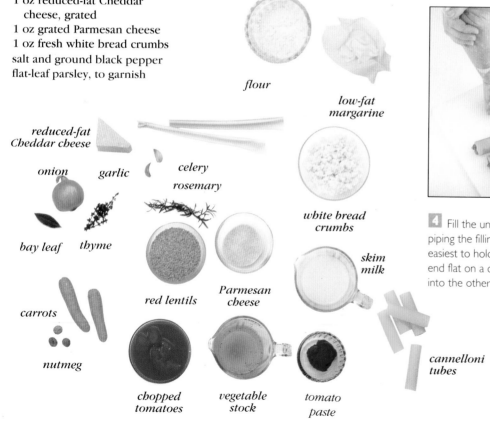

1 To make the filling, put the onion, garlic, carrots and celery into a large saucepan. Add half the stock, cover and cook for 5 minutes or until tender.

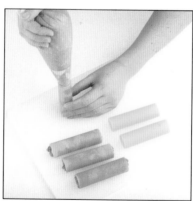

2 Add the lentils, chopped tomatoes, tomato paste, ginger, thyme, rosemary and seasoning. Bring to a boil, cover and cook for 20 minutes. Remove the lid and cook for about 10 minutes until thick and soft. Let cool.

3 To make the sauce, put the margarine, flour, skim milk and bay leaf into a pan and whisk over the heat until thick and smooth. Season with salt, pepper and nutmeg. Discard the bay leaf.

4 Fill the uncooked cannelloni by piping the filling into each tube. (It is easiest to hold them upright with one end flat on a cutting board, while piping into the other end.)

5 Preheat the oven to 350°F. Spoon half the sauce into the bottom of an 8-inch square ovenproof dish. Lay two rows of filled cannelloni on top and spoon over the remaining sauce.

6 Top with the cheeses and bread crumbs. Bake in the preheated oven for 30–40 minutes. Place under broiler to brown the top, if necessary. Garnish with flat-leaf parsley.

Spinach and Ricotta Shells with Pine Nuts

Large pasta shells are designed to hold a variety of delicious stuffings. Few are more pleasing than this mixture of chopped spinach and ricotta cheese.

COOK'S TIP

Choose a large saucepan when cooking pasta and give it an occasional stir to prevent shapes from sticking together. You can use either crushed tomatoes or tomato paste.

Serves 4

INGREDIENTS

12 oz large pasta shells
scant 2 cups crushed tomatoes or tomato paste
10 oz frozen chopped spinach, defrosted
2 oz crustless white bread, crumbled
½ cup milk
3 tbsp olive oil
2¼ cups ricotta cheese
pinch of nutmeg
1 garlic clove, crushed
1 tbsp olive oil
½ tsp black olive paste (optional)
¼ cup freshly grated Parmesan cheese
2 tbsp pine nuts
salt and freshly ground black pepper

olive paste

ricotta cheese

pine nuts

garlic

spinach

pasta shells

1 Bring a large saucepan of salted water to a boil. Toss in the pasta and cook according to the directions on the package. Refresh under cold water, drain and reserve until needed.

2 Pour the crushed tomatoes or paste into a nylon sieve over a bowl and strain to thicken. Place the spinach in another sieve and press out any excess liquid with the back of a spoon.

3 Place the bread, milk and oil in a food processor and combine. Add the spinach and ricotta and season with salt, pepper and nutmeg.

4 Combine the crushed tomatoes with the garlic, olive oil and olive paste if using. Spread the sauce evenly over the bottom of an ovenproof dish.

5 Spoon the spinach mixture into a piping bag fitted with a large plain nozzle and fill the pasta shapes (alternatively fill with a spoon). Arrange the pasta shapes over the sauce.

6 Preheat a moderate broiler. Heat the pasta through in a microwave oven at high power (100%) for 4 minutes. Scatter with Parmesan cheese and pine nuts, and finish under the broiler to brown the cheese.

Cilantro Ravioli with Pumpkin Filling

A stunning herb pasta with a superb creamy pumpkin and roast garlic filling.

Serves 4–6

INGREDIENTS
scant 1 cup flour
2 eggs
pinch of salt
3 tbsp chopped fresh cilantro
cilantro sprigs, to garnish

FOR THE FILLING
4 garlic cloves in their skins
1 lb pumpkin, peeled and seeds removed
½ cup ricotta cheese
4 halves sun-dried tomatoes in olive oil, drained and finely chopped, but reserve 2 tbsp of the oil
freshly ground black pepper

cilantro

egg

garlic

pumpkin

flour

ricotta cheese

sun-dried tomatoes

1 Place the flour, eggs, salt and cilantro into a food processor. Pulse until combined.

2 Place the dough on a lightly floured board and knead well for 5 minutes, until smooth. Wrap in plastic wrap and leave to rest in the refrigerator for 20 minutes.

3 Preheat the oven to 400°F. Place the garlic cloves on a cookie sheet and bake for 10 minutes until softened. Steam the pumpkin for 5–8 minutes until tender and drain well. Peel the garlic cloves and mash into the pumpkin together with the ricotta and drained sun-dried tomatoes. Season with black pepper.

4 Divide the pasta into 4 pieces and flatten slightly. Using a pasta machine, on its thinnest setting, roll out each piece. Leave the sheets of pasta on a clean dish-towel until slightly dried.

5 Using a 3 in crinkle-edged round cutter, stamp out 36 rounds.

6 Top 18 of the rounds with a teaspoonful of mixture, brush the edges with water and place another round of pasta on top. Press firmly around the edges to seal. Bring a large pan of water to a boil, add the ravioli and cook for 3–4 minutes. Drain well and toss into the reserved tomato oil. Serve garnished with cilantro sprigs.

Crescent Spinach Ravioli

Serves 4–6

INGREDIENTS
1 bunch of scallions, finely chopped
1 carrot, coarsely grated
2 garlic cloves, crushed
7 oz low-fat cottage cheese
1 tbsp chopped dill
4 halves sun-dried tomatoes,
    finely chopped
1 oz grated Parmesan cheese
1 recipe basic pasta dough, with
    4 oz frozen spinach, thawed
    and chopped added
egg white, beaten, for brushing
flour, for dusting
salt and ground black pepper
2 halves sun-dried tomatoes, finely
    chopped, and fresh dill,
    to garnish

carrot

dill

sun-dried tomatoes

garlic

scallions

Parmesan cheese

spinach

low-fat cottage cheese

1 Put the scallions, carrot, garlic and cottage cheese into a bowl. Add the chopped dill, tomatoes, seasoning and Parmesan cheese.

2 Roll the spinach pasta into thin sheets, cut into 3-inch rounds with a fluted pastry cutter.

3 Place a small spoonful of filling in the center of each circle. Brush the edges with egg white.

4 Fold each in half to make crescents. Press the edges together to seal. Transfer to a floured dish towel to let rest for 1 hour before cooking.

5 Cook the pasta in a large pan of boiling, salted water for 5 minutes. (Cook in batches to stop them sticking together.) Drain well.

6 Serve the crescents on warmed serving plates and garnish with sun-dried tomatoes and dill.

Herbed Pasta Crescents

Serves 4–6

INGREDIENTS
1 recipe basic pasta dough, with
   3 tbsp chopped fresh
   herbs added
egg white, beaten, for brushing
flour, for dusting
basil leaves, to garnish

FOR THE FILLING
8 oz chopped frozen spinach
1 small onion, finely chopped
pinch of ground nutmeg
4 oz low-fat cottage cheese
1 egg, beaten
1 oz Parmesan cheese
salt and ground black pepper

FOR THE SAUCE
1¼ cups skim milk
1 oz margarine
3 tbsp all-purpose flour
¼ tsp ground nutmeg
2 tbsp chopped fresh herbs
   (chives, basil and parsley)

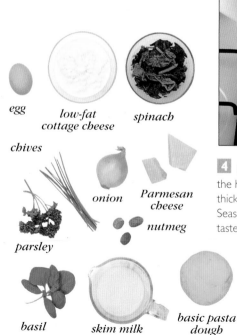

egg

low-fat
cottage cheese

spinach

chives

onion

Parmesan
cheese

nutmeg

parsley

basil

skim milk

basic pasta
dough

margarine

1 To make the filling, put the spinach and onion into a pan, cover and cook slowly to defrost. Remove the lid and increase the heat to boil off any water. Season with salt, pepper and nutmeg. Turn the spinach into a bowl and cool slightly. Add the cottage cheese, beaten egg and Parmesan cheese.

2 Roll the herb pasta into thin sheets. Cut into 3-inch rounds with a fluted pastry cutter.

3 Place a spoonful of filling in the centre of each round. Brush the edges with egg white. Fold each in half (to make crescents). Press the edges together to seal. Transfer to a floured dish towel and let rest for 1 hour before cooking the pasta.

4 Put all the sauce ingredients (except the herbs) into a pan. With a whisk, thicken over medium heat until smooth. Season with salt, pepper and nutmeg to taste. Stir in the herbs.

5 Cook the pasta in a large pan of boiling, salted water for 3 minutes (cook in batches to stop them from sticking together). Drain thoroughly.

6 Serve the crescents on warmed serving plates and pour over the herb sauce. Garnish with basil leaves and serve at once.

Fried Noodles with Bean Sprouts and Asparagus

Soft fried noodles contrast beautifully with crisp bean sprouts and asparagus.

Serves 2

INGREDIENTS
4 oz dried egg noodles
4 tbsp vegetable oil
1 small onion, chopped
1 in piece of fresh ginger, peeled and grated
2 garlic cloves, crushed
6 oz young asparagus spears, trimmed
4 oz bean sprouts
4 scallions, sliced
3 tbsp soy sauce
salt and freshly ground black pepper

onion

scallions

garlic cloves

fresh ginger

soy sauce

bean sprouts

egg noodles

asparagus spears

1 Bring a pan of salted water to a boil. Add the noodles, and cook for 2–3 minutes, until just tender. Drain, and toss in 2 tbsp of the oil.

2 Heat the remaining oil in a wok or frying pan until very hot. Add the onion, ginger and garlic, and stir-fry for 2–3 minutes. Add the asparagus, and stir-fry for 2–3 minutes more.

3 Add the noodles and bean sprouts and stir-fry for 2 minutes.

4 Stir in the scallions and soy sauce. Season to taste, adding salt sparingly as the soy sauce will probably supply enough salt in itself. Stir-fry for 1 minute, then serve at once.

Five-spice Vegetable Noodles

Vary this vegetable stir-fry by substituting mushrooms, bamboo shoots, beansprouts, snow peas or water chestnuts for some or all of the vegetables suggested below.

Serves 2–3

INGREDIENTS

8 oz dried egg noodles
2 tbsp sesame oil
2 carrots
1 celery stalk
1 small fennel bulb
2 zucchini, halved and sliced
1 red chili, seeded and chopped
1 in piece of fresh ginger, grated
1 garlic clove, crushed
1½ tsp Chinese five-spice powder
½ tsp ground cinnamon
4 scallions, sliced
¼ cup warm water
1 red chili, seeded and sliced,
   to garnish (optional)

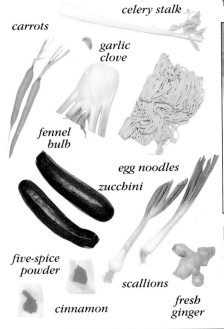

carrots
celery stalk
garlic clove
fennel bulb
egg noodles
zucchini
scallions
five-spice powder
cinnamon
fresh ginger

1 Bring a large pan of salted water to a boil. Add the noodles, and cook for 2–3 minutes until just tender. Drain the noodles, return them to the pan, and toss in a little of the oil. Set aside.

2 Cut the carrot and celery into julienne. Cut the fennel bulb in half, and cut out the hard core. Cut into slices. Then cut the slices into julienne.

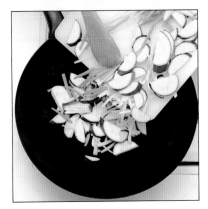

3 Heat the remaining oil in a wok or frying pan until very hot. Add all the vegetables, including the chili, and stir-fry for 7–8 minutes.

4 Add the ginger and garlic, and stir-fry for 2 minutes. Then add the spices. Cook for 1 minute. Add the scallions. Stir-fry for 1 minute. Pour in the warm water, and cook for 1 minute. Stir in the noodles, and toss well together. Serve sprinkled with sliced red chili, if desired.

Noodles with Asparagus and Saffron Sauce

The asparagus, wine and cream give a distinctly French flavor to this elegant and delicious noodle dish.

Serves 4

INGREDIENTS
1 lb young asparagus
2 tbsp butter
2 shallots, finely chopped
2 tbsp white wine
1 cup heavy cream
pinch of saffron threads
grated zest and juice of ½ lemon
1 cup garden peas
12 oz somen noodles
½ bunch chervil, roughly chopped
salt and freshly ground black pepper
grated Parmesan cheese (optional)

asparagus

saffron

shallots

butter

heavy cream

white wine

lemon

peas

somen noodles

COOK'S TIP
Frozen peas can easily be used instead of fresh peas. Add to the asparagus after 3–4 minutes and cook until tender.

1 Cut off the asparagus tips (about 2-inch lengths), then slice the remaining spears into short rounds. Soak the saffron in 2 tablespoons boiling water for a few minutes, until softened.

Melt the butter in a saucepan, add the shallots and cook over low heat for 3 minutes, until soft. Add the white wine, cream and saffron infusion. Bring to a boil, reduce the heat and simmer gently for 5 minutes, or until the sauce thickens to a coating consistency. Add the lemon zest and juice, with salt and pepper to taste.

2 Bring a large saucepan of lightly salted water to a boil. Blanch the asparagus tips, scoop them out and add them to the sauce, then cook the peas and short asparagus rounds in the boiling water until just tender. Scoop them out and add to the sauce.

3 Cook the somen noodles in the same water until just tender, following the directions on the package. Drain, place in a wide pan and pour the sauce over the top.

4 Toss the noodles with the sauce and vegetables, adding the chervil and more salt and pepper if needed. Finally, sprinkle with the grated Parmesan, if using, and serve hot.

Egg Noodle Stir-fry

The thick egg noodles and potatoes, along with the vegetables, make this a satisfying and healthy main dish. If possible, use fresh egg noodles, which are available at most large supermarkets.

Serves 4

INGREDIENTS
2 eggs
1 teaspoon chili powder
1 teaspoon ground turmeric
¼ cup oil
1 large onion, finely sliced
2 red chilies, seeded and finely sliced
1 tablespoon light soy sauce
2 large cooked potatoes, cut into small cubes
6 pieces fried bean curd, sliced
1 cup bean sprouts
4 ounces green beans, blanched
12 ounces fresh thick egg noodles
salt and freshly ground black pepper
sliced scallions, to garnish

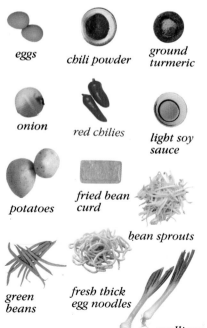

eggs   *chili powder*   *ground turmeric*

onion   *red chilies*   *light soy sauce*

potatoes   *fried bean curd*   *bean sprouts*

green beans   *fresh thick egg noodles*   *scallions*

COOK'S TIP
Ideally, wear gloves when preparing chilies; if you don't, certainly wash your hands thoroughly afterward. Keep your hands away from your eyes, as chilies will sting them.

1 Beat the eggs lightly, then strain them into a bowl. Heat a lightly greased omelet pan. Pour in half of the beaten egg just to cover the bottom of the pan. When the egg is set, carefully turn the omelet over and briefly cook the other side.

2 Slide the omelet onto a plate, blot with paper towels, roll up and cut into narrow strips. Make a second omelet in the same way and slice. Set the omelet strips aside for the garnish.

3 In a cup, mix together the chili powder and turmeric. Form a paste by stirring in a little water. Heat the oil in a wok or large frying pan. Sauté the onion until soft. Reduce the heat and add the chili paste, sliced chilies and soy sauce. Cook for 2–3 minutes.

4 Add the potatoes and cook for about 2 minutes, mixing well with the chilies. Add the bean curd, then the bean sprouts, green beans and noodles.

5 Gently stir-fry until the noodles are evenly coated and heated through. Take care not to break up the potatoes or the bean curd. Season with salt and pepper. Serve hot, garnished with the omelet strips and scallion slices.

Stir-fried Bean Curd with Noodles

This is a satisfying dish that is both tasty and easy to make.

Serves 4

INGREDIENTS
8 oz firm bean curd
peanut oil, for deep-frying
6 oz medium egg noodles
1 tbsp sesame oil
1 tsp cornstarch
2 tsp dark soy sauce
2 tbsp Chinese rice wine
1 tsp sugar
6–8 scallions, cut diagonally into
    1-inch lengths
3 garlic cloves, sliced
1 green chili, seeded and sliced
4 oz Chinese cabbage leaves,
    coarsely shredded (about 2 cups)
¼ cup bean sprouts
½ cup cashew nuts, toasted

bean curd

egg noodles

sesame oil

dark soy sauce

garlic

Chinese cabbage

scallions

green chili

bean sprouts

cashew nuts

1 If in water, drain the bean curd and pat dry with paper towels. Cut it into 1-inch cubes. Half-fill a wok with peanut oil and heat to 350°F. Deep-fry the bean curd in batches for 1–2 minutes, until golden and crisp. Drain on paper towels. Carefully pour all but 2 tablespoons of the oil from the wok.

2 Cook the noodles. Rinse them thoroughly under cold water and drain well. Toss in 2 teaspoons of the sesame oil and set aside. In a bowl, blend together the cornstarch, soy sauce, rice wine, sugar and remaining sesame oil.

3 Reheat the 2 tablespoons of peanut oil and, when hot, add the scallions, garlic, chili, cabbage and bean sprouts. Stir-fry for 1–2 minutes.

4 Add the bean curd, noodles and cornstarch mixture. Cook, stirring, for about 1 minute, until well mixed. Sprinkle the cashew nuts over. Serve at once.

Noodles with Ginger and Cilantro

Here is a simple noodle dish that goes well with most Asian dishes. It can also be served as a snack for two or three people.

Serves 4

INGREDIENTS
handful of cilantro
8 oz dried egg noodles
3 tbsp oil
2-inch piece fresh ginger root, cut into fine shreds
6–8 scallions, cut into shreds
2 tbsp light soy sauce
salt and freshly ground black pepper

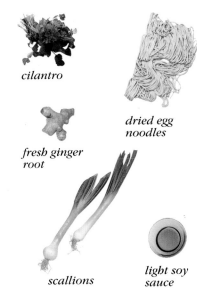

cilantro

dried egg noodles

fresh ginger root

scallions

light soy sauce

1 Strip the leaves from the cilantro stalks. Pile them on a chopping board and coarsely chop them using a cleaver or large, sharp knife.

2 Cook the noodles according to the package instructions. Rinse under cold water, drain well and then toss in 1 tablespoon of the oil.

3 Heat a wok until hot, add the remaining oil and swirl it around. Add the ginger and stir-fry for a few seconds, then add the noodles and scallions. Stir-fry for 3–4 minutes, until hot.

4 Sprinkle the soy sauce, cilantro and seasoning over. Toss well and serve at once.

COOK'S TIP
As with many Thai, Singaporean or Malaysian dishes, for best results use peanut oil. Alternatively, cook vegetables in sunflower oil, but toss noodles in sesame oil.

Deep-fried Zucchini with Chili Sauce

Crunchy coated zucchini are great served with a fiery tomato sauce.

Serves 2

INGREDIENTS
1 tbsp olive oil
1 onion, finely chopped
1 red chili, seeded and finely diced
2 tsp hot chili powder
14 oz can chopped tomatoes
1 vegetable bouillon cube
$1/4$ cup hot water
1 lb zucchini
$2/3$ cup milk
$1/2$ cup all-purpose flour
oil for deep-frying
salt and freshly ground black pepper

TO SERVE
lettuce leaves
watercress sprigs
slices of seeded bread
thyme sprigs, to garnish

zucchini
chopped tomatoes
onion
red chili
all-purpose flour
bouillon cube
milk
chili powder

1 Heat the oil in a pan. Add the onion, and cook for 2–3 minutes. Add the chili. Stir in the chili powder, and cook for 30 seconds.

2 Add the tomatoes. Crumble in the bouillon cube, and stir in the water. Cover and cook for 10 minutes.

3 Meanwhile, remove the ends from the zucchini. Cut them into $1/4$ in slices.

4 Pour the milk into one shallow dish, and spread out the flour in another. Dip the zucchini first in the milk, then into the flour, until well-coated.

5 Heat the oil for deep-frying to 350°F or until a cube of bread, when added to the oil, browns in 30–45 seconds. Add the zucchini slices in batches, and deep-fry for 3–4 minutes until crisp. Drain on paper towels.

6 Place two or three lettuce leaves on each serving plate. Add a few sprigs of watercress, and fan out the bread slices to one side. Season the sauce, spoon some on to each plate, top with the zucchini and garnish with the sprigs of thyme. Serve at once with a crisp salad and bread.

Cumin-spiced Large Zucchini and Spinach

A great way to enjoy the giant zucchini that escaped in the garden is with spinach and cream.

Serves 2

INGREDIENTS

1 lb zucchini
2 tbsp vegetable oil
2 tsp cumin seeds
1 small red chili, seeded and
  finely chopped
2 tbsp water
2 oz tender, young spinach leaves
6 tbsp light cream
salt and freshly ground black pepper

spinach
leaves

cumin
seeds

large
zucchini

light cream

red chili

1 Peel the zucchini, and cut it in half. Scoop out the seeds. Cut the flesh into ½ in cubes.

2 Heat the oil in a large frying pan. Add the cumin seeds and the chopped chili. Cook for 1 minute.

3 Add the zucchini and water to the pan. Cover with foil or a lid, and simmer for 8 minutes, stirring occasionally, until the zucchini is just tender. Remove the cover, and cook for 2 minutes more or until most of the water has evaporated.

4 Put the spinach leaves in a colander. Rinse well under cold water, drain and pat dry with paper towels. Tear into rough pieces.

5 Add the spinach to the zucchini. Replace the cover, and cook gently for 1 minute.

6 Stir in the cream, and cook over a high heat for 2 minutes. Add salt and pepper to taste, and serve. An Indian rice dish would be a good accompaniment. As an alternative, serve with naan bread.

Chili Beans with Basmati Rice

Red kidney beans, tomatoes and chili make a great combination. Serve with pasta or pita bread instead of rice, if you prefer.

Serves 4

INGREDIENTS
2 cups basmati rice
2 tbsp olive oil
1 large onion, chopped
1 garlic clove, crushed
1 tbsp hot chili powder
1 tbsp all-purpose flour
1 tbsp tomato paste
14 oz can chopped tomatoes
14 oz can red kidney beans, drained
²/₃ cup hot vegetable stock
chopped fresh parsley, to garnish
salt and freshly ground black pepper

basmati rice

chopped tomatoes

chili powder

onion

tomato paste

garlic clove

bouillon cube

red kidney beans

all-purpose flour

1 Wash the rice several times under cold running water. Drain well. Bring a large pan of water to a boil. Add the rice, and cook for 10–12 minutes, until tender. Meanwhile, heat the oil in a frying pan. Add the onion and garlic, and cook for 2 minutes.

2 Stir the chili powder and flour into the onion and garlic mixture. Cook for 2 minutes, stirring frequently.

3 Stir in the tomato paste and chopped tomatoes. Rinse the kidney beans under cold water, drain well, and add to the pan with the hot vegetable stock. Cover and cook for 12 minutes, stirring occasionally.

4 Season the chili sauce with salt and pepper. Drain the rice, and serve at once, with the chili beans, sprinkled with a little chopped fresh parsley.

Spicy Cauliflower and Potato Salad

A delicious, cold vegetable salad with a hot and spicy dressing.

Serves 2–3

INGREDIENTS
1 cauliflower
2 potatoes
1½ tsp caraway seeds
1 tsp ground coriander
½ tsp hot chili powder
juice of 1 lemon
4 tbsp olive oil
salt and freshly ground black pepper

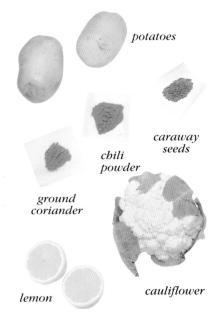

potatoes

chili powder

caraway seeds

ground coriander

lemon

cauliflower

1 Break the cauliflower into small florets. Peel the potatoes, and cut them into chunks.

2 Bring a large pan of water to a boil. Add the cauliflower florets and potato chunks, and cook for 8 minutes until they are just tender.

3 Meanwhile, heat a nonstick frying pan. Add the caraway seeds, and fry, shaking the pan constantly, for 1 minute. Turn the roasted seeds into a bowl, and add the ground coriander and chili powder, with salt and pepper to taste. Stir in the lemon juice and olive oil. Mix to a paste.

4 Drain the vegetables well. Add them to the bowl, and toss to coat in the chili dressing. Serve at once, with hot pita bread or brown rice.

Bengali-style Vegetables

A hot, dry curry using spices that do not require long, slow cooking.

Serves 4

INGREDIENTS

½ cauliflower, broken into small florets
1 large potato, peeled and cut into 1 in dice
4 oz green beans, trimmed
2 zucchini, halved lengthwise and sliced
2 green chilies
1 in piece of fresh ginger, peeled
½ cup plain yogurt
2 tsp ground coriander
½ tsp ground turmeric
2 tbsp ghee or vegetable oil
½ tsp garam masala
1 tsp cumin seeds
2 tsp sugar
pinch each of ground cloves, ground cinnamon and ground cardamom
salt and freshly ground black pepper

1 Bring a large pan of water to a boil. Add the cauliflower and potato, and cook for 5 minutes. Add the beans and zucchini, and cook for 2–3 minutes.

2 Meanwhile, cut the chilies in half, remove the seeds, and coarsely chop the flesh. Finely chop the ginger. Mix the chilies and ginger in a small bowl.

green chili

cumin seeds

green beans

fresh ginger

cauliflower florets

potato

plain yogurt

sugar

ground turmeric

ground coriander

ghee

ground cinnamon

zucchini

ground cloves   garam masala

3 Drain the vegetables, and turn them into a bowl. Add the chili and ginger mixture, with the yogurt, ground coriander and turmeric. Season with plenty of salt and pepper, and mix well.

4 Heat the ghee or oil in a large frying pan. Add the vegetable mixture, and cook over a high heat for 2 minutes, stirring from time to time.

5 Stir in the garam masala and cumin seeds, and cook for 2 minutes.

6 Stir in the sugar and remaining spices, and cook for 1 minute or until all the liquid has evaporated.

COOK'S TIP
If ghee is not available, you can clarify your own butter. Melt ¼ cup butter slowly in a small pan. Remove from the heat, and leave for about 5 minutes. Then pour off the clear yellow clarified butter, leaving the sediment in the pan.

Mushroom and Okra Curry with Fresh Mango Relish

This simple but delicious curry with its fresh gingery mango relish is best served with plain basmati rice.

Serves 4

INGREDIENTS
4 garlic cloves, roughly chopped
1 in piece of fresh ginger root, peeled **and roughly chopped**
1–2 red chilies, seeded and chopped
¾ cup cold water
1 tbsp sunflower oil
1 tsp coriander seeds
1 tsp cumin seeds
1 tsp ground cumin
2 green cardamom pods, seeds removed and ground
pinch of ground turmeric
1 × 14 oz can chopped tomatoes
1 lb mushrooms, halved or quartered if large
8 oz okra, trimmed and cut into ½ in slices
2 tbsp chopped fresh cilantro
basmati rice, to serve

FOR THE MANGO RELISH
1 large ripe mango, about 1¼ lb in weight
1 small garlic clove, crushed
1 onion, finely chopped
2 tsp grated fresh ginger root
1 fresh red chili, seeded and finely chopped
pinch of salt and sugar

onion

garlic

coriander seeds

ginger

mushrooms

mango

okra

red chilies

chopped tomatoes

cumin seeds

turmeric

cardamom pods

1 For the mango relish, peel the mango and cut off the flesh from the pit.

2 In a bowl mash the mango flesh with a fork or pulse in a food processor, and mix in the rest of the relish ingredients. Set to one side.

3 Place the garlic, ginger, chili and 3 tbsp of the water into a blender and blend until smooth.

4 Heat the sunflower oil in a large pan. Add the whole coriander and cumin seeds and allow them to sizzle for a few seconds. Add the ground cumin, ground cardamom and turmeric and cook for 1 minute more.

5 Add the paste from the blender, the tomatoes, remaining water, mushrooms and okra. Stir to mix well and bring to a boil. Reduce the heat, cover, and simmer for 5 minutes.

6 Remove the cover, turn up the heat slightly and cook for another 5–10 minutes until the okra is tender. Stir in the fresh cilantro and serve with rice and the mango relish.

Aloo Gobi

Cauliflower and potatoes are encrusted with Indian spices in this delicious recipe.

Serves 4

INGREDIENTS

1 lb potatoes, cut into
   1-inch chunks
2 tbsp oil
1 tsp cumin seeds
1 green chili, finely chopped
1 lb cauliflower, broken
   into florets
1 tsp ground coriander
1 tsp ground cumin
¼ tsp cayenne pepper
½ tsp ground turmeric
½ tsp salt
chopped cilantro, to garnish
tomato and onion salad and pickle,
   to serve

oil

ground
coriander

cayenne
pepper

ground
cumin

cumin
seeds

ground
turmeric

salt

cauliflower

green
chili

potatoes

VARIATION

Try using sweet potatoes instead of ordinary potatoes for a tasty variation with a sweeter flavor.

1 Parboil the potatoes in a large saucepan of boiling water for 10 minutes. Drain well and set aside.

2 Heat the oil in a large frying pan and fry the cumin seeds for 2 minutes, until they begin to sputter. Add the chili and fry for another minute.

3 Add the cauliflower florets and fry, stirring, for 5 minutes.

4 Add the potatoes and the ground spices and salt and cook for another 7–10 minutes, or until both the vegetables are tender. Garnish with cilantro and serve with tomato and onion salad and pickle.

Masala Okra

Okra, or "ladies' fingers" are a popular Indian vegetable. In this recipe they are stir-fried with a dry, spicy masala to make a delicious side dish.

Serves 4

INGREDIENTS
1 lb okra
½ tsp ground turmeric
1 tsp cayenne pepper
1 tbsp ground cumin
1 tbsp ground coriander
¼ tsp salt
¼ tsp sugar
1 tbsp lemon juice
1 tbsp dried coconut
2 tbsp chopped cilantro
3 tbsp oil
½ tsp cumin seeds
½ tsp black mustard seeds
chopped fresh tomatoes, to garnish
poppadums, to serve

black mustard seeds *lemon juice* *ground coriander* *cumin seeds*

ground cumin

cayenne pepper

sugar

ground turmeric *okra*

dried coconut

salt

cilantro

1 Wash, dry and trim the okra. In a bowl, mix together the turmeric, cayenne pepper, cumin, ground coriander, salt, sugar, lemon juice, dried coconut and the cilantro.

2 Heat the oil in a large frying pan. Add the cumin seeds and mustard seeds and fry for about 2 minutes, or until they begin to sputter.

3 Add the spice mixture and continue to fry for 2 minutes.

4 Add the okra, cover, and cook over low heat for 10 minutes, or until tender. Garnish with chopped fresh tomatoes and serve with poppadums.

COOK'S TIP

When buying okra, choose firm, brightly colored, unblemished pods that are less than 4 inches long.

Mixed Vegetable Curry

A good all-round vegetable curry that goes well with most Indian dishes. You can use any combination of vegetables that are in season for this basic recipe.

Serves 4

INGREDIENTS
2 tbsp oil
½ tsp black mustard seeds
½ tsp cumin seeds
1 onion, thinly sliced
2 curry leaves
1 green chili, finely chopped
1-inch piece ginger root,
    finely chopped
2 tbsp curry paste
1 small cauliflower, broken
    into florets
1 large carrot, thickly sliced
4 oz green beans, cut into
    1-inch lengths
¼ tsp ground turmeric
¼ tsp cayenne pepper
½ tsp salt
2 tomatoes, finely chopped
2 oz frozen peas, thawed
²/₃ cup vegetable broth
nan bread, to serve
fresh curry leaves, to garnish

curry paste
peas
vegetable broth
black mustard seeds
cayenne pepper
cauliflower
ground turmeric
cumin seeds
tomatoes
ginger
green beans
carrot
curry leaves
onion
green chili

1 Heat the oil in a large saucepan and fry the mustard seeds and cumin seeds for 2 minutes, until they begin to sputter.

2 Add the onion and the curry leaves and fry for 5 minutes.

3 Add the chili and ginger and fry for 2 minutes. Stir in the curry paste and fry for 3–4 minutes.

4 Add the cauliflower, carrot and green beans and cook for 4–5 minutes. Add the turmeric, cayenne pepper, salt and tomatoes and cook for 2–3 minutes.

5 Add the thawed peas and cook for another 2–3 minutes.

6 Add the broth. Cover and simmer over low heat for 10–13 minutes or until all the vegetables are tender. Serve, garnished with curry leaves.

Spicy French Fries with Sesame Seeds

This recipe is a variation of the well-known dish Bombay Potatoes, in which the potatoes are fried to give them a crispy texture, and then tossed in spices and sesame seeds.

Serves 4

INGREDIENTS
2 lb potatoes
oil, for deep-frying
¼ tsp ground turmeric
¼ tsp cayenne pepper
¼ tsp salt
2 tbsp oil
¼ tsp black mustard seeds
1 green chili, finely chopped
1 garlic clove, crushed
2 tbsp sesame seeds

oil

black mustard seeds

sesame seeds

ground turmeric

cayenne pepper

green chili

potatoes

garlic

salt

2 Heat the oil for deep-frying to 325°F. Fry the potatoes in batches for 5 minutes, until golden. Drain well on plenty of paper towels.

1 Cut the potatoes into thick strips.

3 Put the potatoes in a bowl and sprinkle over the turmeric, cayenne pepper and salt. Cool, then toss the strips in the spices until evenly coated.

4 Heat the 2 tablespoons oil in a large saucepan and fry the mustard seeds for 2 minutes until they sputter. Add the chili and garlic and fry for 2 minutes.

5 Add the sesame seeds and fry for 3–4 minutes or until the seeds begin to brown. Remove from the heat.

6 Add the sesame seed mixture to the potatoes and toss together to coat evenly. Serve cold, or reheat for 5 minutes in an oven preheated to 400°F.

COOK'S TIP
Make sure the potato strips are as uniform in size as possible to ensure that they cook evenly.

Zucchini Curry

Thickly sliced zucchini are combined with authentic Indian spices for a delicious, colorful vegetable curry.

Serves 4

INGREDIENTS

1½ lb zucchini
3 tbsp oil
½ tsp cumin seeds
½ tsp mustard seeds
1 onion, thinly sliced
2 garlic cloves, crushed
¼ tsp ground turmeric
¼ tsp cayenne pepper
1 tsp ground coriander
1 tsp ground cumin
½ tsp salt
1 tbsp tomato paste
14-oz can chopped tomatoes
⅔ cup water
1 tbsp chopped cilantro
1 tsp garam masala

oil   *mustard seeds*   *chopped tomatoes*

ground cumin   *cumin seeds*   *cayenne pepper*

garam masala   *tomato paste*   *onion*

ground turmeric   *ground coriander*

salt   *garlic*   *zucchini*   *cilantro*

1 Trim the ends from the zucchini then cut into ½-inch thick slices.

2 Heat the oil in a large saucepan and fry the cumin and mustard seeds for 2 minutes.

3 Add the onion and garlic and fry for about 5–6 minutes.

4 Add the turmeric, cayenne pepper, coriander, cumin and salt and fry for about 2–3 minutes.

5 Add the sliced zucchini all at once, and cook for 5 minutes.

6 Mix together the tomato paste and chopped tomatoes and add to the saucepan with the water. Cover and simmer for 10 minutes, until the sauce thickens. Stir in the cilantro and garam masala, then cook for 5 minutes or until the zucchini are tender.

Vegetable Kashmiri

This is a delicious vegetable curry, in which fresh mixed vegetables are cooked in a spicy, aromatic yogurt sauce.

Serves 4

INGREDIENTS
2 tsp cumin seeds
8 black peppercorns
2 green cardamom pods, seeds only
2-inch cinnamon stick
½ tsp grated nutmeg
3 tbsp oil
1 green chili, chopped
1-inch piece ginger root, grated
1 tsp cayenne pepper
½ tsp salt
2 large potatoes, cut into
    1-inch chunks
8 oz cauliflower, broken into
    florets
8 oz okra, thickly sliced
⅔ cup plain yogurt
⅔ cup vegetable broth
toasted flaked almonds and cilantro
    sprigs, to garnish

vegetable broth
oil
cayenne pepper
black peppercorns
cauliflower
potatoes
cumin seeds
cinnamon stick
plain yogurt
salt
nutmeg
ginger
okra
cardamom pods
green chili

1 Grind the cumin seeds, peppercorns, cardamom seeds, cinnamon stick and nutmeg to a fine powder using a mortar and pestle or spice grinder.

2 Heat the oil in a large saucepan and fry the chili and ginger for 2 minutes, stirring all the time.

3 Add the cayenne pepper, salt and ground spice mixture and fry for about 2–3 minutes, stirring constantly to prevent the spices from sticking.

4 Stir in the potatoes, cover, and cook for 10 minutes over low heat, stirring from time to time.

5 Add the cauliflower and okra and cook for 5 minutes.

6 Add the yogurt and broth. Bring to a boil, then reduce the heat. Cover and simmer for 20 minutes, or until all the vegetables are tender. Garnish with toasted almonds and cilantro sprigs.

Red Cabbage in Port and Red Wine

A sweet and sour, spicy red cabbage dish, with the added crunch of pears and walnuts.

Serves 6

INGREDIENTS
1 tbsp walnut oil
1 onion, sliced
2 whole star anise
1 tsp ground cinnamon
pinch of ground cloves
1 lb red cabbage, finely shredded
2 tbsp dark brown sugar
3 tbsp red wine vinegar
1¼ cups red wine
⅔ cup port
2 pears, cut into ½ in cubes
½ cup raisins
salt and freshly ground black pepper
½ cup walnut halves

1 Heat the oil in a large pan. Add the onion and cook gently for about 5 minutes until softened.

brown sugar

red cabbage

pears

onion *raisins*

walnut halves

star anise

red wine vinegar

port

red wine

2 Add the star anise, cinnamon, cloves and cabbage and cook for about 3 minutes more.

3 Stir in the sugar, vinegar, red wine and port. Cover the pan and simmer gently for 10 minutes, stirring occasionally.

4 Stir in the cubed pears and raisins and cook for a further 10 minutes or until the cabbage is tender. Season to taste. Mix in the walnut halves and serve.

Beet and Celeriac Gratin

Beautiful ruby-red slices of beets and celeriac make a stunning light accompaniment to any main course dish.

Serves 6

INGREDIENTS
12 oz raw beets
12 oz celeriac
4 thyme sprigs
6 juniper berries, crushed
salt and freshly ground black pepper
½ cup fresh orange juice
½ cup vegetable stock

celeriac

orange juice

juniper berries

beet

thyme

1 Preheat the oven to 375°F. Scrub, peel and slice the beets very finely. Scrub, quarter and peel the celeriac and slice very finely.

2 Fill a 10 in diameter, cast iron, ovenproof or flameproof frying pan with alternate layers of beet and celeriac slices, sprinkling with the thyme, juniper and seasoning between each layer.

3 Mix the orange juice and stock together and pour over the gratin. Place over a medium heat and bring to a boil. Boil for 2 minutes.

4 Cover with foil and place in the oven for 15–20 minutes. Remove the foil and raise the oven temperature to 400°F. Cook for a further 10 minutes until tender and bubbling.

Roasted Plum Tomatoes with Garlic

These are so simple to prepare, yet taste absolutely wonderful. Use a large, shallow earthenware dish that will allow the tomatoes to sear and char in a hot oven.

Serves 4

INGREDIENTS
8 plum tomatoes
12 garlic cloves
¼ cup extra virgin olive oil
3 bay leaves
salt and ground black pepper
3 tablespoons fresh oregano leaves, to garnish

plum tomatoes *garlic* *olive oil*

oregano *bay leaves*

1 Preheat the oven to 450°F. Halve the plum tomatoes, leaving a small part of the green stem intact, if possible, for decoration.

2 Select an ovenproof dish that will hold all the tomatoes snugly in a single layer. Place the tomatoes in the dish with the cut side facing upward, and push the whole, unpeeled garlic cloves between them.

3 Brush the tomatoes with the oil, add the bay leaves and sprinkle black pepper over the top.

4 Bake for about 45 minutes, until the tomatoes have softened and are sizzling in the dish. They should be charred around the edges. Season with salt and a little more black pepper, if needed. Garnish with the fresh oregano leaves and serve immediately.

VARIATION

For a sweet alternative, use red or yellow bell peppers instead of the tomatoes. Cut each pepper in half and remove all the seeds before placing, cut side up, in an ovenproof dish.

COOK'S TIP

Select ripe, juicy tomatoes without any blemishes to get the best flavor out of this dish.

Zucchini with Onion and Garlic

Use a good-quality olive oil and sunflower oil. The olive oil gives the dish a delicious fragrance without overpowering the zucchini.

Serves 4

INGREDIENTS
1 tbsp olive oil
1 tbsp sunflower oil
1 large onion, chopped
1 garlic clove, finely chopped
6–7 small zucchini, cut into
    ½-inch slices
⅔ cup vegetable broth
½ tsp chopped fresh oregano
salt and ground black pepper
chopped fresh parsley, to garnish

garlic

zucchini

olive oil

broth

sunflower oil

oregano

onion

parsley

1 Heat the olive and sunflower oils together in a large frying pan and add the chopped onion and garlic. Fry over medium heat for 5–6 minutes, until the onion has softened and is beginning to brown.

2 Add the zucchini slices and fry for about 4 minutes, until they just begin to be flecked with brown, stirring frequently.

3 Stir in the broth, oregano and seasoning and simmer gently for 8–10 minutes, or until the liquid has almost evaporated.

4 Spoon the zucchini into a warmed serving dish, sprinkle with chopped parsley and serve.

COOK'S TIP

Zucchini are very popular in Italy, grown in many kitchen gardens. They make a lovely summer dish, and take very little time to prepare. If you can find them, choose small zucchini, which tend to be much sweeter than the larger ones.

Herbed Baked Tomatoes

Dress up sliced, sweet tomatoes with fresh herbs and a crisp bread crumb topping.

Serves 4–6

INGREDIENTS

1½ lb (about 8) large red and yellow
   tomatoes
2 tsp red wine vinegar
½ tsp whole grain mustard
1 garlic clove, crushed
2 tsp chopped fresh parsley
2 tsp chopped fresh chives
½ cup fresh fine white bread
   crumbs
salt and freshly ground black pepper
sprigs of Italian parsley, to garnish

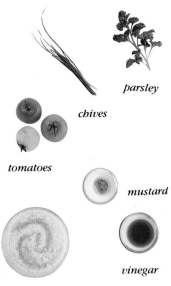

parsley

chives

tomatoes

mustard

vinegar

bread crumbs

1 Preheat the oven to 400°F. Thickly slice the tomatoes and arrange half of them in a 3¾ cup ovenproof dish, overlapping the slices.

2 Mix the vinegar, mustard, garlic clove and seasoning together. Stir in 2 tsp of cold water. Sprinkle the tomatoes with half the parsley and chives, then drizzle over half the dressing.

3 Lay the remaining tomato slices on top, overlapping them slightly. Drizzle with the remaining dressing.

4 Sprinkle over the bread crumbs. Bake in the preheated oven for 25 minutes or until the topping is golden. Sprinkle with the remaining parsley and chives. Serve immediately garnished with sprigs of Italian parsley.

Zucchini in Citrus Sauce

If baby zucchini are unavailable, you can use larger ones, but they should be cooked whole so that they don't absorb too much water. Halve them lengthwise and cut into 4 in lengths.

Serves 4

INGREDIENTS
12 oz baby zucchini
4 scallions, finely sliced
1 in fresh ginger root, grated
2 tbsp cider vinegar
1 tbsp light soy sauce
1 tsp soft light brown sugar
3 tbsp vegetable stock
finely grated rind and juice of ½
    lemon and ½ orange
1 tsp cornstarch

orange

zucchini

lemon

ginger

scallions

1 Cook the zucchini in lightly salted boiling water for 3-4 minutes, or until just tender. Drain well.

2 Meanwhile put all the remaining ingredients, except the cornstarch, into a small saucepan and bring to a boil. Simmer for 3 minutes.

3 Blend the cornstarch with 2 tsp of cold water and add to the sauce. Bring to a boil, stirring continuously, until the sauce has thickened.

4 Pour the sauce over the zucchini and gently heat, shaking the pan to coat evenly. Transfer to a warmed serving dish and serve.

Mixed Mushroom Ragu

These mushrooms are delicious served hot or cold
and can be made up to two days in advance.

Serves 4

INGREDIENTS
1 small onion, finely chopped
1 garlic clove, crushed
1 tsp coriander seeds, crushed
2 tbsp red wine vinegar
1 tbsp soy sauce
1 tbsp dry sherry
2 tsp tomato paste
2 tsp light brown sugar
⅔ cup vegetable stock
4 oz baby white mushrooms
4 oz cremini mushrooms, quartered
4 oz oyster mushrooms, sliced
salt and freshly ground black pepper
sprig of fresh cilantro, to garnish

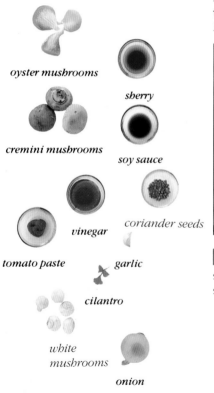

oyster mushrooms

sherry

cremini mushrooms

soy sauce

vinegar

coriander seeds

tomato paste   *garlic*

cilantro

white mushrooms

onion

1 Put the first nine ingredients into a large saucepan. Bring to a boil and reduce the heat. Cover and simmer for 5 minutes.

2 Uncover the saucepan and simmer for 5 more minutes, or until the liquid has reduced by half.

3 Add the baby white and cremini mushrooms and simmer for 3 minutes Stir in the oyster mushrooms and cook for a further 2 minutes.

4 Remove the mushrooms with a slotted spoon and transfer them to a serving dish.

5 Boil the juices for about 5 minutes, or until reduced to about 5 tbsp. Season well with salt and pepper.

6 Allow to cool for 2-3 minutes, then pour over the mushrooms. Serve hot or well chilled, garnished with fresh cilantro.

Baked Onions with Sun-Dried Tomatoes

This wonderfully simple vegetable dish of baked onions brings together the flavors of a hot Italian summer—tomatoes, fresh herbs and olive oil.

Serves 4

INGREDIENTS
1 lb small onions, peeled
2 tsp chopped fresh rosemary or
   1 tsp dried rosemary
2 garlic cloves, chopped
1 tbsp chopped fresh parsley
½ cup sun-dried tomatoes in oil,
   drained and chopped
6 tbsp olive oil
1 tbsp white wine vinegar
salt and ground black pepper

olive oil

garlic

rosemary

small onions

sun-dried tomatoes

white wine vinegar

parsley

1 Preheat the oven to 300°F. Grease a shallow baking dish. Drop the onions into a saucepan of boiling water and cook for 5 minutes. Drain in a colander.

2 Spread the onions in the bottom of the prepared baking dish.

VARIATIONS

Other herbs can be used instead of the rosemary and parsley in this dish. Try using shredded fresh basil, which will enhance the flavor of the sun-dried tomatoes, or fresh thyme, which complements the flavor of baked onions perfectly. If you can find small red onions, these would make a nice change, or even mix the two colors.

3 Combine the rosemary, garlic, parsley, salt and pepper in a small mixing bowl and sprinkle the mixture evenly over the onions in the dish.

4 Sprinkle the chopped sun-dried tomatoes over the onions. Drizzle the olive oil and vinegar on top.

5 Cover the dish with a sheet of foil and bake for 45 minutes, basting occasionally. Remove the foil and bake for about 15 minutes more, until the onions are golden brown all over. Serve immediately from the dish.

Broiled Eggplant Bundles

These are delicious little bundles of tomatoes, mozzarella cheese and fragrant fresh basil, wrapped in slices of eggplant.

Serves 4

INGREDIENTS
2 large, long eggplant
8 oz mozzarella cheese
2 plum tomatoes
16 large basil leaves
2 tbsp olive oil
salt and ground black pepper

FOR THE DRESSING
¼ cup olive oil
1 tsp balsamic vinegar
1 tbsp sun-dried tomato
    paste
1 tbsp lemon juice

FOR THE GARNISH
2 tbsp pine nuts, toasted
torn basil leaves

eggplant
mozzarella cheese
basil
lemon
balsamic vinegar
tomato paste
plum tomatoes
olive oil
pine nuts

1 To make the dressing, whisk together the olive oil, vinegar, sun-dried tomato paste and lemon juice. Season to taste and set aside.

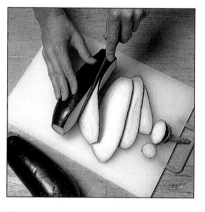

2 Remove the stalks from the eggplants and cut the eggplants lengthwise into thin slices—the aim is to get 16 slices total (each about ¼ inch thick), disregarding the first and last slices. (If you have a mandoline, it will cut perfect, even slices for you; otherwise use a sharp, long-bladed knife.)

3 Bring a large pan of salted water to a boil and cook the eggplant slices for about 2 minutes, or until just softened. Drain the sliced eggplant, then dry on paper towels. Set aside.

4 Cut the cheese into thin slices. Cut each tomato into eight slices, not counting the first and last slices.

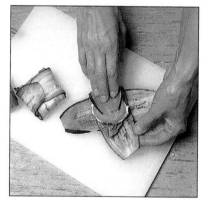

5 Take two eggplant slices and place on a baking sheet or in a large flameproof dish, forming a cross. Place a slice of tomato in the center of the cross, season with salt and pepper, then add a basil leaf, followed by a slice of cheese, another basil leaf, a slice of tomato and more seasoning.

6 Fold the ends of the eggplant slices around the cheese and tomato filling to make a neat bundle. Repeat with the rest of the assembled ingredients to make eight bundles. Chill the bundles for about 20 minutes.

7 Preheat the broiler. Brush the bundles with olive oil and cook for about 5 minutes on each side, or until golden. Serve hot, with the dressing, and sprinkled with pine nuts and basil.

Radicchio and Belgian Endive Gratin

Radicchio and Belgian endive take on a different flavor when cooked in this way. The creamy sauce combines wonderfully with the bitter leaves.

Serves 4

INGREDIENTS
2 heads radicchio
2 heads Belgian endive
½ cup sun-dried tomatoes in oil,
    drained and roughly chopped,
    oil reserved
salt and ground black pepper

FOR THE SAUCE
2 tbsp butter
2 tbsp all-purpose flour
1 cup milk
pinch of grated nutmeg
2 oz (½ cup) grated Emmenthal
    cheese
chopped fresh parsley,
    to garnish

radicchio
Emmenthal cheese
butter
Belgian endive
flour
sun-dried tomatoes
milk
nutmeg
parsley

1 Preheat the oven to 350°F. Grease a 5-cup baking dish. Trim the radicchio and Belgian endive and discard any damaged or wilted leaves. Quarter them lengthwise and arrange in the baking dish. Sprinkle the sun-dried tomatoes on top and brush the leaves liberally with oil from the sun-dried tomato jar. Sprinkle with salt and pepper and cover with foil. Bake for 15 minutes, then remove the foil and bake for another 10 minutes, until the vegetables are softened.

COOK'S TIP

In Italy, radicchio and Belgian endive are often grilled on an outdoor barbecue. To do this, simply prepare the vegetables as above and brush with olive oil. Place cut side down on the grill for 7–10 minutes, until browned. Turn and grill for about 5 more minutes, or until the other side is browned.

2 Make the béchamel sauce. Place the butter in a small saucepan and melt over medium heat. When the butter is foaming, add the flour and cook for 1 minute, stirring. Remove from the heat and gradually add the milk, whisking constantly. Return to the heat, bring to a boil and simmer for 2–3 minutes, until the mixture thickens.

3 Season the sauce to taste and add the grated nutmeg.

4 Pour the sauce over the vegetables and sprinkle with the grated cheese. Bake for 20 minutes, or until golden brown. Serve immediately, garnished with the chopped parsley.

Gorgonzola, Cauliflower and Walnut Gratin

This cauliflower dish is covered with a bubbly blue cheese sauce topped with chopped walnuts and cooked under the broiler.

Serves 4

INGREDIENTS
1 large cauliflower, broken into florets
2 tbsp butter
1 medium onion, finely chopped
3 tbsp flour
scant 2 cups milk
5 oz Gorgonzola or other blue cheese, cut into pieces
½ tsp celery salt
pinch of cayenne papper
¾ cup chopped walnuts
pinch of salt
fresh parsley, to garnish
4 oz green salad, to serve

onion

butter

Gorgonzola

walnuts

cauliflower

1 Bring a large saucepan of salted water to a boil and cook the cauliflower for 6 minutes. Drain and place in a flameproof gratin dish.

2 Heat the butter in a heavy saucepan. Add the onion and cook over a gentle heat to soften without coloring. Stir in the flour, then remove from the heat. Stir in the milk a little at a time until absorbed by the flour, stirring continuously. Add the cheese, celery salt and cayenne pepper. Simmer and stir to thicken.

3 Preheat a moderate broiler. Spoon the sauce over the cauliflower, scatter with chopped walnuts and broil until golden. Garnish with the parsley and serve with a crisp green salad.

VARIATION

For a delicious alternative, substitute cauliflower with 2½ lb fresh broccoli or combine both together.

Leek and Caraway Gratin with a Carrot Crust

Tender leeks are mixed with a creamy caraway sauce and a crunchy carrot topping.

Serves 4–6

INGREDIENTS

1½ lb leeks, cut into 2 in pieces
⅔ cup fresh vegetable stock or water
3 tbsp dry white wine
1 tsp caraway seeds
pinch of salt
1¼ cups skim milk, or as required
2 tbsp butter
¼ cup all-purpose flour

FOR THE TOPPING

2 cups fresh whole-wheat
   breadcrumbs
2 cups grated carrot
2 tbsp chopped fresh parsley
3 oz Jarlsberg cheese, coarsely grated
2 tbsp slivered almonds

parsley

vegetable stock

Jarlsberg

leek

breadcrumbs

butter

1 Place the leeks in a large pan. Add the stock or water, wine, caraway seeds and salt. Bring to a simmer, cover and cook for 5–7 minutes until the leeks are just tender.

2 With a slotted spoon, transfer the leeks to an ovenproof dish. Reduce the remaining liquid to half then make the amount up to 1½ cups with skim milk.

3 Preheat the oven to 350°F. Melt the butter in a saucepan, stir in the flour and cook without allowing it to color for 1–2 minutes. Gradually add the stock and milk, stirring well after each addition, until you have a smooth sauce. Simmer for 5–6 minutes then pour over the leeks in the dish.

4 Mix all the topping ingredients together in a bowl and sprinkle over the leeks. Bake for 20–25 minutes until golden.

Carrot Mousse with Mushroom Sauce

The combination of fresh vegetables in this impressive yet easy-to-make mousse make healthy eating a pleasure.

Serves 4

INGREDIENTS
12 oz carrots, roughly chopped
1 small red bell pepper, seeded and
    roughly chopped
3 tbsp vegetable stock or water
2 eggs
1 egg white
½ cup quark or low fat cream cheese
1 tbsp chopped fresh tarragon
salt and freshly ground black pepper
sprig of fresh tarragon, to garnish
boiled rice and leeks, to serve

FOR THE MUSHROOM SAUCE
2 tbsp low fat spread
6 oz mushrooms, sliced
2 tbsp flour
1 cup skim milk

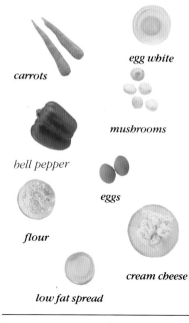

carrots
egg white
mushrooms
bell pepper
eggs
flour
cream cheese
low fat spread

1 Preheat the oven to 375°F. Line the bases of four ⅔ cup ramekin dishes with non-stick baking paper. Put the carrots and red pepper in a small saucepan with the vegetable stock or water. Cover and cook for 5 minutes, or until tender. Drain well.

2 Lightly beat the eggs and egg white together. Mix with the quark or low fat cream cheese. Season to taste. Purée the cooked vegetables in a food processor or blender. Add the cheese mixture and process for a few seconds more until smooth. Stir in the chopped tarragon.

3 Divide the carrot mixture between the prepared ramekin dishes and cover with foil. Place the dishes in a roasting pan half-filled with hot water. Bake in the oven for 35 minutes, or until set.

4 For the mushroom sauce, melt 1 tbsp of the low fat spread in a frying pan. Add the mushrooms and gently sauté for 5 minutes, until soft.

5 Put the remaining low fat spread in a small saucepan together with the flour and milk. Cook over medium heat, stirring all the time, until the sauce thickens. Stir in the mushrooms and season to taste.

6 Turn out each mousse onto a serving plate. Spoon over a little sauce and serve the remainder separately. Garnish with a sprig of fresh tarragon and serve with boiled rice and leeks.

Spring Vegetable Stir-fry

A colorful, dazzling medley of fresh and sweet young vegetables.

Serves 4

INGREDIENTS
1 tbsp peanut oil
1 garlic clove, sliced
1 in piece of fresh ginger root, finely chopped
4 oz baby carrots
4 oz patty pan squash
4 oz baby corn
4 oz green beans, topped and tailed
4 oz sugar-snap peas, topped and tailed
4 oz young asparagus, cut into 3 in pieces
8 scallions, trimmed and cut into 2 in pieces
4 oz cherry tomatoes

FOR THE DRESSING
juice of 2 limes
1 tbsp honey
1 tbsp soy sauce
1 tsp sesame oil

1 Heat the peanut oil in a wok or large frying pan.

2 Add the garlic and ginger and stir-fry over a high heat for 1 minute.

3 Add the carrots, patty pan squash, baby corn and beans and stir-fry for another 3–4 minutes.

4 Add the sugar-snap peas, asparagus, scallions and cherry tomatoes and stir-fry for a further 1–2 minutes.

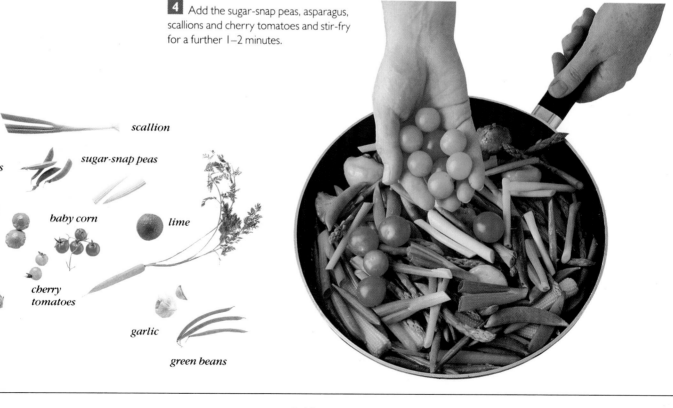

scallion

asparagus

sugar-snap peas

patty pan squash

baby corn

lime

ginger

cherry tomatoes

garlic

green beans

5 Mix the dressing ingredients together and add to the pan.

6 Stir well then cover the pan. Cook for 2–3 minutes more until the vegetables are just tender but still crisp.

COOK'S TIP
Stir-fries take only moments to cook so prepare this dish at the last minute.

Black Bean and Vegetable Stir-fry

The secret of a quick stir-fry is to prepare all the ingredients first. This colorful vegetable mixture is coated in a classic Chinese sauce.

Serves 4

INGREDIENTS
8 scallions
2 cups white mushrooms
1 red bell pepper
1 green bell pepper
2 large carrots
4 tbsp sesame oil
2 garlic cloves, crushed
4 tbsp black bean sauce
6 tbsp warm water
8 oz beansprouts
salt and freshly ground black pepper

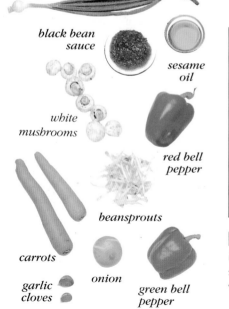

scallions

black bean sauce

sesame oil

white mushrooms

red bell pepper

beansprouts

carrots

garlic cloves

onion

green bell pepper

1 Thinly slice the scallions and button mushrooms. Set them to one side in separate bowls.

2 Cut both the bell peppers in half. Remove the seeds, and slice the flesh into thin strips.

3 Cut the carrots in half. Cut each half into thin strips lengthwise. Stack the slices, and cut through them to make very fine strips.

4 Heat the oil in a large wok or frying pan until very hot. Add the scallions and garlic, and stir-fry for 30 seconds.

5 Add the mushrooms, bell peppers and carrots. Stir-fry for 5–6 minutes over a high heat until the vegetables are just beginning to soften.

6 Mix the black bean sauce with the water. Add to the wok or pan, and cook for 3–4 minutes. Stir in the beansprouts, and stir-fry for 1 minute more, until all the vegetables are coated in the sauce. Season to taste. Serve at once.

COOK'S TIP
For best results the oil in the wok must be very hot before adding the vegetables.

Zucchini and Asparagus en Papillote

An impressive dinner party accompaniment, these puffed paper parcels should be broken open at the table by each guest, so that the wonderful aroma can be fully appreciated.

Serves 4

INGREDIENTS
2 medium zucchini
1 medium leek
8 oz young asparagus, trimmed
4 tarragon sprigs
4 whole garlic cloves, unpeeled
salt and freshly ground black pepper
1 egg, beaten

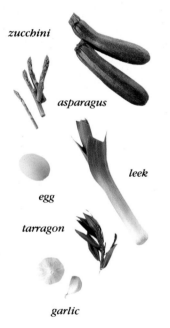

zucchini

asparagus

leek

egg

tarragon

garlic

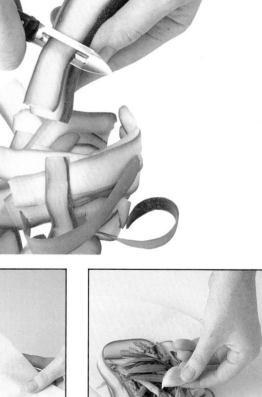

1 Preheat the oven to 400°F. Using a potato peeler slice the zucchini lengthwise into thin strips.

2 Cut the leek into very fine julienne strips and cut the asparagus evenly into 2 in lengths.

3 Cut out 4 sheets of parchment paper 12 × 15 in in size and fold each in half. Draw a large curve to make a heart shape when unfolded. Cut along the inside of the line and open out.

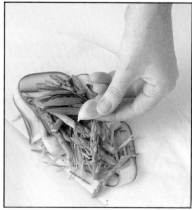

4 Divide the zucchini, asparagus and leek evenly between each paper heart, positioning the filling on one side of the fold line, and topping each with a sprig of tarragon and an unpeeled garlic clove. Season to taste.

COOK'S TIP
Experiment with other vegetables and herbs such as sugar-snap peas and mint or baby carrots and rosemary. The possibilities are endless.

5 Brush the edges lightly with the beaten egg and fold over.

6 Pleat the edges together so that each parcel is completely sealed. Lay the parcels on a cookie sheet and cook for 10 minutes. Serve immediately.

Broccoli and Chestnut Terrine

Served hot or cold, this versatile terrine is equally suitable for a dinner party as for a picnic.

Serves 4–6

INGREDIENTS
1 lb broccoli, cut into small florets
8 oz cooked chestnuts, roughly
    chopped
1 cup fresh whole-wheat breadcrumbs
4 tbsp low-fat plain yogurt
2 tbsp Parmesan cheese, finely grated
salt, grated nutmeg and freshly ground
    black pepper
2 eggs, beaten

yogurt

breadcrumbs

broccoli

chestnuts

egg

Parmesan

1 Preheat the oven to 350°F. Line a 2 lb loaf pan with a generous layer of parchment paper.

2 Blanch or steam the broccoli for 3–4 minutes until just tender. Drain well. Reserve ¼ of the smallest florets and chop the rest finely.

3 Mix together the chestnuts, breadcrumbs, yogurt and Parmesan, and season to taste.

4 Fold in the chopped broccoli, reserved florets and the beaten eggs.

5 Spoon the broccoli mixture into the prepared pan.

6 Place in a roasting pan and pour in boiling water to come halfway up the sides of the loaf pan. Bake for 20–25 minutes. Remove from the oven and tip out onto a plate or tray. Serve cut into even slices.

Baked Squash

A creamy, sweet and nutty filling makes the perfect topping for tender buttery squash.

Serves 4

INGREDIENTS
2 butternut or acorn squash, 1¼ lb
    each
1 tbsp olive oil
¾ cup canned corn kernels, drained
½ cup unsweetened chestnut purée
5 tbsp low-fat yogurt
salt and freshly ground black pepper
¼ cup fresh goat cheese
chopped chives, to garnish

yogurt

chestnut purée

corn

butternut squash

goat cheese

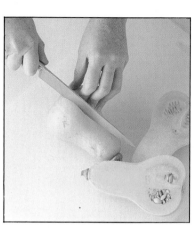

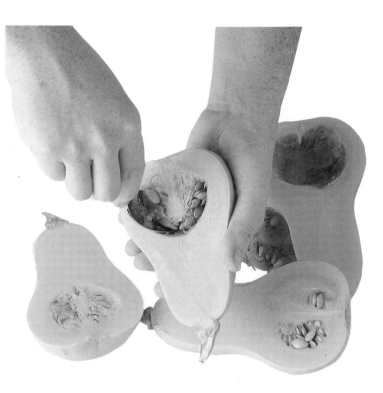

1 Preheat the oven to 350°F. Cut the squash in half lengthwise.

2 Scoop out the seeds with a spoon and discard.

3 Place the squash halves on a cookie sheet and brush the flesh lightly with the oil. Bake in the oven for 30 minutes.

4 Mix together the corn, chestnut purée and yogurt in a bowl. Season to taste.

5 Remove the squash from the oven and divide the chestnut mixture between them, spooning it into the hollows.

COOK'S TIP
Use mozzarella or other mild, soft cheeses in place of goat cheese. The cheese can be omitted entirely for a lower-fat alternative.

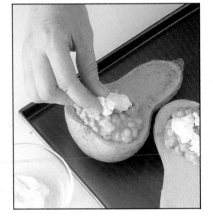

6 Top each half with ¼ of the goat cheese and return to the oven for a further 10–15 minutes. Garnish with chopped chives.

Mushrooms with Leeks and Stilton

Upturned mushrooms make perfect containers for this leek and Stilton filling.

Serves 2–3

INGREDIENTS
1 leek, thinly sliced
6 flat mushrooms
2 garlic cloves, crushed
2 tbsp chopped fresh parsley
½ cup butter, softened
4 oz Stilton cheese
freshly ground black pepper
frisée and tomato halves, to garnish

leek

butter

flat mushrooms

parsley

Stilton cheese

garlic cloves

1 Put the leek slices in a small pan with a little water. Cover, and cook for about 5 minutes until tender. Drain. Refresh under cold water, and drain again.

2 Remove the stalks from the flat mushrooms, and set them aside. Put the mushroom caps, hollows uppermost, on an oiled baking sheet.

3 Put the mushroom stalks, garlic and parsley in a food processor or blender. Process for 1 minute. Turn into a bowl. Add the leek and butter, and season with freshly ground black pepper to taste. Preheat the broiler.

4 Crumble the Stilton into the mushroom mixture, and mix well. Divide the Stilton mixture among the mushroom caps, and broil for 6–7 minutes until bubbling. Serve garnished with frisée lettuce and halved tomatoes, if desired.

Tomato and Okra Stew

Okra is an unusual and delicious vegetable. It releases a sticky sap when cooked, which helps to thicken the stew.

Serves 4

INGREDIENTS
1 tbsp olive oil
1 onion, chopped
12 oz jar pimientos, drained
2 x 14 oz cans chopped tomatoes
10 oz okra
2 tbsp chopped fresh parsley
salt and freshly ground black pepper

parsley

chopped tomatoes

pimientos

onion

okra

1 Heat the oil in a pan. Add the onion, and cook for 2–3 minutes.

2 Coarsely chop the pimientos, and add to the onion. Add the chopped tomatoes, and mix well.

3 Cut the tops off the okra, and cut into halves or quarters if large. Add to the tomato sauce in the pan. Season with plenty of salt and pepper.

4 Bring the vegetable stew to a boil. Then lower the heat, cover the pan, and simmer for 12 minutes until the vegetables are tender and the sauce has thickened. Stir in the chopped parsley, and serve at once.

Vegetable Kebabs with Mustard and Honey

A colorful mixture of vegetables and tofu, skewered, glazed and broiled until tender.

Serves 4

INGREDIENTS
1 yellow bell pepper
2 small zucchini
8 oz piece of firm tofu
8 cherry tomatoes
8 white mushrooms
1 tbsp whole-grain mustard
1 tbsp clear honey
2 tbsp olive oil
salt and freshly ground black pepper

TO SERVE
4 portions cooked mixed rice
  and wild rice
lime segments
flat leaf parsley

1 Cut the pepper in half, and remove the seeds. Cut each half into quarters, and cut each quarter in half.

2 Remove the ends from the zucchini and peel them decoratively. Then cut each zucchini into eight chunks.

3 Cut the tofu into pieces of a similar size to the vegetables.

zucchini

cherry tomatoes

yellow bell pepper

clear honey

whole-grain mustard

white mushrooms

tofu

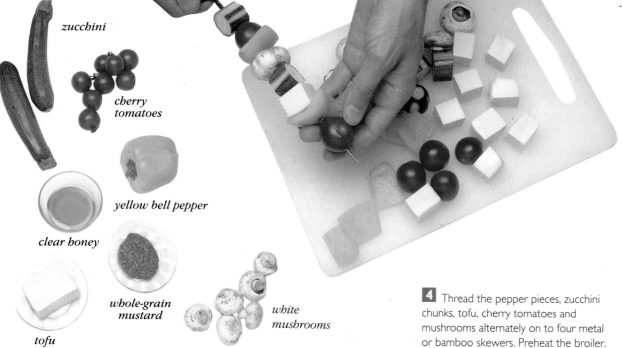

4 Thread the pepper pieces, zucchini chunks, tofu, cherry tomatoes and mushrooms alternately on to four metal or bamboo skewers. Preheat the broiler.

5 Whisk the mustard, honey and olive oil in a small bowl. Add salt and pepper to taste.

6 Put the kebabs on to a baking sheet. Brush with the mustard and honey glaze. Cook under the broiler for 8 minutes, turning once or twice during cooking. Serve with a mixture of long grain and wild rice, and garnish with lime segments and parsley.

COOK'S TIP
If using bamboo skewers, soak them in a bowl of cold water before threading, to prevent them burning when placed under the broiler.

Potato, Broccoli and Red Bell Pepper Stir-fry

A hot and hearty stir-fry of vegetables with just a hint of fresh ginger.

Serves 2

INGREDIENTS

1 lb potatoes
3 tbsp peanut oil
¼ cup butter
1 small onion, chopped
1 red bell pepper, seeded and
  chopped
8 oz broccoli, broken into florets
1 in piece of fresh ginger, peeled
  and grated
salt and freshly ground black pepper

red bell pepper   *butter*

broccoli   *onion*

fresh ginger   *potatoes*

COOK'S TIP

Although a wok is the preferred pan for stir-frying, for this recipe, a flat frying pan is best to cook the potatoes quickly.

1 Peel the potatoes, and cut them into ½ in dice.

2 Heat the oil in a large frying pan, and add the potatoes. Cook for 8 minutes over a high heat, stirring and tossing occasionally, until the potatoes are browned and just tender.

3 Drain off the oil. Add the butter to the potatoes in the pan. As soon as it melts, add the onion and red bell pepper. Stir-fry for 2 minutes.

4 Add the broccoli florets and ginger to the pan. Stir-fry for 2–3 minutes more, taking care not to break up the potatoes. Add salt and pepper to taste, and serve at once.

Bubble and Squeak with Fried Eggs

Originally made with meat and cabbage in England centuries ago, this dish was named for its noisy cooking.

Serves 2

INGREDIENTS
½ Savoy cabbage
¼ cup butter
1 small onion, finely chopped
1 lb mashed potato
1 tbsp chopped fresh parsley
1 tbsp vegetable oil
2 eggs
salt and freshly ground black pepper
2 tomatoes, halved, to serve

eggs

mashed potato

butter

onion

Savoy cabbage

parsley

1 Cut out and discard the hard core of the cabbage. Strip off and discard the outer layer of leaves. Finely slice the remaining cabbage, and set aside.

2 Melt the butter in a large frying pan. Add the onion, and fry for 2–3 minutes until just tender. Reduce the heat slightly. Add the cabbage, and cook, stirring constantly, for 2–3 minutes.

3 Add the mashed potato to the pan. Stir to combine. Cook for 5–6 minutes until the mixture starts to brown. Stir in the chopped parsley, and add salt and pepper to taste. Transfer the mixture to a serving dish, and keep hot.

4 Wipe the pan clean. Heat the oil, and fry the eggs until just set. Serve the bubble and squeak on individual plates, adding a fried egg and two tomato halves to each portion. Sprinkle with black pepper.

Potato, Spinach and Pine Nut Gratin

Pine nuts add a satisfying crunch to this gratin of wafer-thin potato slices and spinach in a creamy cheese sauce.

Serves 2

INGREDIENTS
1 lb potatoes
1 garlic clove, crushed
3 scallions, thinly sliced
²/₃ cup light cream
1 cup milk
8 oz frozen chopped spinach, thawed
4 oz Cheddar cheese, grated
¹/₄ cup pine nuts
salt and freshly ground black pepper

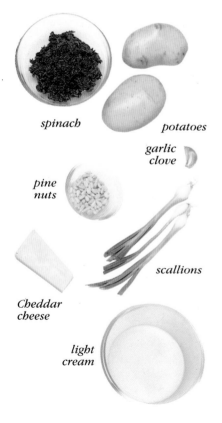

spinach

potatoes

garlic clove

pine nuts

scallions

Cheddar cheese

light cream

1 Peel the potatoes, and cut them carefully into wafer-thin slices. Spread them out in a large, heavy-bottomed, nonstick frying pan.

2 Sprinkle the crushed garlic and sliced scallions evenly over the potatoes.

3 Pour the cream and milk over the potatoes. Place the pan over a gentle heat. Cover, and cook for 8 minutes or until the potatoes are tender.

4 Using both hands, squeeze the spinach dry. Add the spinach to the potatoes, mixing lightly. Cover the pan, and cook for 2 minutes more.

5 Add salt and pepper to taste, then spoon the mixture into a shallow casserole. Preheat the broiler.

6 Sprinkle the grated cheese and pine nuts over the spinach mixture. Heat under the broiler for 2–3 minutes until the topping is golden. A simple lettuce and tomato salad makes an excellent accompaniment to this dish.

Spinach and Potato Galette

Creamy layers of potato, spinach and herbs make a
warming supper dish.

Serves 6

INGREDIENTS
2 lb large potatoes
1 lb fresh spinach
2 eggs
14 oz (1¾ cups) low-fat cream
  cheese
1 tbsp grainy mustard
3 tbsp chopped fresh herbs (e.g.
  chives, parsley, chervil or sorrel)
salt and freshly ground black pepper

mustard

parsley

cream
cheese

spinach

egg

potatoes

chives

cherry tomatoes

chervil

sorrel

COOK'S TIP
Choose firm white or red skinned
boiling potatoes for this dish.

1 Preheat the oven to 350°F. Line a
deep 9 in cake pan with parchment
paper. Place the potatoes in a large pot
and cover with cold water. Bring to a boil
and cook for 10 minutes. Drain well and
allow to cool slightly before peeling and
slicing thinly.

2 Wash the spinach well and place in a
large pot with only the water that is
clinging to the leaves. Cover and cook,
stirring once, until the spinach has just
wilted. Drain well in a sieve and squeeze
out the excess moisture. Chop finely.

3 Beat the eggs with the cream cheese
and mustard then stir in the chopped
spinach and fresh herbs.

4 Place a layer of the sliced potatoes in
the lined pan, arranging them in
concentric circles. Top with a spoonful of
the cream cheese mixture and spread
out. Continue layering, seasoning with salt
and pepper as you go, until all the
potatoes and the cream cheese mixture
are used up.

5 Cover the pan with a piece of foil and
place in a roasting pan.

6 Fill the roasting pan with enough
boiling water to come halfway up the
sides, and cook in the oven for 45–50
minutes. Turn out onto a plate and serve
hot or cold.

Potato Gratin

Don't rinse the potato slices before layering because
the starch makes a thick sauce during cooking.

Serves 4

INGREDIENTS
1 garlic clove
5 large baking potatoes, peeled
3 tbsp freshly grated Parmesan
 cheese
2½ cups vegetable stock
pinch of freshly grated nutmeg
salt and ground black pepper

potatoes

Parmesan cheese

stock

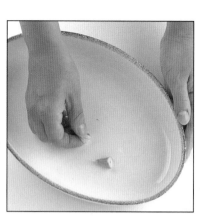

1 Preheat the oven to 400°F. Halve the
garlic clove and rub over the base and
sides of a gratin dish measuring about
8 × 12 in.

2 Slice the potatoes very thinly and
arrange a third of them in the dish.
Sprinkle with a little grated cheese, salt
and freshly ground black pepper. Pour
over some of the stock to prevent the
potatoes from discoloring.

3 Continue layering the potatoes and
cheese as before, then pour over the rest
of the stock. Sprinkle with the nutmeg.

4 Bake in the oven for 1¼-1½ hours
or until the potatoes are tender and the
tops well browned.

VARIATION

For a potato and onion gratin, thinly
slice one medium onion and layer
with the potato.

Cheese and Onion Pie

This inexpensive supper dish is made substantial with the addition of rolled oats.

Serves 4

INGREDIENTS

2 large onions, thinly sliced
1 garlic clove, crushed
⅔ cup vegetable stock
3 cups rolled oats
1 cup grated Edam cheese
2 tbsp chopped fresh parsley
2 eggs, lightly beaten
1 medium potato, peeled
salt and freshly ground black pepper
coleslaw and tomatoes, halved,
    to serve

rolled oats

Edam cheese

eggs

onion

parsley

potato

1 Preheat the oven to 350°F. Line the base of a 8 in sandwich pie pan with non-stick baking paper. Put the onions, garlic clove and stock into a heavy saucepan and simmer until the stock has reduced entirely.

2 Spread the oats on a baking sheet and toast in the oven for 10 minutes. Mix with the onions, cheese, parsley, eggs, salt and freshly ground black pepper.

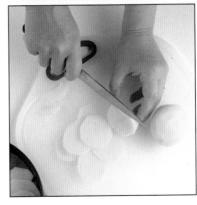

3 Thinly slice the potato and use it to line the base of the pan. Spoon in the oat mixture. Cover with a piece of foil.

4 Bake in the preheated oven for 35 minutes. Turn out onto a baking sheet and remove the lining paper. Put under a preheated hot broiler to brown the potatoes. Cut into wedges and serve hot with coleslaw and halved tomatoes.

Potato Gnocchi with Hazelnut Sauce

These delicate potato dumplings are dressed with a creamy hazelnut sauce.

Serves 4

INGREDIENTS
1½ lb large potatoes
1 cup flour

FOR THE HAZELNUT SAUCE
½ cup skinned, roasted hazelnuts
1 garlic clove, roughly chopped
½ tsp grated lemon rind
½ tsp lemon juice
2 tbsp sunflower oil
scant ¾ cup low-fat ricotta cheese
salt and freshly ground black pepper

lemon

potatoes

flour

hazelnuts   *ricotta cheese*

garlic

1 Place ⅓ cup of the hazelnuts in a blender with the garlic, grated lemon rind and juice. Blend until coarsely chopped. Gradually add the oil and blend until smooth. Spoon into a bowl and mix in the ricotta cheese. Season to taste.

2 Place the potatoes in a pan of cold water. Bring to a boil and cook for 20–25 minutes. Drain well in a colander.

When cool, peel and purée the potatoes while still warm by passing them through a food mill into a bowl.

3 Add the flour a little at a time (you may not need all the flour as potatoes vary in texture). Stop adding flour when the mixture is smooth and slightly sticky. Add salt to taste.

4 Roll out the mixture onto a floured board, into a long sausage about ½ in in diameter. Cut into ¾ in lengths.

5 Take 1 piece at a time and press it on to a floured fork. Roll each piece slightly while pressing it along the prongs and off the fork. Flip onto a floured plate or tray. Continue with the rest of the mixture.

COOK'S TIP
A light touch is the key to making soft gnocchi, so handle the dough as little as possible to prevent the mixture from becoming tough.

6 Bring a large pan of water to a boil and drop in 20–25 pieces at a time. They will rise to the surface very quickly. Let them cook for 10–15 seconds more, then lift them out with a slotted spoon. Drop into a dish and keep warm. Continue with the rest of the gnocchi. To heat the sauce, place in a heatproof bowl over a pot of simmering water and heat gently, being careful not to let the sauce curdle. Pour the sauce over the gnocchi. Roughly chop the remaining hazelnuts and scatter over the sauce.

Parmesan and Poached Egg Salad with Croûtons

Soft poached eggs, hot garlic croûtons and cool, crisp salad leaves make an unforgettable combination.

Serves 2

INGREDIENTS

¹/₂ small loaf white bread
5 tbsp extra virgin olive oil
2 eggs
4 oz mixed salad greens
2 garlic cloves, crushed
¹/₂ tbsp white wine vinegar
1 oz Parmesan cheese

Parmesan cheese

mixed salad greens

white bread

garlic cloves

eggs

1 Remove the crust from the bread. Cut the bread into 1 in cubes.

2 Heat 2 tbsp of the oil in a frying pan. Cook the bread for about 5 minutes, tossing the cubes occasionally, until they are golden brown.

3 Meanwhile, bring a pan of water to a boil. Carefully slide in the eggs, one at a time. Gently poach the eggs for 4 minutes until lightly cooked.

4 Divide the salad greens between two plates. Remove the croûtons from the pan, and arrange them over the leaves. Wipe the pan clean with paper towels.

5 Heat the remaining oil in the pan, add the garlic and vinegar, and cook over high heat for 1 minute. Pour the warm dressing over each salad.

COOK'S TIP

Add a dash of vinegar to the water before poaching the eggs. This helps to keep the whites together. To make sure that a poached egg has a good shape, swirl the water with a spoon, whirlpool-fashion, before sliding in the egg.

6 Place a poached egg on each salad. Sprinkle with shavings of Parmesan and freshly ground black pepper, if desired.

Classic Greek Salad

If you have ever visited Greece, you'll know that a Greek salad with a chunk of bread makes a delicious, filling meal.

Serves 4

INGREDIENTS
1 Romaine lettuce
$1/2$ cucumber, halved lengthwise
4 tomatoes
8 scallions
$1/3$ cup Greek black olives
4 oz feta cheese
6 tbsp white wine vinegar
$1/2$ cup extra virgin olive oil
salt and freshly ground black pepper

tomatoes

Romaine lettuce

feta cheese

white wine vinegar

black olives

cucumber

scallions

COOK'S TIP
The salad can be assembled in advance and chilled, but add the lettuce and dressing just before serving. Keep the dressing at room temperature as chilling deadens its flavor.

1 Tear the lettuce leaves into pieces, and place them in a large mixing bowl. Slice the cucumber, and add to the bowl.

2 Cut the tomatoes into wedges, and put them into the bowl.

3 Slice the scallions. Add them to the bowl with the olives, and toss well.

4 Cut the feta cheese into cubes, and add to the salad.

5 Put the vinegar, olive oil and seasoning into a small bowl, and whisk well. Pour the dressing over the salad, and toss to combine. Serve at once, with olives and chunks of bread, if desired.

Belgian Endive, Fruit and Nut Salad

Mildly bitter endive is wonderful with sweet fruit, and is especially delicious when complemented by a creamy curry sauce.

Serves 4

INGREDIENTS
3 tbsp mayonnaise
1 tbsp strained, plain yogurt
1 tbsp mild curry paste
6 tbsp light cream
$^1/_2$ iceberg lettuce
2 heads of Belgian endive
$^1/_2$ cup cashews
1$^1/_4$ cups flaked coconut
2 red apples
$^1/_2$ cup currants

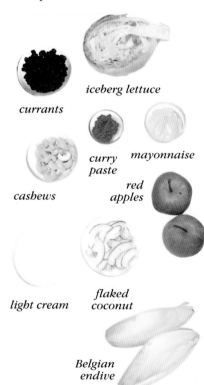

currants

iceberg lettuce

curry paste

mayonnaise

cashews

red apples

light cream

flaked coconut

Belgian endive

1 Mix the mayonnaise, yogurt, curry paste and light cream in a small bowl. Cover, and chill until required.

2 Tear the iceberg lettuce into pieces, and put into a salad bowl.

3 Cut the root end off each head of Belgian endive, and discard. Slice the endive, and add it to the salad bowl.

4 Preheat the broiler. Toast the cashews for 2 minutes until they are golden. Turn into a bowl, and set aside. Spread out the coconut flakes on a baking sheet. Broil for 1 minute.

5 Quarter the apples, and cut out the cores. Slice the apples, and add to the lettuce with the cashews, flaked coconut, and currants.

COOK'S TIP
Watch the coconut and cashews very carefully when broiling, as they brown very fast.

6 Spoon the dressing over the salad. Toss lightly, and serve.

Broiled Bell Pepper Salad

Broiled bell peppers are delicious served hot
with a sharp dressing. You can also eat them cold.

Serves 2

INGREDIENTS
1 red bell pepper
1 green bell pepper
1 yellow or orange bell pepper
¹/₂ radicchio, separated into leaves
¹/₂ frisée, separated into leaves
1¹/₂ tsp white wine vinegar
2 tbsp extra virgin olive oil
6 oz goat cheese
salt and freshly ground black pepper

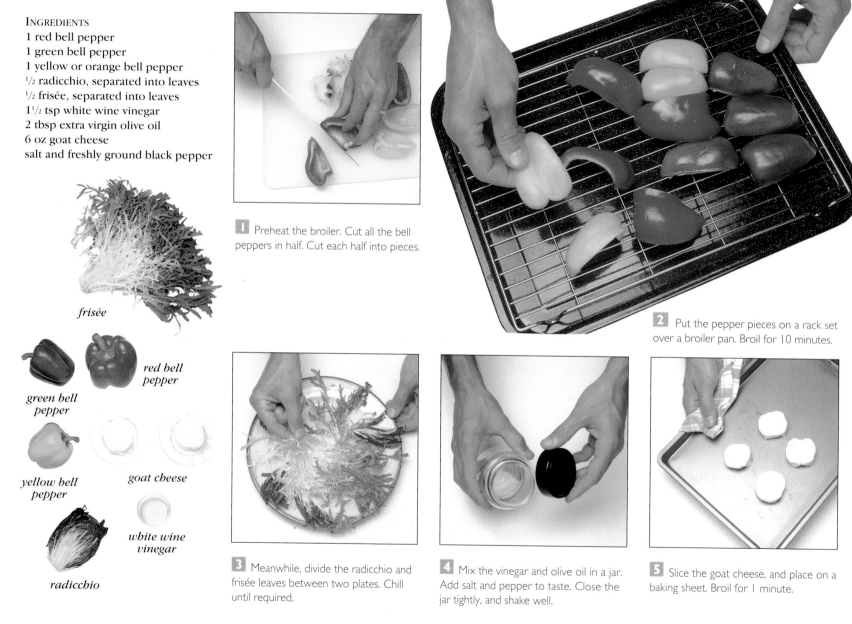

frisée

green bell pepper

red bell pepper

yellow bell pepper

goat cheese

white wine vinegar

radicchio

1 Preheat the broiler. Cut all the bell peppers in half. Cut each half into pieces.

2 Put the pepper pieces on a rack set over a broiler pan. Broil for 10 minutes.

3 Meanwhile, divide the radicchio and frisée leaves between two plates. Chill until required.

4 Mix the vinegar and olive oil in a jar. Add salt and pepper to taste. Close the jar tightly, and shake well.

5 Slice the goat cheese, and place on a baking sheet. Broil for 1 minute.

6 Arrange the peppers and broiled goat cheese on the salads. Pour over the dressing, and grind a little extra black pepper over each.

COOK'S TIP
Broil the bell peppers until they just start to blacken around the edges – don't let them burn.

Sesame Noodle Salad with Hot Peanuts

An orient-inspired salad with crunchy vegetables and a light soy dressing. The hot peanuts make a surprisingly successful union with the cold noodles.

Serves 4

INGREDIENTS
12 oz egg noodles
2 carrots, peeled and cut into fine
  julienne strips
½ cucumber, peeled and cut into
  ½ in cubes
4 oz celeriac, peeled and cut into fine
  julienne strips
6 scallions, finely sliced
8 canned water chestnuts, drained
  and finely sliced
6 oz beansprouts
1 small fresh green chili, seeded and
  finely chopped
2 tbsp sesame seeds, to serve
1 cup peanuts, to serve

FOR THE DRESSING
1 tbsp dark soy sauce
1 tbsp light soy sauce
1 tbsp honey
1 tbsp rice wine or dry sherry
1 tbsp sesame oil

1 Preheat the oven to 400°F. Cook the egg noodles in boiling water, following the instructions on the side of the package.

2 Drain the noodles, refresh in cold water, then drain again.

3 Mix the noodles with all of the prepared vegetables.

celeriac

beansprouts

green chili

scallion

sesame seeds

water chestnuts

cucumber

peanuts

noodles

carrot

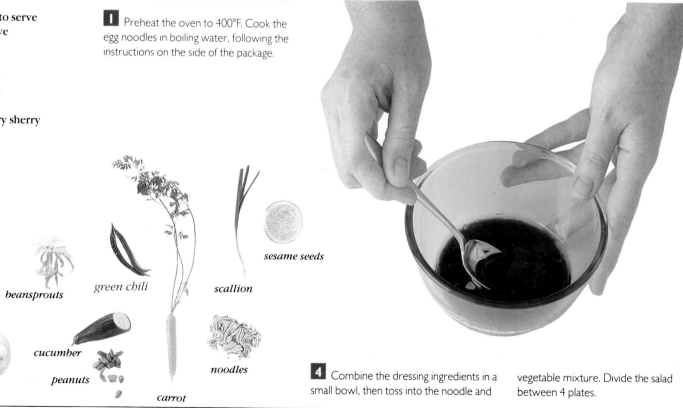

4 Combine the dressing ingredients in a small bowl, then toss into the noodle and vegetable mixture. Divide the salad between 4 plates.

5 Place the sesame seeds and peanuts on separate cookie sheets and place in the oven. Take the sesame seeds out after 5 minutes and continue to cook the peanuts for a further 5 minutes until evenly browned.

6 Sprinkle the sesame seeds and peanuts evenly over each portion and serve at once.

Green Lentil and Cabbage Salad

This warm crunchy salad makes a satisfying meal if served with crusty French bread or whole-wheat rolls.

Serves 4–6

INGREDIENTS
1 cup green lentils
6 cups cold water
1 garlic clove
1 bay leaf
1 small onion, peeled and studded
    with 2 cloves
1 tbsp olive oil
1 red onion, finely sliced
2 garlic cloves, crushed
1 tbsp thyme leaves
12 oz cabbage, finely shredded
finely grated rind and juice of 1 lemon
1 tbsp raspberry vinegar
salt and freshly ground black pepper

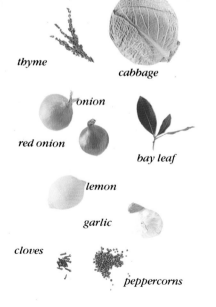

thyme

cabbage

onion

red onion

bay leaf

lemon

garlic

cloves

peppercorns

1 Rinse the lentils in cold water and place in a large pan with the water, peeled garlic clove, bay leaf and clove-studded onion. Bring to a boil and cook for 10 minutes. Reduce the heat, cover the pan and simmer gently for 15–20 minutes. Drain and remove the onion, garlic and bay leaf.

2 Heat the oil in a large pan. Add the red onion, garlic and thyme and cook for 5 minutes until softened.

3 Add the cabbage and cook for 3–5 minutes until just cooked but still crunchy.

4 Stir in the cooked lentils, lemon rind and juice and the raspberry vinegar. Season to taste and serve.

Tabouli with Fennel and Pomegranate

A fresh salad originating in the Middle East, with the added crunchiness of fennel and sweet pomegranate seeds. It is perfect for a summer lunch.

Serves 6

INGREDIENTS
1 cup bulgur wheat
2 fennel bulbs
1 small fresh red chili, seeded and
    finely chopped
1 celery stalk, finely sliced
2 tbsp olive oil
finely grated rind and juice of 2
    lemons
6–8 scallions, chopped
6 tbsp chopped fresh mint
6 tbsp chopped fresh parsley
1 pomegranate, seeds removed
salt and freshly ground black pepper

lemon

red chili

celery

bulgur wheat

scallion

fennel

pomegranate

parsley

mint

1 Place the bulgur wheat in a bowl and pour over enough cold water to cover. Leave to stand for 30 minutes.

2 Drain the wheat through a sieve, pressing out any excess water using a spoon.

3 Halve the fennel bulbs and cut into very fine slices.

4 Mix all the remaining ingredients together, including the soaked bulgur wheat and fennel. Season well, cover, and set aside for 30 minutes before serving.

Zucchini Puffs with Salad and Balsamic Dressing

This unusual salad consists of deep-fried zucchini, flavored with mint, and served warm on a bed of salad greens with a balsamic dressing.

Serves 2

INGREDIENTS
1 lb zucchini
1½ cups fresh white bread crumbs
1 egg
pinch of cayenne pepper
1 tbsp chopped fresh mint
oil for deep-frying
3 tbsp balsamic vinegar
3 tbsp extra virgin olive oil
7 oz mixed salad greens
salt and freshly ground black pepper

zucchini

white bread crumbs

balsamic vinegar

mixed salad greens

egg

mint

1 Remove the ends from the zucchini. Coarsely grate them, and put into a colander. Squeeze out the excess water. Then put the zucchini into a bowl.

2 Add the bread crumbs, egg, cayenne, mint and seasoning. Mix well.

3 Shape the zucchini mixture into balls, about the size of walnuts.

4 Heat the oil for deep-frying to 350°F or until a cube of bread, when added to the oil, browns in 30–40 seconds. Deep-fry the zucchini balls in batches for 2–3 minutes. Drain on paper towels.

5 Whisk the vinegar and oil together, and season well.

6 Put the salad greens in a bowl, and pour over the dressing. Add the zucchini puffs, and toss lightly together. Serve at once, while the puffs are still crisp.

Vegetable and Satay Salad

Baby new potatoes, tender vegetables and crunchy chick-peas are smothered in a creamy peanut dressing.

Serves 4

INGREDIENTS
1 lb baby new potatoes
1 small head cauliflower, broken
  into small florets
8 oz green beans, trimmed
14 oz can chick-peas, drained
4 oz watercress sprigs
4 oz beansprouts
8 scallions, sliced
4 tbsp crunchy peanut butter
²/₃ cup hot water
1 tsp chili sauce
2 tsp brown sugar
1 tsp soy sauce
1 tsp lime juice

cauliflower

watercress

soy
sauce

scallions

crunchy
peanut butter

brown
sugar

chick-
peas

beansprouts

chili
sauce

green
beans

lime

baby new
potatoes

1 Put the potatoes into a pan, and add water just to cover. Bring to a boil, and cook for 10–12 minutes or until the potatoes are just tender when pierced with the point of a sharp knife. Drain, and refresh under cold running water. Drain once again.

2 Meanwhile, bring another pan of salted water to a boil. Add the cauliflower, and cook for 5 minutes. Then add the beans, and cook for 5 minutes more. Drain both vegetables, refresh under cold water, and drain once more.

3 Put the cauliflower and beans into a large bowl, and add the chick-peas. Halve the potatoes, and add. Toss lightly. Mix the watercress, beansprouts and scallions together. Divide among four plates, and pile the vegetables on top.

4 Put the peanut butter into a bowl, and stir in the water. Add the chili sauce, brown sugar, soy sauce and lime juice. Whisk well, then drizzle the dressing over the vegetables.

Vegetables à la Greque

This simple salad is made with winter vegetables, but you can vary it according to the season.

Serves 4

INGREDIENTS

¾ cup white wine
1 tsp olive oil
2 tbsp lemon juice
2 bay leaves
sprig of fresh thyme
4 juniper berries
1 lb leeks, trimmed and cut into 1 in
    lengths
1 small cauliflower, broken into
    florets
4 celery stalks, sliced on the diagonal
2 tbsp chopped fresh parsley
salt and freshly ground black pepper

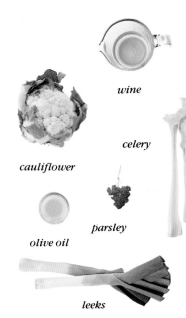

wine

celery

cauliflower

parsley

olive oil

leeks

1 Put the wine, oil, lemon juice, bay leaves, thyme and juniper berries into a large, heavy saucepan and bring to a boil. Cover and leave to simmer for 20 minutes.

2 Add the leeks, cauliflower and celery. Simmer very gently for 5–6 minutes or until just tender.

COOK'S TIP

Choose a dry or medium-dry white wine for this dish.

3 Remove the vegetables with a slotted spoon and transfer them to a serving dish. Briskly boil the cooking liquid for 15-20 minutes, or until reduced by half. Strain.

4 Stir the parsley into the liquid and season to taste. Pour over the vegetables and leave to cool. Chill in the refrigerator for at least 1 hour before serving.

Fruit and Fiber Salad

Fresh, fast and filling, this salad makes a great starter, supper or snack.

Serves 4–6

INGREDIENTS
8 oz red or white cabbage or a
   mixture of both
3 medium carrots
1 pear
1 red-skinned apple
7 oz can lima beans,
   drained
¼ cup chopped dates

FOR THE DRESSING
½ tsp dry English mustard
2 tsp honey
2 tbsp orange juice
1 tsp white wine vinegar
½ tsp paprika
salt and freshly ground black pepper

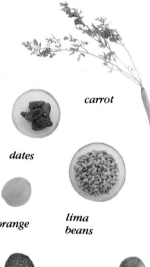
carrot

dates

lima
beans

orange

cabbage

pear

apple

1 Shred the cabbage very finely, discarding any tough stalks.

2 Cut the carrots into very thin strips, about 2 in long.

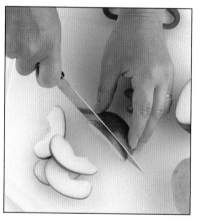

3 Quarter, core and slice the pear and apple, leaving the skin on.

4 Put the fruit and vegetables in a bowl with the beans and dates. Mix well.

5 For the dressing, blend the mustard with the honey until smooth. Add the orange juice, vinegar, paprika and seasoning and mix well.

6 Pour the dressing over the salad and toss to coat. Chill in the refrigerator for 30 minutes before serving.

Bulgur and Mint Salad with Fresh Vegetables

Also known as cracked wheat, burghul or pourgouri, the bulgur has been partially cooked, so it requires only a short soaking before serving.

Serves 4

INGREDIENTS
1⅔ cups bulgur
4 tomatoes
4 small zucchini, thinly sliced lengthwise
4 scallions, sliced on the diagonal
8 dried apricots, chopped
¼ cup raisins
juice of 1 lemon
2 tbsp tomato juice
3 tbsp chopped fresh mint
1 garlic clove, crushed
salt and freshly ground black pepper
sprig of fresh mint, to garnish

zucchini *bulgur*

tomatoes

lemon

scallions

1 Put the bulgur into a large bowl. Add enough cold water to come 1 in above the level of the wheat. Leave the bulgur to soak for 30 minutes, then drain well and squeeze out any excess water in a clean dish towel.

2 Meanwhile plunge the tomatoes into boiling water for 1 minute and then into cold water. Slip off the skins. Halve, remove the seeds and cores and roughly chop the flesh.

3 Stir the chopped tomatoes, sliced zucchini, scallions, apricots, and raisins into the bulgur.

4 Put the lemon and tomato juice, mint, garlic clove and seasoning into a small bowl and whisk together with a fork. Pour over the salad and mix well. Chill in the refrigerator for at least 1 hour. Serve garnished with a sprig of mint.

Fresh Spinach and Avocado Salad

Young, tender spinach leaves make a change from lettuce and are delicious served with avocado, cherry tomatoes and radishes in a tofu sauce.

Serves 2–3

INGREDIENTS
1 large avocado
juice of 1 lime
8 oz fresh baby spinach leaves
4 oz cherry tomatoes
4 scallions, sliced
½ cucumber
2 oz radishes, sliced

FOR THE DRESSING
4 oz soft silken tofu
3 tbsp milk
2 tsp prepared mustard
½ tsp white wine vinegar
pinch of cayenne
salt and freshly ground black pepper

tofu *scallions* *spinach leaves*

avocado *cherry tomatoes*

cayenne *white wine vinegar* *mustard* *lime* *cucumber*

radishes *milk*

1 Cut the avocado in half, remove the pit, and strip off the skin. Cut the flesh into slices. Transfer to a plate, drizzle over the lime juice, and set aside.

2 Wash and dry the spinach leaves. Put them in a mixing bowl.

COOK'S TIP
Use soft silken tofu rather than the block variety. It can be found in most supermarkets in the vegetable or refrigerated sections.

3 Cut the larger cherry tomatoes in half, and add all the tomatoes to the mixing bowl, with the scallions. Cut the cucumber into chunks, and add to the bowl with the sliced radishes.

4 Make the dressing. Put the tofu, milk, mustard, wine vinegar and cayenne in a food processor or blender. Add salt and pepper to taste. Process for 30 seconds until smooth. Scrape the dressing into a bowl, and add a little extra milk if you like a thinner dressing. Sprinkle with a little extra cayenne, and garnish with radish roses and herb sprigs, if desired.

New Spring Salad

This chunky salad makes a satisfying meal. Use other spring vegetables, if you like.

Serves 4

INGREDIENTS

1½ lb small new potatoes, halved
14 oz can fava beans, drained
4 oz cherry tomatoes
½ cup walnut halves
2 tbsp white wine vinegar
1 tbsp whole-grain mustard
4 tbsp olive oil
pinch of sugar
8 oz young asparagus spears,
  trimmed
6 scallions, trimmed
salt and freshly ground black pepper
baby spinach leaves, to serve

*new
potatoes*

*asparagus
spears*

*whole-grain
mustard*

fava beans

*cherry
tomatoes*

scallions

walnut halves

1 Put the potatoes in a pan. Cover with cold water, and bring to a boil. Cook for 10–12 minutes, until tender. Meanwhile, turn the fava beans into a bowl. Cut the tomatoes in half, and add them to the bowl with the walnuts.

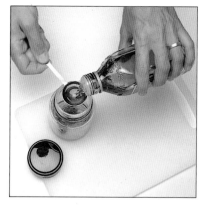

2 Put the white wine vinegar, mustard, olive oil and sugar into a jar. Add salt and pepper to taste. Close the jar tightly, and shake well.

3 Add the asparagus to the potatoes, and cook for 3 minutes more. Drain the cooked vegetables well. Cool under cold running water, and drain again. Thickly slice the potatoes, and cut the scallions into halves.

4 Add the asparagus, potatoes and scallions to the bowl containing the fava bean mixture. Pour the dressing over the salad, and toss well. Serve on a bed of baby spinach leaves.

Carrot, Raisin and Apricot Coleslaw

A tasty, high-fiber coleslaw, combining cabbage, carrots and dried fruit in a light yogurt dressing.

Serves 6

INGREDIENTS

3 cups finely shredded white
  cabbage
1½ cups coarsely grated carrots
1 red onion, sliced
3 celery stalks, sliced
1 cup raisins
3 oz dried apricots, chopped
8 tbsp reduced-calorie
  mayonnaise
6 tbsp low-fat plain yogurt
2 tbsp chopped fresh
  mixed herbs
salt and ground black pepper

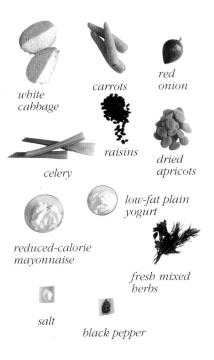

white cabbage *carrots* *red onion* *raisins* *dried apricots* *celery* *reduced-calorie mayonnaise* *low-fat plain yogurt* *fresh mixed herbs* *salt* *black pepper*

1 Put the cabbage and carrots in a large bowl.

2 Add the onion, celery, raisins and apricots and mix well.

3 In a small bowl, mix together the mayonnaise, yogurt, herbs and seasoning.

COOK'S TIP
Use other dried fruit such as golden raisins and dried pears or peaches in place of the dark raisins and apricots.

4 Add the mayonnaise dressing to the cabbage mixture and toss the ingredients together to mix. Cover and chill for several hours before serving.

Curried New Potato and Green Bean Salad

Tender new potatoes and green beans tossed together in a subtly flavored light dressing make this salad ideal for serving with broiled vegetables and fresh whole-wheat bread.

Serves 6

INGREDIENTS

1½ cups green beans, trimmed and halved
1½ lb cooked baby new potatoes
2 bunches scallions, chopped
⅔ cup golden raisins
3 oz dried pears, finely chopped
6 tbsp reduced-calorie mayonnaise
4 tbsp low-fat plain yogurt
2 tbsp sheep's milk yogurt (if available)
1 tbsp tomato paste
1 tbsp curry paste
2 tbsp chopped fresh chives
salt and ground black pepper

green beans   baby new potatoes

scallions

golden raisins   dried pears

                     reduced-calorie mayonnaise

low-fat plain yogurt   sheep's milk yogurt   tomato paste

curry paste   chives

salt   black pepper

1 Cook the beans in boiling water for about 5 minutes, until tender. Rinse under cold running water to cool them quickly, drain and set aside.

2 Put the potatoes, beans, scallions, golden raisins and pears in a bowl and mix together.

3 In a small bowl, mix together the mayonnaise, yogurts, tomato paste, curry paste, chives and seasoning.

4 Add the dressing to the potato mixture and toss the ingredients together to mix. Cover and allow to stand for at least 1 hour before serving.

Cannellini Bean Purée with Broiled Radicchio

The slightly bitter flavors of the radicchio and Belgian endive make a wonderful marriage with the creamy citrus flavored bean purée.

Serves 4

INGREDIENTS
14 oz can cannellini beans
3 tbsp low-fat ricotta cheese
finely grated rind and juice of 1
   large orange
1 tbsp finely chopped fresh rosemary
4 heads of Belgian endive
2 medium radicchio
1 tbsp walnut oil

chicory

ricotta cheese

cannellini beans

rosemary

radicchio

orange

1 Drain the beans, rinse, and drain again. Purée the beans in a blender or food processor with the ricotta cheese, orange juice and rosemary. Set aside.

2 Cut the endive in half lengthwise.

3 Cut each radicchio into 8 wedges.

4 Lay out the endive and radicchio on a baking tray and brush with walnut oil. Grill for 2–3 minutes. Serve with the sauce and scatter over the orange rind.

COOK'S TIP
Other suitable beans to use are navy, mung or fava beans.

Fruity Rice Salad

An appetizing and colorful rice salad combining many different flavors, ideal for a packed lunch.

Serves 4–6

INGREDIENTS

1 cup mixed brown and
  wild rice
1 yellow bell pepper,
  seeded and diced
1 bunch scallions, chopped
3 stalks celery, chopped
1 large beefsteak tomato, chopped
2 green apples, chopped
¾ cup dried apricots, chopped
⅔ cup raisins
**2 tbsp unsweetened
  apple juice**
2 tbsp dry sherry
2 tbsp light soy sauce
dash of Tabasco sauce
2 tbsp chopped fresh parsley
**1 tbsp chopped fresh
  rosemary**
salt and ground black pepper

*mixed brown
and wild rice* *yellow bell
pepper* *scallions*

celery *beefsteak
tomato* *apples*

*dried
apricots* *raisins*

*unsweetened
apple juice* *dry sherry* *light soy
sauce*

*Tabasco
sauce* *fresh
parsley* *fresh
rosemary*

1 Cook the rice in a large saucepan of lightly salted boiling water for about 30 minutes (or according to the instructions on the package), until tender. Rinse the rice under cold running water to cool quickly and drain thoroughly.

2 Place the pepper, scallions, celery, tomato, apples, apricots, raisins and the cooked rice in a serving bowl and mix well.

3 In a small bowl, mix together the apple juice, sherry, soy sauce, Tabasco sauce, herbs and seasoning.

4 Pour the dressing over the rice mixture and toss the ingredients together to mix. Serve immediately, or cover and chill in the refrigerator before serving.

Bulgur and Fava Bean Salad

This appetizing salad is ideal served with fresh, crusty whole-wheat bread and homemade chutney, and for non-vegetarians it can be served as an accompaniment to broiled lean meat or fish.

Serves 6

INGREDIENTS
2 cups bulgur
8 oz frozen fava beans
1 cup frozen baby peas
8 oz cherry tomatoes, halved
1 scallion, chopped
1 red bell pepper, seeded and diced
2 oz snow peas, chopped
2 oz watercress
1 tbsp chopped fresh parsley
1 tbsp chopped fresh basil
1 tbsp chopped fresh thyme
salt and ground black pepper
fat-free French dressing

bulgur

*frozen fava
beans*

*frozen
baby
peas*

*cherry
tomatoes*

scallions

*red bell
pepper*

snow peas

watercress

*fresh
parsley*

fresh basil

*fresh
thyme*

*fat-free
French
dressing*

salt

black pepper

1 Soak and cook the bulgur according to the package instructions. Drain thoroughly and put into a serving bowl.

2 Meanwhile, cook the fava beans and baby peas in boiling water for about 3 minutes, until tender. Drain thoroughly and add to the prepared bulgur.

3 Add the cherry tomatoes, scallion, pepper, snow peas and watercress to the bulgur mixture and mix.

4 Add the herbs, seasoning and French dressing to taste, tossing the ingredients together. Serve immediately, or cover and chill in the refrigerator before serving.

COOK'S TIP
Use cooked couscous, brown rice or whole-wheat pasta in place of the bulgur.

Basic Pizza Dough

This simple bread base is rolled out thinly for a
traditional pizza recipe.

MAKES

1 × 10–12 in round pizza
   base
4 × 5 in round pizza bases
1 × 12 × 7 in oblong pizza
   base

INGREDIENTS

1½ cups bread flour
¼ tsp salt
1 tsp rapid-rise dried yeast
½–⅔ cups lukewarm water
1 tbsp olive oil

1 Sift the flour and salt into a large
mixing bowl.

2 Stir in the yeast.

3 Make a well in the center of the dry
ingredients. Pour in the water and oil and
mix with a spoon to a soft dough.

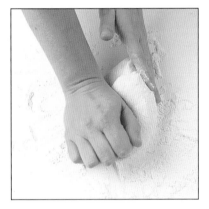

4 Knead the dough on a lightly floured
surface for about 10 minutes until smooth
and elastic.

5 Place the dough in a greased bowl
and cover with plastic wrap. Let rise in a
warm place for about 1 hour or until the
dough has doubled in size.

6 Punch down the dough. Turn on to a
lightly floured surface and knead again for
2–3 minutes. Roll out as required and
place on a greased baking sheet. Pinch up
the dough to make a rim. The dough is
now ready for topping.

Deep-dish Pizza Dough

This recipe produces a deep and spongy base.

MAKES
1 × 10 in deep-dish pizza base

INGREDIENTS
2 cups bread flour
½ tsp salt
1 tsp rapid-rise dried yeast
⅔ cup lukewarm water
2 tbsp olive oil

Follow the method for Basic Pizza Dough. When the dough has doubled in size, punch down and knead for 2–3 minutes. Roll out the dough to fit a greased 10 in deep-dish pizza pan or square cake pan. Let the dough prove for 10 minutes, then add the topping. Alternatively, shape and place on a greased baking sheet.

Whole-wheat Pizza Dough

INGREDIENTS
3 oz/¾ cup whole-wheat flour
¾ cup bread flour
¼ tsp salt
1 tsp rapid-rise dried yeast
½–⅔ cup lukewarm water
1 tbsp olive oil

Follow the method for Basic Pizza Dough. You may have to add a little extra water to form a soft dough, depending on the absorbency of the flour.

Cornmeal Pizza Dough

INGREDIENTS
1½ cups bread flour
¼ cup cornmeal
¼ tsp salt
1 tsp rapid-rise dried yeast
½–⅔ cup lukewarm water
1 tbsp olive oil

Follow the method for Basic Pizza Dough.

Biscuit Pizza Dough

The joy of using a biscuit mixture is it's quick to make and uses pantry ingredients.

MAKES
1 × 10 in round pizza base
1 × 12 × 7 in oblong pizza
base

INGREDIENTS
1 cup self-rising flour
1 cup self-rising whole-wheat
flour
pinch of salt
4 tbsp butter, diced
⅔ cup milk

1 Mix together the flours and salt in a mixing bowl. Rub in the butter until the mixture resembles fine bread crumbs.

2 Add the milk and mix with a wooden spoon to a soft dough.

3 Knead lightly on a lightly floured surface until smooth. The dough is now ready to use.

Superquick Pizza Dough

If you're really pressed for time, try a packaged pizza dough mix. For best results roll out the dough to a 10–12 in circle; this is slightly larger than stated on the package, but it does produce a perfect thin, crispy base. For a deep-dish version use two packets.

ALSO MAKES
4 × 5 in round pizza bases
1 × 12 × 7 in oblong pizza
base

INGREDIENTS
1 × 5 oz package pizza base mix
½ cup lukewarm water

1 Empty the contents of the package into a mixing bowl.

2 Pour in the water and mix with a wooden spoon to a soft dough.

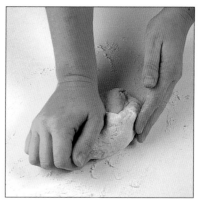

3 Turn the dough on to a lightly floured surface and knead for 5 minutes until smooth and elastic. The dough is now ready to use.

Tomato Sauce

Tomato sauce forms the basis of the topping in many of the recipes. Make sure it is well seasoned and thick before spreading it over the base. It will keep fresh in a covered container in the refrigerator for 3 days.

COVERS
1 × 10–12 in round pizza
   base
1 × 12 × 7 in oblong pizza
   base

INGREDIENTS
1 tbsp olive oil
1 onion, finely chopped
1 garlic clove, crushed
1 × 14 oz can chopped tomatoes
1 tbsp tomato paste
1 tbsp chopped fresh mixed herbs,
   such as parsley, thyme, basil and
   oregano
pinch of sugar
salt and black pepper

1 Heat the oil in a pan, add the onion and garlic and gently sauté for about 5 minutes until softened.

2 Add the tomatoes, tomato paste, herbs, sugar and seasoning.

3 Simmer, uncovered, stirring occasionally for 15–20 minutes or until the tomatoes have reduced to a thick pulp. Leave to cool.

Flavored Oils

For extra flavor brush these over the pizza base before adding the topping. They also form a kind of protective seal that keeps the crust crisp and dry.

CHILI

INGREDIENTS
⅔ cup olive oil
2 tsp tomato paste
1 tbsp dried red chili flakes

1 Heat the oil in a pan until very hot but not smoking. Stir in the tomato paste and red chili flakes. Leave to cool.

2 Pour the chili oil into a small jar or bottle. Cover and store in the refrigerator for up to one week.

GARLIC

INGREDIENTS
3–4 whole garlic cloves
½ cup olive oil

1 Peel the garlic cloves and put them into a small jar or bottle.

2 Pour in the oil, cover and refrigerate for up to 1 week.

Margherita Pizza

(Tomato, Basil and Mozzarella)
This classic pizza is simple to prepare. The sweet flavour of sun-ripened tomatoes works wonderfully with the basil and mozzarella.

Serves 2–3

INGREDIENTS
1 pizza base, about 10–12 in
　diameter
2 tbsp olive oil
1 quantity Tomato Sauce
5 oz mozzarella
2 ripe tomatoes, thinly sliced
6–8 fresh basil leaves
2 tbsp freshly grated Parmesan
black pepper

basil

mozzarella

Parmesan

olive oil

Tomato Sauce

tomatoes

1 Preheat the oven to 425°F. Brush the pizza base with 1 tbsp of the oil and then spread over the Tomato Sauce.

2 Cut the mozzarella into thin slices.

3 Arrange the sliced mozzarella and tomatoes on top of the pizza base.

4 Roughly tear the basil leaves, add and sprinkle with the Parmesan. Drizzle over the remaining oil and season with black pepper. Bake for 15–20 minutes until crisp and golden. Serve immediately.

Marinara Pizza

(Tomato and Garlic)
The combination of garlic, good quality olive oil and oregano give this pizza an unmistakably Italian flavor.

Serves 2–3

INGREDIENTS
4 tbsp olive oil
1½ lb plum tomatoes, peeled, seeded
  and chopped
1 pizza base, about 10–12 in
  diameter
4 garlic cloves, cut into slivers
1 tbsp chopped fresh oregano
salt and black pepper

olive oil

oregano

plum tomatoes

garlic

1 Preheat the oven to 425°F. Heat 2 tbsp of the oil in a pan. Add the tomatoes and cook, stirring frequently for about 5 minutes until soft.

2 Place the tomatoes in a strainer and leave to drain for about 5 minutes.

3 Transfer the tomatoes to a food processor or blender and purée until smooth.

4 Brush the pizza base with half the remaining oil. Spoon over the tomatoes and sprinkle with garlic and oregano. Drizzle over the remaining oil and season. Bake for 15–20 minutes until crisp and golden. Serve immediately.

Fiorentina Pizza

Spinach is the star ingredient of this pizza. A grating of nutmeg to heighten its flavor gives this pizza its unique character.

Serves 2–3

INGREDIENTS
6 oz fresh spinach
3 tbsp olive oil
1 small red onion, thinly sliced
1 pizza base, about 10–12 in diameter
1 quantity Tomato Sauce
freshly grated nutmeg
5 oz mozzarella
1 large egg
1 oz Gruyère, grated

mozzarella

Gruyère

Tomato Sauce

spinach

red onion

nutmeg

egg

1 Preheat the oven to 425°F. Remove the stems from the spinach and wash the leaves in plenty of cold water. Drain well and pat dry with paper towels.

2 Heat 1 tbsp of the oil and fry the onion until soft. Add the spinach and continue to fry until just wilted. Drain off any excess liquid.

3 Brush the pizza base with half the remaining oil. Spread over the Tomato Sauce, then top with the spinach mixture. Grate some nutmeg over.

4 Thinly slice the mozzarella and arrange over the spinach. Drizzle the remaining oil over. Bake for 10 minutes, then remove from the oven.

5 Make a small well in the center and drop the egg into the hole.

6 Sprinkle over the Gruyère and return to the oven for a further 5–10 minutes until crisp and golden. Serve immediately.

Chili, Tomato and Spinach Pizza

This richly flavored topping with a hint of spice makes a colorful and satisfying pizza.

Serves 3

INGREDIENTS

1–2 fresh red chilies
3 tbsp tomato oil (from jar of sun-dried tomatoes)
1 onion, chopped
2 garlic cloves, chopped
2 oz (drained weight) sun-dried tomatoes in oil
14 oz can crushed tomatoes
1 tbsp tomato paste
6 oz fresh spinach
1 pizza base, 10–12 in diameter
3 oz smoked Gouda cheese, grated
3 oz sharp Cheddar, grated
salt and black pepper

1 Seed and finely chop the chilies.

2 Heat 2 tbsp of the tomato oil in a pan, add the onion, garlic and chilies and gently fry for about 5 minutes until they are soft.

3 Coarsely chop the sun-dried tomatoes. Add to the pan with the crushed tomatoes, tomato paste and seasoning. Simmer uncovered, stirring occasionally, for 15 minutes.

smoked Gouda cheese

crushed tomatoes

sharp Cheddar

sun-dried tomatoes

spinach

onion

garlic

red chilies

tomato oil

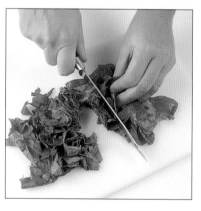

4 Remove the stems from the spinach and wash the leaves in plenty of cold water. Drain well and pat dry with paper towels. Coarsely chop the spinach.

5 Stir the spinach into the sauce. Cook, stirring, for a further 5–10 minutes until the spinach has wilted and no excess moisture remains. Leave to cool.

6 Meanwhile, preheat the oven to 425°F. Brush the pizza base with the remaining tomato oil, then spoon the sauce over. Sprinkle the cheeses over and bake for 15–20 minutes until crisp and golden. Serve immediately.

Three-cheese Pizza

You can use any combination of cheese you like. Edam and Cheddar both have good flavors and melting properties.

Serves 3–4

INGREDIENTS
3 tbsp olive oil
3 medium onions, sliced
1 pizza base, 10–12 in diameter
4 small tomatoes, peeled, seeded and
    cut into thin wedges
2 tbsp chopped fresh basil
4 oz Saga Blue
5 oz mozzarella
4 oz Red Leicester
black pepper
fresh basil leaves, to garnish

tomatoes

mozzarella

basil

Saga Blue

Red Leicester

olive oil

onions

1 Preheat the oven to 425°F. Heat 2 tbsp of the oil in a frying pan, add the onions and gently fry for about 10 minutes, stirring occasionally. Remove from the heat and let cool.

2 Brush the pizza base with the remaining oil. Spoon the onions and tomatoes over, then scatter the basil leaves over.

3 Thinly slice the cheeses and arrange over the tomatoes and onions.

4 Grind over plenty of black pepper and bake for 15–20 minutes until crisp and golden. Garnish with basil leaves and serve immediately.

Tomato, Fennel and Parmesan Pizza

This pizza relies on the winning combination of tomatoes, fennel and Parmesan. The fennel adds both a crisp texture and a distinctive flavor.

Serves 2–3

INGREDIENTS
1 fennel bulb
3 tbsp Garlic Oil
1 pizza base, 10–12 in diameter
1 quantity Tomato Sauce
2 tbsp chopped fresh Italian parsley
2 oz mozzarella, grated
2 oz Parmesan, grated
salt and black pepper

Italian parsley

mozzarella

Parmesan

Tomato Sauce

fennel bulb

Garlic Oil

1 Preheat the oven to 425°F. Trim and quarter the fennel lengthwise. Remove the core and slice each quarter of fennel thinly.

2 Heat 2 tbsp of the Garlic Oil in a frying pan and sauté the fennel for 4–5 minutes until just tender. Season.

3 Brush the pizza base with the remaining Garlic Oil and spread over the Tomato Sauce. Spoon the fennel on top and scatter the Italian parsley over.

4 Mix together the mozzarella and Parmesan and sprinkle over. Bake for 15–20 minutes until crisp and golden. Serve immediately.

Spring Vegetable and Pine Nut Pizza

This colorful pizza is well worth the time it takes to prepare. You can vary the ingredients according to availability.

Serves 2–3

INGREDIENTS
1 pizza base, 10–12 in diameter
3 tbsp Garlic Oil
1 quantity Tomato Sauce
4 scallions
2 zucchini
1 leek
4 oz asparagus tips
1 tbsp chopped fresh oregano
2 tbsp pine nuts
2 oz mozzarella, grated
2 tbsp freshly grated Parmesan
black pepper

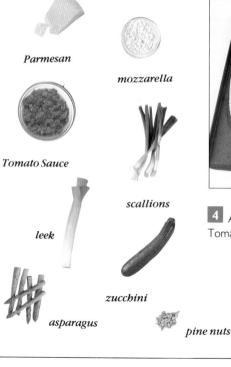

Parmesan

mozzarella

Tomato Sauce

scallions

leek

zucchini

asparagus

pine nuts

1 Preheat the oven to 425°F. Brush the pizza base with 1 tbsp of the Garlic Oil, then spread the Tomato Sauce over.

2 Slice the scallions, zucchini, leek and asparagus.

3 Heat half the remaining Garlic Oil in a frying pan and stir-fry the vegetables for 3–5 minutes.

4 Arrange the vegetables over the Tomato Sauce.

5 Sprinkle the oregano and pine nuts over the pizza.

6 Mix together the mozzarella and Parmesan and sprinkle over. Drizzle the remaining Garlic Oil over and season with black pepper. Bake for 15–20 minutes until crisp and golden. Serve immediately.

Roasted Vegetable and Goat Cheese Pizza

Here is a pizza which incorporates the smoky flavors of oven-roasted vegetables with the distinctive taste of goat cheese.

Serves 3

INGREDIENTS

1 eggplant, cut into thick chunks
2 small zucchini, sliced lengthwise
1 red bell pepper, quartered and seeded
1 yellow bell pepper, quartered and seeded
1 small red onion, cut into wedges
6 tbsp Garlic Oil
1 pizza base, 10–12 in diameter
1 × 14 oz can chopped tomatoes, drained well
1 × 4 oz goat cheese (with rind)
1 tbsp chopped fresh thyme
black pepper
green olive tapenade, to serve

1 Preheat the oven to 425°F. Place the eggplant, zucchini, peppers and onion in a large roasting pan. Brush with 4 tbsp of the Garlic Oil. Roast for about 30 minutes until lightly charred, turning the peppers halfway through cooking. Remove from the oven and set aside.

2 When the peppers are cool enough to handle, peel off the skins and cut the flesh into thick strips.

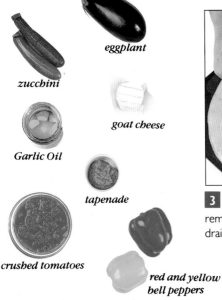

eggplant

zucchini

goat cheese

Garlic Oil

tapenade

crushed tomatoes

red and yellow bell peppers

3 Brush the pizza base with half the remaining Garlic Oil and spread over the drained tomatoes.

4 Arrange the roasted vegetables on top of the pizza.

5 Cube the goat cheese and arrange on top. Scatter the thyme over.

COOK'S TIP

If you place the roasted peppers in a paper bag while they cool, peeling off the skins becomes easier.

6 Drizzle the remaining Garlic Oil over and season with black pepper. Bake for 15–20 minutes until crisp and golden. Spoon the tapenade over to serve.

New Potato, Rosemary and Garlic Pizza

New potatoes, smoked mozzarella, rosemary and garlic make the flavor of this pizza unique. For a delicious variation, use sage instead of rosemary.

Serves 2–3

INGREDIENTS
12 oz new potatoes
3 tbsp olive oil
2 garlic cloves, crushed
1 pizza base, 10–12 in diameter
1 red onion, thinly sliced
5 oz smoked mozzarella, grated
2 tsp chopped fresh rosemary
salt and black pepper
2 tbsp freshly grated Parmesan, to garnish

olive oil

new potatoes

red onion

Parmesan

smoked mozzarella

rosemary

garlic

1 Preheat the oven to 425°F. Cook the potatoes in boiling salted water for 5 minutes. Drain well. When cool, peel and slice thinly.

2 Heat 2 tbsp of the oil in a frying pan. Add the sliced potatoes and garlic and fry for 5–8 minutes until tender.

3 Brush the pizza base with the remaining oil. Scatter the onion over, then arrange the potatoes on top.

4 Sprinkle over the mozzarella and rosemary. Grind over plenty of black pepper and bake for 15–20 minutes until crisp and golden. Remove from the oven and sprinkle the Parmesan over to serve.

Fresh Herb Pizza

Cut this pizza into thin wedges and serve as part of a mixed antipasti.

Serves 8

INGREDIENTS
4 oz mixed fresh herbs, such as
   parsley, basil and oregano
3 garlic cloves, crushed
½ cup heavy cream
1 pizza base, 10–12 in diameter
1 tbsp Garlic Oil
4 oz Pecorino, grated
salt and black pepper

heavy cream

Garlic Oil

Pecorino

basil

parsley

garlic

1 Preheat the oven to 425°F. Chop the herbs in a food processor if you have one.

2 In a bowl mix together the herbs, garlic, cream and seasoning.

3 Brush the pizza base with the Garlic Oil, then spread the herb mixture over.

4 Sprinkle the Pecorino over. Bake for 15–20 minutes until crisp and golden and the topping is still moist. Cut into thin wedges and serve immediately.

Tomato, Pesto and Black Olive Pizza

These individual pizzas take very little time to put together. Marinating the tomatoes gives them extra flavor.

Serves 4

INGREDIENTS
2 plum tomatoes
1 garlic clove, crushed
4 tbsp olive oil
1 quantity Basic or Superquick Pizza Dough
2 tbsp red pesto
5 oz mozzarella, thinly sliced
4 pitted black olives, chopped
1 tbsp chopped fresh oregano
salt and black pepper
oregano leaves, to garnish

red pesto

mozzarella

oregano

plum tomatoes

black olives

1 Slice the tomatoes thinly crosswise, then cut each slice in half. Place the tomatoes in a shallow dish with the garlic. Drizzle 2 tbsp of the oil over and season. Let marinate for 15 minutes.

2 Meanwhile, preheat the oven to 425°F. Divide the dough into four pieces and roll out each one on a lightly floured surface to a 5 in circle. Place well apart on two greased baking sheets, then pinch up the dough edges to make a rim. Brush the pizza bases with half the remaining oil and spread over the pesto.

3 Drain the tomatoes, then arrange a fan of alternate slices of tomatoes and mozzarella on each base.

4 Sprinkle over the olives and oregano. Drizzle over the remaining oil on top and bake for 15–20 minutes until crisp and golden. Garnish with the oregano leaves and serve immediately.

Red Onion, Gorgonzola and Sage Pizza

This topping combines the richness of Gorgonzola with the earthy flavors of sage and sweet red onions.

Serves 4

INGREDIENTS
1 quantity Basic or Superquick Pizza
   Dough
2 tbsp Garlic Oil
2 small red onions
5 oz Gorgonzola
2 garlic cloves
2 tsp chopped fresh sage
black pepper

sage

Gorgonzola

garlic

Garlic Oil

red onions

1 Preheat the oven to 425°F. Divide the dough into eight pieces and roll out each one on a lightly floured surface to a small oval about ¼ in thick. Place well apart on two greased baking sheets and prick with a fork. Brush the bases of each oval well with 1 tbsp of the Garlic Oil.

2 Halve, then slice the onions into thin wedges. Scatter over the pizza bases.

3 Remove the rind from the Gorgonzola. Cut the cheese into small cubes, then scatter it over the onions.

4 Cut the garlic lengthwise into thin strips and sprinkle over, along with the sage. Drizzle the remaining oil on top and grind over plenty of black pepper. Bake for 10–15 minutes until crisp and golden. Serve immediately.

Mini Pizzas

For a quick supper dish try these delicious little pizzas made with fresh and sun-dried tomatoes.

Makes 4

INGREDIENTS
1 × 5 oz package pizza mix
8 halves sun-dried tomatoes in olive
    oil, drained
½ cup black olives, pitted
8 oz ripe tomatoes, sliced
¼ cup goat cheese
2 tbsp fresh basil leaves

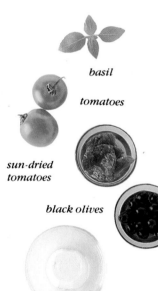

basil

tomatoes

*sun-dried
tomatoes*

black olives

goat cheese

1 Preheat the oven to 400°F. Make up the pizza base following the instructions on the side of the package.

2 Divide the dough into 4 and roll each piece out to a 5 in disc. Place on a lightly oiled cookie sheet.

3 Place the sun-dried tomatoes and olives in a blender or food processor and blend until smooth. Spread the mixture evenly over the pizza bases.

4 Top with the tomato slices and crumble over the goat cheese. Bake for 10–15 minutes. Sprinkle with the fresh basil and serve.

Quattro Formaggi Pizzas

Rich and tasty, these individual pizzas are very quick to assemble and the aroma of melting cheese is irresistible.

Serves 4

INGREDIENTS
1 quantity Basic or Superquick Pizza Dough
1 tbsp Garlic Oil
½ small red onion, very thinly sliced
2 oz Saga Blue
2 oz mozzarella
2 oz Gruyère, grated
2 tbsp freshly grated Parmesan
1 tbsp chopped fresh thyme
black pepper

red onion

mozzarella

Parmesan

Garlic Oil

Saga Blue

Gruyère

thyme

1 Preheat the oven to 425°F. Divide the dough into four pieces and roll out each one on a lightly floured surface into a 5 in circle. Place well apart on two greased baking sheets, then pinch up the dough edges to make a thin rim. Brush with Garlic Oil and top with the red onion.

2 Cut the Saga Blue and mozzarella into cubes and scatter over the bases.

3 Mix together the Gruyère, Parmesan and thyme and sprinkle over.

4 Grind over plenty of black pepper. Bake for 15–20 minutes until crisp and golden and the cheese is bubbling. Serve immediately.

Wild Mushroom Pizzettes

Serve these extravagant pizzas as an appetizer. Fresh wild mushrooms add a distinctive flavor to the topping but a mixture of cultivated mushrooms such as shiitake, oyster and cremini mushrooms would do just as well.

Serves 4

INGREDIENTS
3 tbsp olive oil
12 oz fresh wild mushrooms, washed and sliced
2 shallots, chopped
2 garlic cloves, finely chopped
2 tbsp chopped fresh mixed thyme and Italian parsley
1 quantity Basic or Superquick Pizza Dough
1½ oz Gruyère, grated
2 tbsp freshly grated Parmesan
salt and black pepper

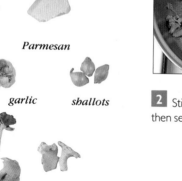

Gruyère
Italian parsley
olive oil
thyme
Parmesan
garlic *shallots*
wild mushrooms

1 Preheat the oven to 425°F. Heat 2 tbsp of the oil in a frying pan. Add the mushrooms, shallots and garlic and fry over a moderate heat until all the juices have evaporated.

2 Stir in half the herbs and seasoning, then set aside to cool.

3 Divide the dough into four pieces and roll out each one on a lightly floured surface to a 5 in circle. Place well apart on two greased baking sheets, then pinch up the dough edges to form a thin rim. Brush the pizza bases with the remaining oil and top with the wild mushroom mixture.

4 Mix together the Gruyère and Parmesan, then sprinkle over. Bake for 15–20 minutes until crisp and golden. Remove from the oven and sprinkle the remaining herbs over to serve.

Feta, Roasted Garlic and Oregano Pizzas

This is a pizza for garlic lovers! Mash down the cloves as you eat – they should be soft and will have lost their pungency.

Serves 4

INGREDIENTS

1 medium garlic head, unpeeled
3 tbsp olive oil
1 medium red bell pepper, quartered
    and seeded
1 medium yellow bell pepper,
    quartered and seeded
2 plum tomatoes
1 quantity Basic or Superquick Pizza
    Dough
6 oz feta, crumbled
black pepper
1–2 tbsp chopped fresh oregano, to
    garnish

oregano

feta

plum tomatoes

olive oil

red and yellow
bell peppers

garlic head

1 Preheat the oven to 425°F. Break the head of garlic into cloves, discarding the outer papery layers. Toss in 1 tbsp of the oil.

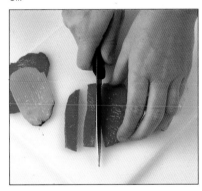

2 Place the peppers skin-side up on a baking sheet and broil until the skins are evenly charred. Place in a covered bowl for 10 minutes, then peel off the skins. Cut the flesh into strips.

3 Put the tomatoes in a bowl and pour boiling water over. Leave for 30 seconds, then plunge into cold water. Peel, seed and coarsely chop the flesh. Divide the dough into four pieces and roll out each one on a lightly floured surface to a 5 in circle.

4 Place the dough circles well apart on two greased baking sheets, then pinch up the dough edges to form a thin rim. Brush with half the remaining oil and scatter the chopped tomatoes over. Top with the peppers, crumbled feta and garlic cloves. Drizzle over the remaining oil and season with black pepper. Bake for 15–20 minutes until crisp and golden. Garnish with chopped oregano and serve immediately.

French Bread Pizzas with Artichokes

Crunchy French bread makes an ideal base for these quick pizzas.

Serves 4

INGREDIENTS
1 tbsp sunflower oil
1 onion, chopped
1 green bell pepper, seeded and
  chopped
7 oz can chopped tomatoes
1 tbsp tomato paste
$^{1}/_{2}$ French stick
14 oz can artichoke hearts, drained
4 oz mozzarella cheese, sliced
1 tbsp poppy seeds
salt and freshly ground black pepper

mozzarella cheese

French stick

tomato paste

chopped tomatoes

green bell pepper

poppy seeds

onion

artichoke hearts

1 Heat the oil in a frying pan. Add the chopped onion and bell pepper, and cook for 4 minutes until just softened.

2 Stir in the chopped tomatoes and tomato paste. Cook for 4 minutes. Remove from the heat, and add salt and pepper to taste.

3 Cut the piece of French stick in half lengthwise. Cut each half in four to give eight pieces in all.

4 Spoon a little of the pepper and tomato mixture over each piece of bread. Preheat the broiler.

5 Slice the artichoke hearts. Arrange them on top of the pepper and tomato mixture. Cover with the mozzarella slices, and sprinkle with the poppy seeds.

6 Arrange the French bread pizzas on a rack over a broiler pan, and broil for 6–8 minutes until the cheese melts and is beginning to brown. Serve at once.

Eggplant, Shallot and Sun-dried Tomato Calzone

Eggplant, shallots and sun-dried tomatoes make an unusual filling for calzone. Add more or less red chili flakes, depending on personal taste.

Serves 2

INGREDIENTS
3 tbsp olive oil
3 shallots, chopped
4 baby eggplant
1 garlic clove, chopped
2 oz (drained weight) sun-dried
  tomatoes in oil, chopped
¼ tsp dried red chili flakes
2 tsp chopped fresh thyme
1 quantity Basic or Superquick Pizza
  Dough
3 oz mozzarella, cubed
salt and black pepper
1–2 tbsp freshly grated Parmesan, to
  serve

Parmesan

thyme

mozzarella

olive oil

baby eggplant

shallots

red chili flakes

1 Preheat the oven to 425°F. Heat 2 tbsp of the oil in a frying pan. Add the shallots and cook until soft. Trim the eggplant, then cut into small cubes.

2 Add the eggplant to the shallots with the garlic, sun-dried tomatoes, red chili flakes, thyme and seasoning. Cook for 4–5 minutes, stirring frequently, until the eggplant is beginning to soften. Remove from the heat and let cool.

3 Divide the dough in half and roll out each piece on a lightly floured surface to a 7 in circle.

4 Spread the eggplant mixture over half of each circle, leaving a 1 in border, then scatter the mozzarella over.

5 Dampen the edges with water, then fold over the other half of dough to enclose the filling. Press the edges firmly together to seal. Place on two greased baking sheets.

6 Brush with half the remaining oil and make a small hole in the top of each to allow the steam to escape. Bake for 15–20 minutes until golden. Remove from the oven and brush with the remaining oil. Sprinkle the Parmesan over and serve immediately.

Spinach and Ricotta Panzerotti

These make great party food to serve with drinks or as tasty appetizers for a crowd.

Makes 20–24

INGREDIENTS
4 oz frozen chopped spinach,
    defrosted and squeezed dry
2 oz ricotta
2 oz freshly grated Parmesan
generous pinch freshly grated nutmeg
2 quantities Basic or Superquick Pizza
    Dough
1 egg white, lightly beaten
vegetable oil for deep-frying
salt and black pepper

nutmeg

ricotta

vegetable oil

egg

frozen spinach

Parmesan

1 Place the spinach, ricotta, Parmesan, nutmeg and seasoning in a bowl and beat until smooth.

2 Roll out the dough on a lightly floured surface to about ⅛ in thick. Using a 3 in plain round cutter stamp out 20–24 circles.

3 Spread a teaspoon of spinach mixture over one half of each circle.

4 Brush the edges of the dough with a little egg white.

5 Fold the dough over the filling and press the edges firmly together to seal.

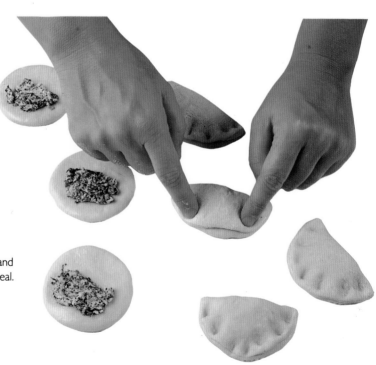

COOK'S TIP

Do serve these as soon as possible after frying, they will become much less appetizing if left to cool.

6 Heat the oil in a large heavy pan or deep-fat fryer to 350°F. Deep-fry the panzerotti a few at a time for 2–3 minutes until golden. Drain on paper towels and serve immediately.

DESSERTS

Fresh Fig, Apple, and Date Salad

Sweet Mediterranean figs and dates combine especially well with crisp dessert apples. A hint of almond serves to unite the flavors.

Serves 4

INGREDIENTS
6 large apples
juice of ½ lemon
6 oz fresh dates
1 oz white marzipan
1 tsp orange flower water
4 tbsp plain yogurt
4 green or purple figs
4 almonds, toasted

apples

figs   *almonds*

dates

1 Core the apples. Slice thinly, then cut into fine matchsticks. Toss with lemon juice to keep them white.

2 Remove the pits from the dates and cut the flesh into fine strips, then combine with the apple slices.

3 Soften the marzipan with orange flower water and combine with the yogurt. Mix well.

4 Pile the apples and dates in the center of 4 plates. Remove the stem from each of the figs and divide the fruit into quarters without cutting right through the base. Squeeze the base with the thumb and forefinger of each hand to open up the fruit.

5 Place a fig in the center of the salad, spoon in the yogurt filling, and decorate with a toasted almond.

Strawberries with Raspberry and Passion Fruit Sauce

Fragrant strawberries release their finest flavor when moistened with a sauce of fresh raspberries and scented passion fruit.

Serves 4

INGREDIENTS
12 oz raspberries, fresh or frozen
3 tbsp superfine sugar
1 passion fruit
1½ lb small strawberries
8 plain butter cookies, to serve

cookies

raspberries

passion fruit

strawberries

1 Place the raspberries and sugar in a stain-resistant saucepan and soften over a gentle heat to release the juices. Simmer for 5 minutes. Allow to cool.

2 Halve the passion fruit and scoop out the seeds and juice.

3 Transfer the raspberries into a food processor or blender, add the passion fruit, and blend smoothly.

COOK'S TIP
Berry fruits offer their best flavor when served at room temperature.

4 Force the fruit sauce through a fine nylon strainer to remove the seeds.

5 Fold the strawberries into the sauce, then spoon into 4 stemmed glasses. Serve with plain butter cookies.

Mixed Melon Salad with Wild Strawberries

Ice-cold melon is a delicious way to end a meal. Here several varieties are combined with strongly flavored wild strawberries. If wild berries are not available, use ordinary strawberries or raspberries.

Serves 4

INGREDIENTS
1 cantaloupe or charentais melon
1 galia or Spanish melon
2 lb watermelon
6 oz wild strawberries
4 sprigs fresh mint

COOK'S TIP
Ripe melons should give slightly when pressed at the base, and should give off a fruity, melony scent. Buy carefully if you plan to use the fruit on the day.

wild strawberries

galia melon

mint

cantaloupe

watermelon

1 Halve the cantaloupe, galia, and watermelons.

2 Remove the seeds from the cantaloupe and galia with a spoon.

3 With a melon-baller, take out as many balls as you can from all 3 melons. Combine in a large bowl and refrigerate.

4 Add the wild strawberries and transfer to 4 stemmed glass dishes.

5 Decorate with sprigs of mint.

Winter Fruit Salad

A colorful, refreshing and nutritious fruit salad, which is ideal served with reduced-fat plain yogurt or cream.

Serves 6

INGREDIENTS

**1 can (8 oz) pineapple cubes
  in fruit juice**
scant cup freshly
  squeezed orange juice
scant cup unsweetened apple juice
**2 tbsp orange or
  apple liqueur**
2 tbsp honey (optional)
2 oranges, peeled
2 green-skinned apples, chopped
2 pears, chopped
4 plums, pitted and chopped
12 fresh dates, pitted and chopped
½ cup dried apricots
fresh mint sprigs, to garnish

*pineapple cubes
in fruit juice* *freshly
squeezed
orange juice*

*unsweetened
apple juice* *orange
or apple
liqueur* *honey*

oranges *green-skinned
apples* *pears*

plums *fresh
dates* *dried
apricots*

1 Drain the pineapple, reserving the juice. Put the pineapple juice, orange juice, apple juice, liqueur and honey, if using, in a large serving bowl and stir.

2 Segment the oranges, catching any juice in the bowl, and put the orange segments and pineapple in the fruit juice mixture.

3 Add the apples and pears to the bowl.

COOK'S TIP
Use other unsweetened fruit juices such as pink grapefruit and pineapple juice in place of the orange and apple juice.

4 Stir in the plums, dates and apricots, cover and chill for several hours. Garnish with fresh mint sprigs to serve.

Apricot and Banana Compote

This compote is delicious served on its own or with low-fat custard or ice cream. Served for breakfast, it makes a tasty start to the day.

Serves 4

INGREDIENTS

1 cup dried apricots
1¼ cups unsweetened orange juice
⅔ cup unsweetened apple juice
1 teaspoon ground ginger
3 medium bananas, sliced
¼ cup toasted sliced almonds

dried apricots

unsweetened apple juice

unsweetened orange juice

ground ginger

bananas

toasted sliced almonds

1 Put the apricots in a saucepan with the fruit juices and ginger and stir. Cover, bring to a boil and simmer gently for 10 minutes, stirring occasionally.

2 Set aside to cool, leaving the lid on. Once cool, stir in the sliced bananas.

COOK'S TIP
Use other combinations of dried and fresh fruit such as prunes or figs and apples or peaches.

3 Spoon the fruit and juices into a serving dish.

4 Serve immediately, or cover and chill for several hours before serving. Sprinkle with sliced almonds just before serving.

Apples and Raspberries in Rose Pouchong Syrup

Inspiration for this dessert stems from the fact that the apple and the raspberry belong to the rose family. The subtle flavors are shared here in an infusion of rose-scented tea.

Serves 4

INGREDIENTS
1 tsp rose pouchong tea
1 tsp rose water (optional)
¼ cup sugar
1 tsp lemon juice
5 dessert apples
1½ cups fresh raspberries

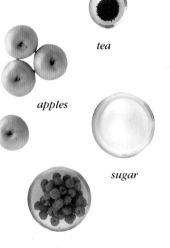

tea

apples

sugar

raspberries

COOK'S TIP

If fresh raspberries are out of season, use the same weight of frozen fruit or a 14 oz can of well drained fruit.

1 Warm a large tea pot. Add the rose pouchong tea and 3¾ cups of boiling water together with the rose water, if using. Allow the tea to stand and infuse for 4 minutes.

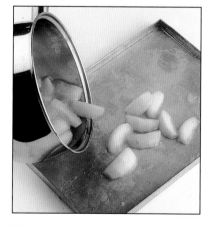

2 Measure the sugar and lemon juice into a stainless steel saucepan. Strain in the tea and stir to dissolve the sugar.

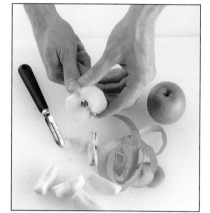

3 Peel and core the apples, then cut into quarters.

4 Poach the apples in the syrup for about 5 minutes.

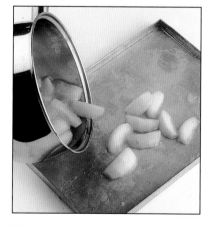

5 Transfer the apples and syrup to a large metal tray and leave to cool to room temperature.

6 Pour the cooled apples and syrup into a bowl, add the raspberries and mix to combine. Spoon into individual glass dishes or bowls and serve warm.

Watermelon Sorbet

A slice of this refreshing sorbet is the perfect way to cool down on a hot sunny day.

Serves 4–6

INGREDIENTS
½ small watermelon, weighing about 2¼ lb
½ cup superfine sugar
4 tbsp cranberry juice or water
2 tbsp lemon juice
sprigs of fresh mint, to decorate

cranberry juice

sugar

watermelon   lemon juice

1 Cut the watermelon into 4–6 equal-sized wedges (depending on the number of servings you require). Scoop out the pink flesh, discarding the seeds but reserving the shell.

2 Line a freezer-proof bowl, about the same size as the melon, with plastic wrap. Arrange the melon skins in the bowl to re-form the shell, fitting them together snugly so that there are no gaps. Put in the freezer.

3 Put the sugar and cranberry juice or water in a saucepan and stir over a low heat until the sugar dissolves. Bring to a boil and simmer for 5 minutes. Leave the sugar syrup to cool.

4 Put the melon flesh and lemon juice in a blender and process to a smooth purée. Stir in the sugar syrup and pour into a freezer-proof container. Freeze for 3–3½ hours, or until slushy.

5 Tip the sorbet into a chilled bowl and whisk to break up the ice crystals. Return to the freezer for another 30 minutes, whisk again, then tip into the melon shell and freeze until solid.

6 Remove from the freezer and leave to defrost at room temperature for 15 minutes. Take the melon out of the bowl and cut into wedges with a warmed sharp knife. Serve with sprigs of fresh mint.

COOK'S TIP

If preferred, this pretty pink sorbet can be served scooped into balls. Do this before the mixture is completely frozen and re-freeze the balls on a baking sheet, ready to serve.

Fresh Orange Granita

A granita is like an Italian ice, but coarser and quite grainy in texture, hence its name. It makes a refreshing dessert after a rich main course, or a cooling treat on a hot summer's day.

Serves 6

INGREDIENTS
4 large oranges
1 large lemon
¾ cup granulated sugar
2 cups water
amaretti cookies, to serve

oranges　　*sugar*

amaretti cookies

lemon

COOK'S TIP
To make the decoration, slice the orange and lemon zest into thin strips. Blanch for 2 minutes, refresh under cold water and dry before using.

1 Thinly pare the zest from the oranges and lemon, trying to avoid the bitter white pith, and set a few pieces aside for decoration. Halve the fruit and squeeze the juice into a pitcher. Set aside.

2 Heat the sugar and water in a heavy saucepan, stirring over low heat, until the sugar dissolves. Bring to a boil, then boil without stirring for about 10 minutes, until a syrup forms. Remove the syrup from the heat, add the orange and lemon zest and shake the pan. Cover and let cool.

3 Strain the sugar syrup into a shallow freezer container and add the fruit juice. Stir well to mix, then freeze, uncovered, for about 4 hours, until slushy.

4 Take the half-frozen mixture from the freezer and mix with a fork. Freeze for 4 more hours, or until hard. To serve, let sit at room temperature for about 10 minutes, then break up with a fork and pile into long-stemmed glasses. Decorate with strips of zest (see Cook's Tip) and serve with amaretti cookies.

Whole-wheat Bread and Banana Yogurt Ice

Serve this tempting yogurt ice with some fresh fruit, such as strawberries, or with wafer cookies, for a light dessert.

Serves 6

INGREDIENTS

2 cups fresh whole-wheat
  bread crumbs
¼ cup light brown sugar
1¼ cups low-fat cold custard
**5 oz low-fat ricotta cheese or
  low-fat cream cheese**
5 oz plain yogurt
4 bananas, mashed
juice of 1 lemon
¼ cup confectioners' sugar, sifted
⅓ cup raisins, chopped
  pared lemon rind, to garnish

fresh whole-wheat bread crumbs

light brown sugar

low-fat cold custard

low-fat ricotta cheese

plain yogurt

bananas

lemon

sugar

raisins

1 Preheat the oven to 400°F. Mix together the bread crumbs and brown sugar and spread the mixture out on a nonstick baking sheet. Bake for about 10 minutes, stirring occasionally, until crisp. Set aside to cool, then break the mixture up into crumbs.

2 Meanwhile, put the custard, ricotta cheese and yogurt in a bowl and mix. Mash the bananas with the lemon juice and add to the custard mixture, mixing well. Fold in the confectioners' sugar.

3 Pour the mixture into a shallow plastic freezer-proof container and freeze for about 3 hours, or until mushy in consistency. Spoon into a chilled bowl and quickly mash with a fork to break down the ice crystals.

4 Add the bread crumb mixture and raisins and mix well. Return to the container, cover and freeze until firm. Soften in the refrigerator for 30 minutes before serving. Garnish with lemon rind.

Brown Bread Ice Cream

This dish sounds homely but tastes heavenly. Toasted whole-wheat bread crumbs have a wonderful nutty flavor, especially when accentuated with hazelnuts.

Serves 6

INGREDIENTS
½ cup roasted and chopped
 hazelnuts, ground
1½ cups fresh whole-wheat
 bread crumbs
4 tbsp raw sugar
3 egg whites
½ cup sugar
1¼ cups heavy cream
few drops of vanilla extract
fresh mint sprigs, to decorate

FOR THE SAUCE
1½ cups black currants
6 tbsp sugar
1 tbsp crème de cassis

hazelnuts

raw sugar

*fresh whole-
wheat bread
crumbs*

eggs

sugar

*heavy
cream*

*vanilla
extract*

*black
currants*

crème de cassis

1 Preheat the broiler. Combine the hazelnuts and bread crumbs on a baking sheet, then sprinkle over the raw sugar. Broil, stirring frequently, until the mixture is crisp and evenly browned. Leave to cool.

2 Whisk the egg whites in a grease-free bowl until stiff, then gradually whisk in the sugar until thick and glossy. Whip the cream until it forms soft peaks and fold into the meringue with the bread crumb mixture and vanilla extract.

3 Spoon the mixture into a 5-cup loaf pan. Smooth the top level, then cover and freeze for several hours, or until firm.

5 To serve, turn out the ice cream onto a plate and cut into slices. Arrange each slice on a serving plate, spoon over a little sauce and decorate with fresh mint sprigs.

4 Meanwhile, make the sauce. Put the black currants in a small bowl with the sugar. Toss gently to mix and leave for 30 minutes. Purée the black currants in a blender or food processor, then press through a nylon sieve into a bowl. Stir in the crème de cassis and chill well.

COOK'S TIP

To string black currants, run a fork down the stalks so that the berries are pulled off by the tines.

Chocolate Chip Banana Crêpes

Serve these delicious crêpes as a dessert topped with cream and toasted almonds.

Makes 16

INGREDIENTS
2 ripe bananas
scant 1 cup milk
2 eggs
1¼ cups self-rising flour
⅓ cup ground almonds
1 tbsp superfine sugar
1 oz plain chocolate chips
butter, for frying
pinch of salt

FOR THE TOPPING
⅔ cup heavy cream
1 tbsp confectioners' sugar
½ cup toasted slivered almonds,
    to decorate

chocolate chips

bananas

flour

eggs

ground almonds

milk

1 In a bowl, mash the bananas with a fork, combine with half of the milk and beat in the eggs. Sift in the flour, ground almonds, sugar and salt. Make a well in the center and pour in the remaining milk. Add the chocolate chips and stir to produce a thick batter.

2 Heat a pat of butter in a nonstick frying pan. Spoon the crêpe mixture into heaps, allowing room for them to spread. When bubbles emerge, turn the crêpes over and cook briefly on the other side.

3 Loosely whip the cream with the confectioners' sugar to sweeten it slightly. Spoon the cream onto crêpes and decorate with slivered almonds.

COOK'S TIP

For banana and blueberry crêpes, replace the chocolate with 1 cup fresh blueberries. Hot crêpes are also delicious when accompanied by ice cream.

Plum, Rum and Raisin Brulée

Crack through the crunchy caramel to find the juicy plums and smooth creamy center of this dessert.

Serves 4

INGREDIENTS
3 tbsp raisins
1 tbsp dark rum
12 oz medium plums (about 6)
juice of 1 orange
1 tbsp honey
2 cups low-fat cream cheese
½ cup sugar

raisins

rum

orange

plums

honey

1 Put the raisins into a small bowl and sprinkle over the rum. Leave to soak for 5 minutes.

2 Quarter the plums and remove their pits. Put into a large, heavy saucepan together with the orange juice and honey. Simmer gently for 5 minutes or until soft. Stir in the soaked raisins. Reserve 1 tbsp of the juice, then divide the rest between four ⅔ cup ramekin dishes.

3 Blend the low-fat cream cheese with the reserved 1 tbsp of plum juice. Spoon over the plums and chill in the refrigerator for 1 hour.

4 Put the sugar into a large, heavy saucepan with 3 tbsp cold water. Heat gently, stirring until the sugar has dissolved. Boil for 15 minutes or until it turns golden brown. Cool for 2 minutes, then carefully pour over the ramekins. Cool and serve.

Raspberry and Passionfruit Puffs

Few desserts are so strikingly easy to make as this one: beaten egg whites and sugar baked in a dish, turned out and served with a handful of soft fruit.

Serves 4

INGREDIENTS
2 tbsp butter, softened
5 egg whites
⅔ cup superfine sugar
2 passionfruit
1 cup ready-made custard from a
   carton or can
milk, as required
6 cups fresh raspberries
confectioners' sugar, for dusting

raspberries

egg whites

passionfruit

confectioners' sugar

VARIATION
If raspberries are out of season, use either fresh, bottled or canned soft berry fruit such as strawberries, blueberries or red currants.

1 Preheat the oven to 350°F. Brush four ½ pint soufflé dishes with a visible layer of soft butter.

2 Whisk the egg whites in a mixing bowl until firm. (You can use an electric mixer.) Add the sugar a little at a time and whisk into a firm meringue.

3 Halve the passionfruit, take out the seeds with a spoon and fold them into the meringue.

4 Turn the meringue out into the prepared dishes, stand in a deep roasting pan which has been half-filled with boiling water and bake for 10 minutes. The meringue will rise above the tops of the soufflé dishes.

5 Turn the puffs out upside-down onto a serving plate.

6 Top with raspberries. Thin the custard with a little milk and pour around the edge. Dredge with confectioners' sugar and serve warm or cold.

Ice Cream Strawberry Shortcake

This simple dessert is an all-time American classic. Make sure you use the freshest, most beautiful berries available. You can substitute whipped cream for the ice cream if you like.

Serves 4

INGREDIENTS
3 × 6 in ready-made sponge cake cases or shortcakes
2 pints/5 cups vanilla or strawberry ice cream
1½ lb hulled fresh strawberries
confectioners' sugar, for dusting

strawberries

vanilla ice cream

sponge cake case

1 If using sponge cake cases, trim the raised edges with a serrated knife.

2 Sandwich the sponge cake cases or shortcakes with two-thirds of the ice cream and the strawberries.

COOK'S TIP

Don't worry if the shortcake falls apart when you cut into it. Messy cakes are best. Ice Cream Strawberry Shortcake can be assembled up to 1 hour in advance and kept in the freezer without spoiling the fruit.

3 Place the remaining ice cream on top, finish with strawberries, dust with confectioners' sugar and serve.

Malted Chocolate and Banana Dip

Malted drinks and "smoothies" are hot, and this delectable dip is perfect served with chunks of fruit.

Serves 4

INGREDIENTS
2 oz semisweet chocolate
2 large ripe bananas
1 tbsp malt extract

semisweet chocolate

bananas

malt extract

 Break the chocolate into pieces and place in a small heatproof bowl. Stand the bowl over a pan of gently simmering water and stir the chocolate occasionally until it melts. Let cool.

2 Cut the bananas into pieces and process them until finely chopped in a blender or food processor.

COOK'S TIP

This smooth dip can be prepared in advance and chilled. When ready to serve, stir in some lightly whipped cream to soften and enrich the mixture.

3 With the motor running, pour in the malt extract, and continue processing until the mixture is thick and frothy.

4 Drizzle in the chocolate in a steady stream and process until well blended. Serve immediately.

Papaya and Coconut Dip

Sweet and smooth papaya teams up well with
rich coconut cream to make a luscious sweet dip.

Serves 6

INGREDIENTS
2 ripe papayas
scant 1 cup crème fraîche
1 piece ginger
fresh coconut, to decorate

papayas

crème fraîche

ginger

fresh coconut

1 Halve each papaya lengthwise, then
scoop out and discard the seeds. Cut a
few slices and reserve for decoration.

2 Scoop out the flesh and process
it until smooth in a blender or a
food processor.

3 Stir in the crème fraîche and process
until well blended. Finely chop the ginger
and stir it into the mixture, then chill until
ready to serve.

4 Pierce a hole in the "eye" of the
coconut and drain the liquid, then break
open the coconut. Hold it securely in
one hand and hit it sharply with a
hammer.

5 Remove the shell from a piece of
coconut, then snap the coconut into
pieces no wider than ¾ in.

6 Use a swivel-bladed vegetable peeler
to shave off ¾-in lengths of coconut.
Scatter these over the dip with the
reserved papaya before serving.

COOK'S TIP

If fresh coconut is not available,
buy shredded coconut and lightly
toast in a hot oven until golden.

Broiled Pineapple with Rum-custard Sauce

Freshly ground black pepper may seem an unusual ingredient to put with pineapple, until you realise that peppercorns are the fruit of a tropical vine. If the idea does not appeal, make the sauce without pepper.

Serves 4

INGREDIENTS
1 ripe pineapple
2 tbsp butter
fresh strawberries, sliced, to serve

FOR THE SAUCE
1 egg
2 egg yolks
2 tbsp superfine sugar
2 tbsp dark rum
½ tsp freshly ground black
   pepper

butter

rum

eggs

pineapple

black pepper

superfine sugar

1 Remove the top and bottom from the pineapple with a serrated knife. Fare away the outer skin from top to bottom, remove the core and cut into slices.

2 Preheat a moderate broiler. Dot the pineapple slices with butter and broil for about 5 minutes.

3 To make the sauce, place all the ingredients in a bowl. Set over a saucepan of simmering water and whisk with a hand-held mixer for about 3–4 minutes or until foamy and cooked. Scatter the strawberries over the pineapple and serve with the sauce.

COOK'S TIP

The sweetest pineapples are picked and exported when ripe. Contrary to popular belief, pineapples do not ripen well after picking. Choose fruit that smells sweet and yields to firm pressure from your thumbs.

344

Oranges with Saffron Yogurt

This is a popular Indian dessert to eat after a hot and spicy curry.

Serves 4

INGREDIENTS

4 large oranges
¼ tsp ground cinnamon
1⅔ cups plain yogurt
2 tsp sugar
3–4 saffron threads
¼ tsp ground ginger
1 tbsp chopped pistachio
    nuts, toasted
fresh lemon balm or mint leaves,
    to decorate

yogurt

saffron threads

sugar

mint leaves

pistachio nuts

oranges

ground cinnamon

ground ginger

1 Slice the bottom off each of the oranges. Working from the top of the orange, cut across the top of the orange and down one side. Follow the contours of the orange. Repeat until all the peel and pith has been removed, reserving any juice. Peel the remaining oranges in the same way.

2 Slice the oranges thinly and remove any seeds. Lay in a single layer, overlapping the slices, on a shallow serving plate. Sprinkle the ground cinnamon over the oranges. Cover the plate with plastic wrap and chill.

3 Mix the yogurt, sugar, saffron and ginger together in a bowl and leave to infuse for 5–10 minutes. Sprinkle with the chopped nuts. To serve, spoon the yogurt and nut mixture over the chilled orange slices and decorate with herbs.

COOK'S TIP

For a more unusual dessert use deliciously juicy blood oranges, which look dramatic and have a wonderful flavor.

Stuffed Peaches with Mascarpone Cream

Mascarpone is a thick, velvety Italian cream cheese, made from cow's milk. It is often used in desserts, or eaten with fresh fruit.

Serves 4

INGREDIENTS
4 large peaches, halved and pitted
¾ cup amaretti cookie crumbs
2 tbsp ground almonds
3 tbsp granulated sugar
1 tbsp unsweetened
  cocoa powder
⅔ cup sweet wine
2 tbsp butter

FOR THE MASCARPONE CREAM
2 tbsp superfine sugar
3 egg yolks
1 tbsp sweet wine
1 cup mascarpone cheese
⅔ cup heavy cream

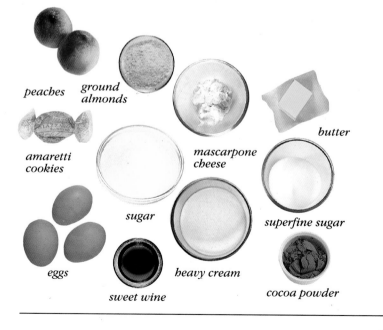

peaches

ground almonds

amaretti cookies

mascarpone cheese

butter

sugar

superfine sugar

eggs

heavy cream

sweet wine

cocoa powder

1 Preheat the oven to 400°F. Using a teaspoon, scoop some of the flesh from the cavities in the peaches to make a reasonable space for stuffing. Chop the scooped-out flesh.

2 Combine the amaretti cookies, ground almonds, sugar, cocoa and peach flesh in a bowl. Add enough wine to make the mixture into a thick paste. Place the peaches in a buttered ovenproof dish and fill them with the amaretti and almond stuffing. Dot with butter, then pour the remaining wine into the dish. Bake for 35 minutes.

3 To make the mascarpone cream, beat the sugar and egg yolks until thick and pale. Stir in the wine, then fold in the mascarpone. Whip the cream until it forms soft peaks and fold into the mixture. Remove the peaches from the oven and let cool. Serve the peaches at room temperature, with the mascarpone cream.

Feather-light Peach Pudding

On chilly days, try this hot fruit pudding with its tantalizing sponge topping.

Serves 4

INGREDIENTS

14 oz can peach slices in
   natural juice
4 tbsp low-fat spread
¼ cup light brown sugar
1 egg, beaten
½ cup whole-wheat
   flour
½ cup flour
1 tsp baking powder
½ tsp ground cinnamon
4 tbsp skim milk
½ tsp vanilla extract
2 tsp confectioner's sugar, for
   dusting
low-fat ready-made custard,
   to serve

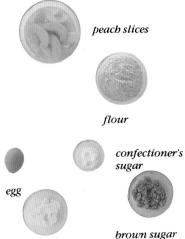

peach slices

flour

*confectioner's
sugar*

egg

brown sugar

*low-fat
custard*

1 Preheat the oven to 350°F. Drain the peaches and put into a 4 cup pie dish with 2 tbsp of the juice.

2 Put all the remaining ingredients, except the confectioner's sugar into a mixing bowl. Beat for 3–4 minutes, until thoroughly combined.

COOK'S TIP

For a simple sauce, blend 1 tsp arrowroot with 1 tbsp peach juice in a small saucepan. Stir in the remaining peach juice from the can and bring to a boil. Simmer for 1 minute until thickened and clear.

3 Spoon the sponge mixture over the peaches and level the top evenly. Cook in the oven for 35-40 minutes, or until springy to the touch.

4 Lightly dust the top with confectioner's sugar and serve hot with the low-fat custard.

Spiced Bread Pudding with Cranberry Sauce

Nutmeg is a warm, aromatic spice and is particularly suited to old-fashioned puddings.

Serves 6–8

INGREDIENTS

¼ cup butter, melted
3 cups milk
3 eggs
½ cup sugar
1 tsp vanilla extract
2 tsp ground cinnamon
½ tsp grated nutmeg
1 day-old French loaf, cubed
½ cup chopped walnuts
½ cup golden raisins

FOR THE CRANBERRY SAUCE

12 oz cranberries, fresh or frozen
finely grated zest and juice of
    1 large orange
2 tbsp sugar

1 Brush the butter generously into the bottom and sides of an ovenproof dish. Pour any remaining butter into the milk. Beat the eggs until light and frothy, then beat in the sugar, vanilla extract, cinnamon and nutmeg. Stir in the milk and mix well.

2 Arrange the bread cubes in the prepared dish, scattering the walnuts and golden raisins over the top.

3 Preheat the oven to 350°F. Pour the custard over the bread, coating each piece thoroughly. Leave to stand for about 45 minutes.

4 Bake the pudding in the oven for 45 minutes until the top is golden and puffy. If the top doesn't brown, increase the oven temperature for the last 10 minutes.

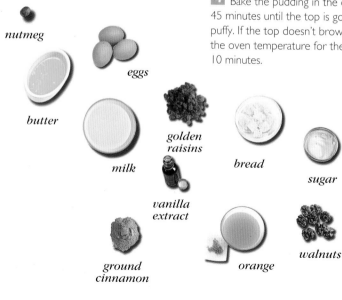

nutmeg

eggs

butter

golden raisins

milk

bread

sugar

vanilla extract

ground cinnamon

orange

walnuts

5 To make the cranberry sauce, put the cranberries into a saucepan with the orange rind and juice and the sugar.

6 Stir over low heat until the sugar dissolves, then cook until the berries pop and the mixture thickens and becomes syrupy. Serve the sauce hot or cold.

Ginger and Lemon Puddings with Custard

The flavors of lemon and ginger complement each other perfectly in these light little puddings.

Serves 8

INGREDIENTS

3 lemons
½ cup drained preserved ginger, plus 2 tbsp syrup from the jar
4 tbsp corn syrup
1½ cups self-rising flour
2 tsp ground ginger
½ cup butter, softened
generous ½ cup sugar
2 eggs, beaten
3–4 tbsp milk

FOR THE VANILLA CUSTARD
⅔ cup milk
⅔ cup heavy cream
1 vanilla bean, split
3 egg yolks
1 tsp cornstarch
2 tbsp sugar

sugar   *corn syrup*

eggs   *lemons*   *butter*   *ground ginger*   *heavy cream*

milk   *vanilla bean*

COOK'S TIP
Use vanilla sugar for additional flavor. Place a vanilla bean in a jar of sugar and leave for at least a week before using.

1 Preheat the oven to 325°F. Grease 8 individual pudding bowls. Set one lemon aside for the sauce. Grate the rind from the remaining lemons and reserve. Remove all the pith from one of the grated lemons and slice into 8 thin rounds. Squeeze the juice from the second grated lemon. Chop the preserved ginger.

2 Mix together 1 tablespoon of the ginger syrup with 2 tablespoons of the corn syrup and 1 teaspoon of the lemon juice. Divide among the greased pudding bowls. Place a slice of lemon in the bottom of each bowl.

3 Sift the flour and ground ginger into a bowl. In a separate bowl, beat the butter and sugar together until pale and fluffy. Beat in the eggs, then fold in the flour mixture. Add enough milk to give a soft consistency, then stir in the lemon rind. Spoon into the pudding bowls.

4 Cover each bowl with foil and stand in a roasting pan. Add boiling water to come halfway up the bowls. Overwrap with foil, sealing well. Bake for 30–45 minutes, until cooked through.

5 To make the lemon and ginger sauce, grate the rind and squeeze the juice from the remaining lemon. Place in a pan with the remaining ginger syrup and corn syrup, bring to a boil, and simmer for 2 minutes. Keep warm.

6 To make the custard, pour the milk and cream into a pan. Add the vanilla bean and heat until almost boiling. Remove from the heat and leave for 10 minutes. Whisk together the egg yolks, cornstarch and sugar, then strain into the milk and cream. Whisk until blended, then return to the clean pan and heat, stirring, until thick. Turn out the puddings, spoon over the sauce and serve with the custard.

Red Berry Sponge Tart

When soft berry fruits are in season, try making this delicious sponge tart. Serve warm from the oven with scoops of vanilla ice cream.

Serves 4

INGREDIENTS
softened butter, for greasing
4 cups soft berry fruits such as
    raspberries, blackberries, black
    currants, red currants, strawberries
    or blueberries
2 eggs, at room temperature
¼ cup superfine sugar, plus extra to
    taste (optional)
1 tbsp flour
¾ cup ground almonds
vanilla ice cream, to serve

1 Preheat the oven to 375°F. Brush a 9 in pie pan with softened butter and line the bottom with a circle of non-stick baking paper. Scatter the fruit in the bottom of the pan with a little sugar if the fruits are tart.

2 Whisk the eggs and sugar together for about 3–4 minutes or until they leave a thick trail across the surface. Combine the flour and almonds, then fold into the egg mixture with a spatula – retaining as much air as possible.

eggs

ground almonds

flour

superfine sugar

red currants

black currants

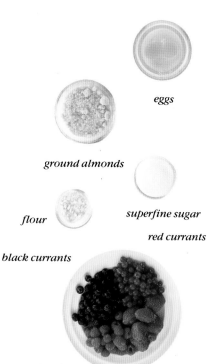

raspberries

strawberries

VARIATION
When berry fruits are out of season, use bottled fruits, but ensure that they are well drained before use.

3 Spread the mixture on top of the fruit base and bake in the preheated oven for 15 minutes. Turn out onto a serving plate and serve with vanilla ice cream.

Pear Tart Tatin with Cardamom

Cardamom is a versatile spice that is good with sweet or savory dishes. It is delicious with pears.

Serves 2–4

INGREDIENTS

¼ cup butter, melted
¼ cup sugar
seeds from 10 cardamom pods
8 oz puff pastry, thawed if frozen
4–5 ripe pears
cream, to serve

sugar   *butter*

cardamom pods   *puff pastry*

pears

1 Preheat the oven to 425°F. Spread the butter over the base of a 7-inch flameproof round pan, sprinkle with the sugar and scatter over the cardamom seeds. Roll out the pastry to a round slightly larger than the pan, prick the pastry lightly and chill.

COOK'S TIP
You will need to use a heavy pan for this recipe. If you do not have a heavy cake pan, use an ovenproof omelet pan.

2 Peel, core and halve the pears lengthwise. Arrange the pears, rounded side down, on the butter and sugar. Set the pan over medium heat until the sugar melts and begins to bubble. If any areas are browning more than others, move the pan, but do not stir.

3 As soon as the sugar has caramelized, quickly remove the pan from the heat, so that the sugar does not burn. Place the pastry on top, tucking the edges down the side of the pan. Bake in the oven for 25 minutes until the pastry is well risen and golden.

4 Leave the tart in the pan for 2–3 minutes until the juices have stopped bubbling. Invert over a plate and shake to release the tart. It may be necessary to slide a spatula underneath the pears to loosen them. Serve the tart warm with cream.

Crunchy Apple and Almond Tart

Generations of cooks have taken pride in making this traditional tart, with its attractive arrangement of tender apples topped with nut crumble.

Serves 8

INGREDIENTS
1½ cups flour
6 tbsp butter, cubed
⅓ cup ground almonds
2 tbsp sugar
1 egg yolk
1 tbsp cold water
¼ tsp almond extract
4 large apples
3 tbsp raisins (optional)
confectioners' sugar, to decorate

FOR THE CRUNCHY TOPPING
1 cup flour
¼ tsp apple pie spice
4 tbsp butter, diced
⅓ cup raw sugar
½ cup sliced almonds

flour

butter

sugar

egg

ground
almonds

almond
extract

raw sugar

apples

raisins

sliced
almonds

1 Process the flour and butter in a food processor until it resembles fine bread crumbs. Stir in the ground almonds and sugar. Whisk the egg yolk, water and almond extract together and add to the dry ingredients to form a dough. Knead lightly, wrap and leave for 20 minutes.

4 Preheat the oven to 375°F. Place a baking sheet in the oven to preheat. Peel, core and slice the apples thinly. Arrange in the pie shell in concentric circles, doming the centre.

2 Meanwhile, make the crunchy topping. Sift the flour and apple pie spice into a bowl and rub in the butter. Stir in the sugar and almonds.

5 Scatter over the raisins, if using. Cover the apples with the crunchy topping, pressing it on lightly. Bake on the hot baking sheet for 25–30 minutes, or until golden brown and the apples are tender when tested with a fine skewer.

3 Roll out the pastry on a lightly floured surface and use it to line a 9-inch loose-bottomed pie pan, taking care to press it neatly into the edges and to make a lip around the top edge. Roll off the excess pastry to neaten the edge. Chill for 15 minutes.

6 Leave the tart to cool in the pan for 10 minutes. Serve warm or cold, dusted with sifted confectioners' sugar.

COOK'S TIP

Do not be tempted to put any sugar with the apples, as this makes them produce too much liquid. All the sweetness necessary is in the pastry and topping.

Ricotta Cheesecake

Low-fat ricotta cheese is excellent for cheesecake fillings because it creates a good, firm texture. Here it is enriched with eggs and cream and enlivened with tangy orange and lemon zest to make a Sicilian-style dessert.

Serves 8

INGREDIENTS

16 oz (2 cups) low-fat
   ricotta cheese
½ cup heavy cream
2 eggs
1 egg yolk
⅓ cup granulated sugar
finely grated zest of 1 orange
finely grated zest of 1 lemon
blanched thin strips of orange and
   lemon zest, to decorate

FOR THE PASTRY

1½ cups all-purpose flour
3 tbsp granulated sugar
pinch of salt
8 tbsp (1 stick) chilled
   butter, diced
1 egg yolk

heavy
cream

ricotta cheese

sugar   flour

eggs

butter   lemon

orange

1 Make the pastry. Sift the flour, sugar and salt onto a cold work surface. Make a well in the center and put in the diced butter and egg yolk. Gradually work the flour into the diced butter and egg yolk, using your fingertips.

2 Gather the dough together, reserve about a quarter for the lattice, then press the rest into a 9-inch fluted tart pan with a removable bottom. Chill the pastry shell for 30 minutes.

3 Meanwhile, preheat the oven to 375°F and make the filling. Put the ricotta, cream, eggs, egg yolk, sugar and grated orange and lemon zests in a large bowl and beat until the ingredients are evenly mixed.

6 Bake the cheesecake for 30–35 minutes, until golden and set. Transfer to a wire rack and let cool thoroughly, then carefully remove the side of the pan and slide the cheesecake onto a serving plate. Decorate with blanched thin strips of orange and lemon zest before serving.

4 Prick the bottom of the pastry shell, then line with foil and fill with baking beans, raw rice or pastry weights. Bake blind for 15 minutes, then transfer to a wire rack, remove the foil and beans and let the pastry shell cool in the pan.

5 Spoon the cheese and cream filling into the pastry shell and level the surface. Roll out the reserved dough and cut into strips. Arrange the strips on top of the filling in a lattice pattern, sticking them in place with water.

VARIATIONS

Add ⅓–⅔ cup finely chopped candied peel to the filling in step 3, or ⅓ cup semisweet chocolate chips.

For a really rich dessert, you can add both candied peel and some grated semisweet chocolate.

Baked Blackberry Cheesecake

This light, low-fat cheesecake is best made with wild blackberries, if they are in season, but cultivated ones will do; or substitute other soft fruit, such as raspberries or blueberries.

Serves 4–6

INGREDIENTS
¼ cup cottage cheese
⅔ cup low-fat plain yogurt
1 tbsp whole-wheat flour
2 tbsp sugar
1 egg, plus 1 egg white
finely grated rind and juice of
    ½ lemon
2 cups fresh or frozen and
    thawed blackberries

cottage cheese

low-fat plain yogurt

whole-wheat flour

sugar

eggs

lemon

blackberries

COOK'S TIP
If you prefer to use canned blackberries, choose those canned in natural juice and drain the fruit well before adding it to the cheesecake mixture. The juice can be served with the cheesecake.

1 Preheat the oven to 350°F. Lightly grease and base-line an 7-inch shallow cake pan.

2 Place the cottage cheese in a food processor and process until smooth. Alternatively, rub it through a sieve. Scrape the smooth mixture into a bowl.

3 Stir in the yogurt, flour, sugar, egg and egg white. Fold in the lemon rind and juice and the blackberries, reserving a few for decoration.

4 Tip the mixture into the prepared pan and level the surface. Bake for 30–35 minutes, or until the mixture is just set. Switch off the oven and leave for a further 30 minutes.

5 Run a knife around the edge of the cheesecake, and then turn it out. Remove the lining paper and place the cheesecake on a warm serving plate.

6 Decorate the cheesecake with the reserved blackberries. Serve warm.

Apple Brown Betty

Crisp, spicy bread crumbs layered with lemony apples make a simply delicious dessert.

Serves 6

INGREDIENTS
1 cup fresh white bread crumbs
4 tbsp butter, plus extra for
  greasing
1 cup light brown sugar
½ tsp ground cinnamon
¼ tsp ground cloves
¼ tsp grated nutmeg
2 lb cooking apples
juice of 1 lemon
¼ cup finely chopped walnuts

fresh white
bread crumbs

butter

light
brown
sugar

ground
cinnamon

grated
nutmeg

cooking apples

lemon

chopped
walnuts

1 Preheat the broiler. Spread out the bread crumbs on a baking sheet or in a roasting pan and toast under the broiler until golden, stirring frequently to color them evenly. Set aside.

2 Preheat the oven to 375°F. Grease a large, deep ovenproof dish with a little butter. Mix the sugar with the spices. Cut the butter into tiny pieces, then set aside.

3 Peel, core, and slice the apples. Toss immediately with the lemon juice to prevent them from turning brown.

4 Sprinkle a thin layer of bread crumbs into the dish. Cover with one-third of the apples and sprinkle with one-third of the sugar and spice mixture. Add another layer of bread crumbs and dot with one-third of the butter. Repeat the layers twice more, sprinkling the nuts on top of the final layer of bread crumbs before dotting the remaining butter over the surface.

5 Bake for 35–40 minutes, until the apples are tender and the top is golden brown. Serve warm.

Pear and Cherry Crunch

A triumph of contrasting textures and flavors, this dessert teams fresh and dried fruit with a nut and crumb topping.

Serves 6

INGREDIENTS

½ cup butter, plus extra for greasing
8 pears
3 tbsp lemon juice
3 cups fresh white bread crumbs
⅔ cup dried cherries or pitted
    prunes, chopped
⅔ cup coarsely chopped hazelnuts
⅔ cup light brown sugar
fresh mint sprigs, to decorate
whipped cream, to serve

butter

pears

lemon

*fresh white
bread crumbs*

prunes

hazelnuts

*light
brown
sugar*

1 Preheat the oven to 375°F. Grease a 8-inch square cake pan. Peel, core and chop the pears. Place them in a bowl and sprinkle them with the lemon juice to prevent them from turning brown.

2 Melt 6 tablespoons of the butter. Stir in the bread crumbs. Spread a scant one-third of the crumb mixture on the bottom of the prepared pan.

3 Top with half the pears. Sprinkle over half the dried cherries or prunes, half the hazelnuts and half the sugar. Repeat the layers, then sprinkle the remaining crumbs over the surface.

4 Dice the remaining butter and dot it over the surface. Bake for 30–35 minutes, until golden. Serve hot, with whipped cream. Decorate each portion with a sprig of fresh mint.

Spiced Apple Cake

Grated apple and chopped dates give this cake a natural sweetness – omit 1 oz of the sugar if the fruit is very sweet.

Serves 8

INGREDIENTS

2 cups self-rising whole-wheat flour
1 tsp baking powder
2 tsp ground cinnamon
1 cup chopped dates
$^1\!/_2$ cup light brown sugar
1 tbsp pear and apple spread
$^1\!/_2$ cup apple juice
2 large eggs
6 tbsp sunflower oil
2 eating apples, cored and grated
1 tbsp chopped walnuts

apple juice

ground cinnamon

sunflower oil

self-rising whole-wheat flour

chopped walnuts

chopped dates

baking powder

light brown sugar

pear and apple spread

eating apples

eggs

1 Preheat the oven to 350°F. Grease and line a deep, round 8 in cake pan with parchment paper. Sift the flour, baking powder and cinnamon into a mixing bowl, stir in the dates, and make a well in the center.

2 Mix the sugar with the pear and apple spread in a small bowl. Gradually stir in the apple juice. Add to the dry ingredients, along with the eggs, oil and apples. Combine thoroughly.

COOK'S TIP

You do not need to peel the apples – the skin adds fiber, and it softens on cooking.

3 Spoon the mixture into the prepared cake pan, sprinkle with the walnuts, and bake for 60–65 minutes, or until a skewer inserted into the center of the cake comes out clean. Transfer to a wire rack, peel off the parchment paper, and let cool.

Apple Crumble Cake

This is a wonderful way of using windfall apples, and it makes a satisfying and tasty treat to serve on a cool fall evening.

Serves 8–10

INGREDIENTS
4 tbsp butter, softened, plus extra
    for greasing
6 tbsp sugar
1 egg, beaten
1 cup self-rising flour
2 large apples
⅓ cup golden raisins

FOR THE TOPPING
¾ cup self-rising flour
½ tsp ground cinnamon
3 tbsp butter
2 tbsp sugar

FOR THE DECORATION
1 red apple, cored, thinly slioced
    and tossed in lemon juice
2 tbsp sugar
ground cinnamon, for sprinkling

butter

sugar

egg

*self-rising
flour*

apples

*golden
raisins*

*ground
cinnamon*

1 Preheat the oven to 350°F. Grease and base-line a deep 7 in springform pan. To make the topping, sift the flour and cinnamon into a mixing bowl. Rub in the butter until the mixture resembles bread crumbs, then stir in the sugar and set aside.

2 Put the butter, sugar, egg and flour into a bowl and beat for 1–2 minutes until smooth. Spoon the batter into the prepared pan.

3 Peel, core and slice the large apples into a bowl. Add the golden raisins. Spread the apple and raisin mixture evenly over the cake batter, then sprinkle with the crumble. Bake for about 1 hour.

4 Leave to cool in the pan for 10 minutes before turning out onto a wire rack and peeling off the lining paper. Serve warm or cool, decorated with slices of red apple and sprinkled with sugar and cinnamon.

COOK'S TIP
This cake can be kept for up to 2 days in an airtight container.

Farmhouse Apple and Raisin Cake

A slice of this tasty, moist fruitcake makes an ideal afternoon treat.

Serves 12

INGREDIENTS

¾ cup reduced-fat spread
¾ cup light brown sugar
3 eggs
2 cups self-rising whole-wheat
  flour, sifted
1 cup self-rising white
  flour, sifted
1 tsp baking powder, sifted
2 tsp pumpkin pie spice
12 oz cooking apples, peeled, cored
  and diced
1 cup golden raisins
5 tbsp skim milk
2 tbsp raw sugar

reduced-fat spread

light brown sugar

eggs

self-rising whole-wheat flour

self-rising white flour

baking powder

pumpkin pie spice

cooking apples

golden raisins

skim milk

raw sugar

1 Preheat the oven to 325°F. Lightly grease a deep 8-inch round loose-bottomed cake pan and line with waxed paper. Put the reduced-fat spread, brown sugar, eggs, flours, baking powder and spice in a bowl and beat together until thoroughly mixed.

2 Fold in the apples, raisins and sufficient milk so that mixture is soft enough to drop from a spoon.

3 Spoon the mixture into the prepared pan and level the surface.

4 Sprinkle the top with raw sugar. Bake for about 1½ hours, until risen, golden brown and firm to the touch. Cool in the pan for a few minutes, then turn out onto a wire rack to cool completely. Serve in slices.

Carrot and Coconut Cake

A satisfying cake made with a delicious combination of flavors.

Serves 10

INGREDIENTS

8 tbsp reduced-fat spread
½ cup superfine sugar
2 eggs
1½ cups self-rising whole-wheat
   flour, sifted
3 cups bran
1 tbsp baking powder, sifted
6 tbsp skim milk, plus more
   if needed
1¾ cups carrots, coarsely grated
4 oz coconut
¼ cup golden raisins
finely grated rind of 1 orange
1–2 tbsp light brown granulated
   sugar, for sprinkling

*reduced-
fat spread*

*superfine
sugar*

eggs

*self-rising
whole-wheat
flour*

bran

*baking
powder*

skim milk

carrots

*diced
coconut*

*golden
raisins*

orange

*light brown
granulated
sugar*

1 Preheat the oven to 350°F. Lightly grease a deep 7-inch round cake pan and line with waxed paper. Put the reduced-fat spread, sugar, eggs, flour, bran, baking powder and milk in a bowl and beat together until thoroughly mixed.

2 Fold in the carrots, coconut, raisins and orange rind. Add milk until mixture is soft enough to drop from a spoon.

3 Spoon the mixture into the prepared pan and level the surface.

4 Sprinkle the top with granulated sugar and bake for about 1 hour, until risen, golden brown and firm to the touch. Cool in the pan for a few minutes, then turn out onto a wire rack to cool completely. Serve in slices.

Nectarine Amaretto Cake

Try this delicious cake with low fat ricotta cheese for dessert, or serve it solo for an afternoon snack. The syrup makes it moist but not soggy.

Serves 8

INGREDIENTS

3 large eggs, separated
³⁄₄ cup superfine sugar
grated rind and juice of 1 lemon
¹⁄₃ cup semolina
¹⁄₃ cup ground almonds
¹⁄₄ cup all-purpose flour
2 nectarines or peaches, halved
   and pitted
4 tbsp Apricot Glaze

FOR THE SYRUP

6 tbsp sugar
6 tbsp water
2 tbsp Amaretto liqueur

Amaretto liqueur

water

eggs

Apricot Glaze

superfine sugar

semolina

lemon

ground almonds

flour

nectarines

1 Preheat the oven to 350°F. Grease an 8 in round cake pan with a removable bottom. Whisk the egg yolks, sugar, lemon rind and juice in a bowl until thick, pale and creamy.

2 Fold in the semolina, almonds and flour until smooth.

COOK'S TIP

To make Apricot Glaze, place a few spoonfuls of apricot jam in a small pan along with a squeeze of lemon juice. Heat the jam, stirring until it is melted. Push through a fine sieve.

3 Whisk the egg whites in a clean bowl until fairly stiff. Using a metal spoon, stir a generous spoonful of the whites into the semolina mixture to lighten it, then fold in the remaining egg whites. Spoon the mixture into the prepared cake pan.

4 Bake for 30–35 minutes, until the center of the cake springs back when lightly pressed. Remove the cake from the oven, and carefully loosen around the edge with a metal spatula. Prick the top of the cake with a skewer, and let cool slightly in the pan.

5 Meanwhile, make the syrup. Heat the sugar and water in a small pan, stirring until dissolved, then boil without stirring for 2 minutes. Add the Amaretto liqueur, and drizzle slowly over the cake.

6 Remove the cake from the pan, and transfer it to a serving plate. Slice the nectarines or peaches, arrange them over the top, and brush with the warm Apricot Glaze.

Spiced Chocolate Cake

This cake is flavored with aromatic cinnamon, cloves, nutmeg and cardamom and makes a perfect end to a meal.

Makes 24

INGREDIENTS

3 eggs
1 cup sugar
½ cup flour
1 tsp ground cinnamon
¼ tsp ground cloves
¼ tsp freshly grated nutmeg
¼ tsp ground cardamom
2½ cups unblanched almonds,
    coarsely ground
2 tbsp candied lemon peel,
    finely chopped
2 tbsp candied orange peel,
    finely chopped
½ cup semisweet chocolate, grated
½ tsp grated lemon zest
½ tsp grated orange zest
2 tsp rosewater

FOR THE FROSTING
1 egg white
2 tsp cocoa powder, mixed with
    1 tbsp boiling water and cooled
1 cup confectioners' sugar
2 tbsp sugar crystals

eggs

almonds   *cinnamon*

nutmeg

cloves   *chocolate*

rose-
water   *candied peel*

orange zest

lemon zest

COOK'S TIP
Do not worry when the top of the cake cracks when you cut it; it is meant to be like that!

1 Preheat the oven to 325°F. Line a 12 x 9-inch jelly-roll pan with rice paper.

2 Whisk the eggs and sugar in a large bowl until thick and pale. Sift in the flour, cinnamon, cloves, nutmeg and cardamom and then stir in all the remaining dry ingredients.

3 Spoon evenly into the prepared pan and brush with the rosewater. Bake for 30–35 minutes until firm. Turn out of the pan.

4 To make the frosting, stir the egg white into the cocoa mixture, sift in the confectioners' sugar and mix. Spread over the cake while still warm. Sprinkle with sugar crystals and then return to the oven for 5 minutes. Cut into squares when cold.

Banana Gingerbread Slices

Bananas make this spicy bread delightfully moist.
The flavor develops on keeping, so wrap the
gingerbread and store it for a few days before
slicing, if possible.

Makes 20 slices

INGREDIENTS
2½ cups all-purpose flour
1 tsp baking soda
4 tsp ground ginger
2 tsp pumpkin pie spice
⅔ cup light brown sugar
4 tbsp sunflower oil
2 tbsp molasses
2 tbsp malt extract
2 large eggs
4 tbsp orange juice
3 ripe bananas
⅔ cup raisins or golden raisins

1 Preheat the oven to 350°F. Lightly grease and line an 11 x 7 in shallow baking pan with parchment paper.

2 Sift together the flour, baking soda and spices into a mixing bowl. Place the sugar in the sifter over the bowl, add some of the flour mixture and rub through the sifter with a wooden spoon.

3 Make a well in the center of the dry ingredients, and add the oil, molasses, malt extract, eggs and orange juice. Mix together thoroughly.

orange juice

malt extract

raisins

flour

pumpkin pie spice

light brown sugar

eggs

sunflower oil

baking soda

ground ginger

bananas

molasses

5 Scrape the mixture into the prepared baking pan. Bake for about 35–40 minutes, or until the center of the gingerbread springs back when lightly pressed.

4 Mash the bananas on a plate. Add the raisins or golden raisins to the mixture, then mix in the mashed bananas.

6 Let the gingerbread cool in the pan for 5 minutes, then turn it out onto a wire rack to cool completely. Transfer to a board, and cut into 20 slices to serve.

COOK'S TIP
If your brown sugar is lumpy, mix it with a little flour and it will be easier to sift.

Chocolate and Banana Brownies

Nuts traditionally give brownies their chewy texture. Here oat bran is used instead, creating a moist, tasty, yet healthy alternative.

Makes 9

INGREDIENTS
5 tbsp reduced fat cocoa powder
1 tbsp superfine sugar
5 tbsp skim milk
3 large bananas, mashed
1 cup light brown sugar
1 tsp vanilla extract
5 egg whites
¾ cup self-rising flour
¾ cup oat bran
1 tbsp confectioner's sugar, for dusting

cocoa powder

vanilla extract

oat bran

egg

bananas

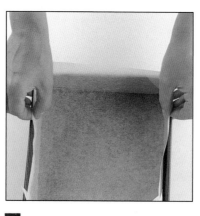

1 Preheat the oven to 350°F. Line a 8 in square pan with non-stick baking paper.

2 Blend the reduced fat cocoa powder and superfine sugar with the skim milk. Add the bananas, brown sugar and vanilla extract.

COOK'S TIP
Store these brownies in an airtight tin for a day before eating – they improve with keeping.

3 Lightly beat the egg whites with a fork. Add the chocolate mixture and continue to beat well. Sift the flour over the mixture and fold in with the oat bran. Pour into the prepared pan.

4 Cook in the preheated oven for 40 minutes or until firm. Cool in the pan for 10 minutes, then turn out onto a wire rack. Cut into 9 squares and lightly dust with confectioner's sugar before serving.

Apricot and Almond Fingers

These almond fingers will stay moist for several days, thanks to the addition of apricots.

Makes 18

INGREDIENTS
2 cups self-rising flour
²/₃ cup light brown sugar
¹/₃ cup semolina
1 cup dried apricots, chopped
2 large eggs
2 tbsp malt extract
2 tbsp honey
4 tbsp skim milk
4 tbsp sunflower oil
few drops of almond extract
2 tbsp sliced almonds

honey

skim milk

sunflower oil

eggs

dried apricots

light brown sugar

self-rising flour

semolina

malt extract

sliced almonds

1 Preheat the oven to 325°F. Lightly grease and line an 11 x 7 in shallow baking pan. Sift the flour into a bowl, and add the brown sugar, semolina, chopped dried apricots and eggs. Add the malt extract, honey, milk, sunflower oil and almond extract. Mix well until the mixture is smooth.

2 Turn the mixture into the prepared pan, spread to the edges, and sprinkle with the sliced almonds.

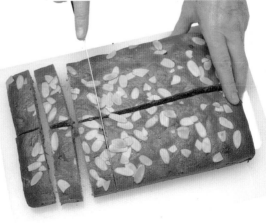

3 Bake for 30–35 minutes, or until the center of the cake springs back when lightly pressed. Transfer to a wire rack to cool. Remove the paper, place the cake on a board, and cut it into eighteen slices with a sharp knife.

Coffee Sponge Drops

These are delicious on their own, but taste even better with a filling of nonfat cream cheese and drained and chopped preserved ginger.

Makes 12

INGREDIENTS
1/2 cup all-purpose flour
1 tbsp instant coffee powder
2 large eggs
6 tbsp superfine sugar

FOR THE FILLING
1/2 cup nonfat cream cheese
1/4 cup chopped stem ginger

instant coffee powder

eggs

flour

superfine sugar

nonfat cream cheese

stem ginger

1 Preheat the oven to 375°F. Line two baking sheets with parchment paper. Make the filling by beating together the cheese and ginger. Refrigerate until ready to use. Sift the flour and instant coffee powder together.

2 Combine the eggs and superfine sugar in a bowl. Beat with a hand-held electric mixer until thick and like a mousse (when the mixer is lifted, a trail should remain on the surface of the mixture for at least 15 seconds).

3 Gently fold in the sifted flour and coffee mixture with a metal spoon, taking care not to knock out any air.

4 Spoon the mixture into a pastry bag fitted with a 1/2 in plain tip. Pipe 1 1/2 in rounds onto the baking sheets. Bake for 12 minutes. Cool on a wire rack, then sandwich together with the filling.

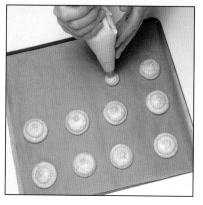

Oaty Crisps

These cookies are very crisp and crunchy – ideal to serve with morning coffee.

Makes 18

INGREDIENTS
1¾ cups rolled oats
½ cup light brown sugar
1 large egg
4 tbsp sunflower oil
2 tbsp malt extract

malt extract

sunflower oil

rolled oats

light brown sugar

egg

1 Preheat the oven to 375°F. Lightly grease two baking sheets. Combine the rolled oats and brown sugar in a bowl, breaking up any lumps in the sugar. Add the egg, sunflower oil and malt extract, mix together well, then let soak for about 15 minutes.

2 Using a teaspoon, place small mounds of the mixture well apart on the prepared baking sheets. Press the mounds into 3 in rounds with the back of a dampened fork.

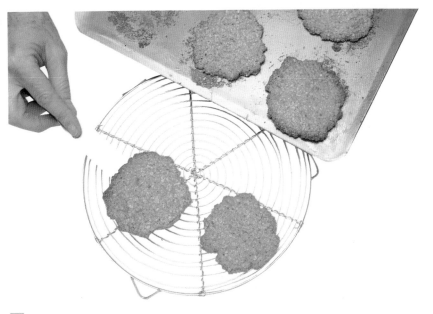

VARIATION
To give these crisp cookies a coarser texture, substitute jumbo oats for some or all of the rolled oats.

3 Bake the cookies for 10–15 minutes until golden brown. Let cool for 1 minute, then remove with a metal spatula, and cool on a wire rack.

Banana and Apricot Chelsea Buns

Old favorites are given a low fat twist with a delectable fruit filling.

Makes 9

INGREDIENTS
6 tbsp warm skim milk
1 tsp dried yeast
pinch of sugar
2 cups white bread flour
2 tsp pumpkin pie spice
$\frac{1}{2}$ tsp salt
2 tbsp margarine
$\frac{1}{4}$ cup sugar
1 large egg, lightly beaten

FOR THE FILLING
1 large ripe banana
1 cup dried apricots
2 tbsp light brown sugar

FOR THE GLAZE
2 tbsp sugar
2 tbsp water

dried yeast

egg

dried apricots

margarine

brown sugar

banana

pumpkin pie spice

sugar

white bread flour

salt

skim milk

COOK'S TIP
Do not leave the buns in the pan for too long or the glaze will stick to the sides, making them very difficult to remove.

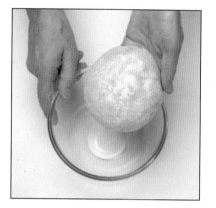

1 Grease a 7 in square cake pan. Put the warm milk in a small pitcher. Sprinkle the yeast on top. Add a pinch of sugar to help activate the yeast, mix well, and let stand for 30 minutes.

2 Sift the flour, spice and salt into a mixing bowl. Work in the margarine, then stir in the sugar. Make a well in the center, then pour in the yeast mixture and the egg. Gradually stir in the flour to make a soft dough. Add milk if needed.

3 Turn the dough out onto a floured surface and knead for 5 minutes until smooth and elastic. Return to the clean bowl, cover with a damp dish towel, and let rise in a warm place or about 2 hours, or until doubled in bulk.

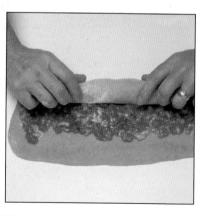

4 Meanwhile prepare the filling. Mash the banana in a bowl. Using kitchen scissors, cut up the apricots and add to the mashed banana with the sugar.

5 Knead the risen dough on a floured surface for 2 minutes, then roll out to a 12 x 9 in rectangle. Spread the banana and apricot filling over the dough, and roll up lengthwise like a jelly roll, with the join underneath.

6 Cut the roll into nine pieces and place, cut-side down, in the prepared pan. Cover and let rise in a warm place for about 30 minutes. Preheat the oven to 400°F.

7 Bake the buns for 20–25 minutes until golden brown and cooked in the center. Meanwhile make the glaze. Mix the sugar and water in a small saucepan. Heat, stirring, until dissolved, then boil for 2 minutes. Brush the glaze over the buns while still hot, then remove the buns from the pan and let cool on a wire rack.

Raspberry Muffins

These muffins are made with baking powder and low fat buttermilk, giving them a light and spongy texture. They are delicious at any time of the day.

Makes 10–12

INGREDIENTS
2½ cups all-purpose flour
1 tbsp baking powder
½ cup sugar
1 large egg
1 cup buttermilk
4 tbsp sunflower oil
1 cup raspberries

egg

buttermilk

sunflower oil

sugar

flour

baking powder

raspberries

1 Preheat the oven to 400°F. Arrange twelve cupcake holders in a deep muffin pan. Sift the flour and baking powder into a mixing bowl, stir in the sugar, then make a well in the center.

2 Stir the egg, buttermilk and sunflower oil together in a bowl, pour into the flour mixture, and stir quickly until just combined.

3 Add the raspberries, and lightly fold them in with a metal spoon. Spoon the mixture into the cupcake holders, filling them two-thirds full.

4 Bake the muffins for 20–25 minutes until golden brown and firm in the middle. Transfer to a wire rack, and serve warm or cold.

Date and Apple Muffins

You'll only need one or two of these wholesome muffins per person, since they are very filling.

Makes 12

INGREDIENTS

1¼ cups self-rising whole-wheat
flour
1¼ cups self-rising white flour
1 tsp ground cinnamon
1 tsp baking powder
2 tbsp margarine
½ cup light brown sugar
1 eating apple
1 cup apple juice
2 tbsp pear and apple spread
1 large egg, lightly beaten
½ cup chopped dates
1 tbsp chopped pecan halves

chopped dates

egg

pecans

self-rising whole-wheat flour

ground cinnamon

light brown sugar

self-rising white flour

apple juice

margarine

pear and apple spread

baking powder

eating apple

1 Preheat the oven to 400°F. Arrange twelve cupcake holders in a deep muffin pan. Put the whole-wheat flour in a mixing bowl. Sift in the white flour with the cinnamon and baking powder. Work in the margarine until the mixture resembles bread crumbs, then stir in the light brown sugar.

2 Quarter and core the apple, finely chop it, and set aside. Stir a little of the apple juice with the pear and apple spread until smooth. Stir in the remaining juice, then add to the flour mixture with the egg. Add the chopped apple to the bowl with the dates. Stir quickly until just combined.

3 Divide the batter evenly among the cupcake holders.

4 Sprinkle the muffins with the chopped pecan halves. Bake for about 20–25 minutes until golden brown and firm in the middle. Remove to a wire rack, and serve while still warm.

Chive and Potato Biscuits

These little treats should be fairly thin, soft and crisp on the outside. Serve them for breakfast.

Makes 20

INGREDIENTS
1 lb potatoes, peeled
1 cup all-purpose flour, sifted
2 tbsp olive oil
2 tbsp chopped chives
salt and freshly ground black pepper
low fat spread, for topping
   (optional)

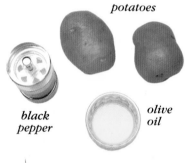

potatoes

black pepper

olive oil

chives

flour

salt

1 Cook the potatoes in a saucepan of boiling, salted water for 20 minutes or until tender, then drain thoroughly. Return the potatoes to the clean pan and mash them. Preheat a griddle or heavy-bottomed frying pan.

2 Add the flour, olive oil and chopped chives with a little salt and pepper to the hot mashed potato in the pan. Mix until a soft dough is formed.

COOK'S TIP
Cook the biscuits over low heat so that the outsides do not burn before the insides are cooked through.

3 Roll out the dough on a well-floured surface to a thickness of $1/4$ in, and stamp out rounds with a 2 in plain cookie cutter. Lightly grease the griddle or pan.

4 Cook the biscuits, in batches, on the hot griddle or frying pan for about 10 minutes, turning once, until they are golden brown on both sides. Keep the heat low. Top with a little low fat spread, if you like, and serve immediately.

Cheese and Chive Biscuits

Feta cheese makes an excellent substitute for butter in these tangy savory biscuits.

Makes 9

INGREDIENTS
1 cup self-rising flour
1 cup self-rising whole-wheat flour
½ tsp salt
3 oz feta cheese
1 tbsp chopped fresh chives
⅔ cup skim milk, plus extra for glazing
¼ tsp cayenne pepper

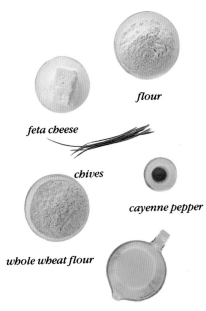

flour

feta cheese

chives

cayenne pepper

whole wheat flour

milk

1 Preheat the oven to 400°F. Sift the flours and salt into a mixing bowl, adding any bran left over from the flour in the sieve.

2 Crumble the feta cheese and rub into the dry ingredients. Stir in the chives, then add the milk and mix to a soft dough.

3 Turn out onto a floured surface and lightly knead until smooth. Roll out to ¾ in thick and stamp out nine biscuits with a 2½ in cookie cutter.

4 Transfer the biscuits to a non-stick baking sheet. Brush with skim milk, then sprinkle over the cayenne pepper. Bake in the oven for 15 minutes, or until golden brown. Serve warm or cold.

Curry Crackers

These spicy, crisp little crackers are very low in fat and are ideal for serving with drinks.

Makes 12

INGREDIENTS
1/2 cup all-purpose flour
1/4 tsp salt
1 tsp curry powder
1/4 tsp chili powder
1 tbsp chopped fresh cilantro
2 tbsp water

fresh cilantro

chili powder

salt

flour

water

curry powder

1 Preheat the oven to 350°F. Sift together the flour and salt into a mixing bowl, then add the curry powder and chili powder. Make a well in the center, and add the chopped fresh cilantro and water. Gradually incorporate the flour, and mix to make a firm dough.

2 Turn onto a lightly floured surface, knead until smooth, then let rest for 5 minutes.

VARIATIONS

Omit the curry and chili powders, and add 1 tbsp caraway, fennel or mustard seeds.

3 Cut the dough into twelve pieces, and knead into small balls. Roll each ball out very thinly to a 4 in round.

4 Arrange the rounds on two ungreased baking sheets, then bake for 15 minutes, turning once during cooking. Cool on a wire rack.

Oat Cakes

Try serving these oat cakes with reduced-fat hard cheeses. They are also delicious topped with thick honey for breakfast.

Makes 8

INGREDIENTS
1 cup medium oatmeal, plus extra
   for sprinkling
1/2 tsp salt
pinch of baking soda
1 tbsp butter
5 tbsp water

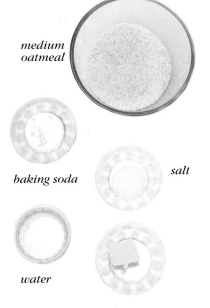

medium oatmeal

baking soda

salt

water

butter

1 Preheat the oven to 300°F. Mix together the oatmeal, salt and baking soda in a mixing bowl.

2 Melt the butter with the water in a small saucepan. Bring to a boil, then add to the oatmeal mixture, and mix to make a moist dough.

COOK'S TIP

To achieve a neat round, place a 10 in plate on top of the oat cake. Cut away any excess dough with a knife, then remove the plate.

3 Turn the dough onto a surface sprinkled with oatmeal, and knead to a smooth ball. Turn a large baking sheet upside down, grease it, sprinkle it lightly with oatmeal, and place the ball of dough on top. Sprinkle the dough with oatmeal, then roll out to a 10 in circle.

4 Cut the circle into eight sections, ease them apart slightly, and bake for about 50–60 minutes until crisp. Let cool on the baking sheet, then remove the oat cakes with a metal spatula.

Pancakes

These little pancakes are delicious with jam.

Makes 18

INGREDIENTS
2 cups self-rising flour
$\frac{1}{2}$ tsp salt
1 tbsp sugar
1 egg, beaten
$1\frac{1}{4}$ cups skim milk

egg

self-rising flour

salt

skim milk

sugar

VARIATION

For a savory version of these scones, omit the sugar and add 2 chopped scallions and 1 tbsp freshly grated Parmesan cheese to the batter. Serve with cottage cheese.

1 Preheat a griddle or heavy frying pan. Sift together the flour and salt into a mixing bowl. Stir in the sugar, and make a well in the center.

2 Add the egg and half the milk, then gradually incorporate the surrounding flour to make a smooth batter. Beat in the remaining milk.

3 Lightly grease the griddle or pan. Drop tablespoons of the batter onto the surface, leaving them until they bubble and the bubbles begin to burst.

4 Turn the pancakes over with a metal spatula, and cook until the bottoms are golden brown. Keep the cooked pancakes warm and moist by wrapping them in a clean napkin while cooking successive batches.

Pineapple and Cinnamon Pancakes

Making the batter with pineapple juice instead of milk cuts down on fat and adds to the flavor.

Makes 24

INGREDIENTS

1 cup self-rising whole-wheat flour
1 cup self-rising white flour
1 tsp ground cinnamon
1 tbsp sugar
1 large egg
1¼ cups pineapple juice
½ cup dried pineapple, chopped

egg

dried pineapple

pineapple juice

sugar

self-rising whole-wheat flour

ground cinnamon

self-rising white flour

1 Preheat a griddle or heavy frying pan. Put the whole-wheat flour in a mixing bowl. Sift in the white flour, add the cinnamon and sugar, and make a well in the center.

2 Add the egg with half the pineapple juice, and gradually incorporate the surrounding flour to make a smooth batter. Beat in the remaining juice with the chopped pineapple.

COOK'S TIP

Pancakes don't keep well so are best eaten freshly cooked.

3 Lightly grease the griddle or pan. Drop tablespoons of the batter onto the surface, leaving them until they bubble and the bubbles begin to burst.

4 Turn the pancakes over with a metal spatula, and cook until the bottoms are golden brown. Keep the cooked pancakes warm and moist by wrapping them in a clean napkin while continuing to cook successive batches.

Malt Loaf

This is a rich and sticky loaf. If it lasts long enough to go stale, try toasting it for a delicious afternoon snack.

Serves 8

INGREDIENTS
⅔ cup warm skim milk
1 tsp dried yeast
pinch of sugar
3 cups all-purpose flour
¼ tsp salt
2 tbsp light brown sugar
generous 1 cup golden raisins
1 tbsp sunflower oil
3 tbsp malt extract

FOR THE GLAZE
2 tbsp sugar
2 tbsp water

golden raisins

malt extract

salt

flour

skim milk

light brown sugar

dried yeast

sunflower oil

1 Place the warm milk in a bowl. Sprinkle the yeast over the top, and add the sugar. Leave for 30 minutes until frothy. Sift the flour and salt into a mixing bowl, stir in the brown sugar and golden raisins, and make a well in the center.

2 Add the yeast mixture with the oil and malt extract. Gradually incorporate the flour, and mix to make a soft dough, adding a little milk, if necessary.

3 Turn onto a floured surface, and knead for about 5 minutes until smooth and elastic. Grease a 9 x 3½ in loaf pan.

4 Shape the dough, and place it in the prepared pan. Cover with a damp dish towel, and let stand in a warm place for 1–2 hours until well risen. Preheat the oven to 375°F.

5 Bake the loaf for 30–35 minutes, or until it sounds hollow when it is tapped on the bottom.

6 Meanwhile, prepare the glaze by dissolving the sugar in the water in a small pan. Bring to a boil, stirring, then lower the heat, and simmer for 1 minute. Place the loaf on a wire rack, and brush with the glaze while still hot. Let the loaf cool before serving.

VARIATION

To make buns, divide the dough into ten pieces, shape into rounds, let rise, then bake for 15–20 minutes. Brush with the glaze while still hot.

Banana and Ginger Quickbread

Serve this quickbread with a low fat spread. The stem ginger adds an interesting flavor.

Serves 6–8

INGREDIENTS
1½ cups self-rising flour
1 tsp baking powder
3 tbsp margarine
⅓ cup dark brown sugar
⅓ cup drained stem
   ginger, chopped
4 tbsp skim milk
2 ripe bananas, mashed

baking powder

stem ginger

dark brown sugar

bananas

self-rising flour

skim milk

margarine

1 Preheat the oven to 350°F. Grease and line a 9 × 3½ in loaf pan. Sift the flour and baking powder into a bowl.

2 Work in the margarine until the mixture resembles bread crumbs.

VARIATION
To make Banana and Golden Raisin Quickbread, add 1 tsp pumpkin pie spice and omit the ginger. Stir in ⅔ cup golden raisins.

3 Stir in the sugar. Add the ginger, milk and bananas, and mix to a soft batter.

4 Spoon into the prepared pan, and bake for 40–45 minutes. Run a metal spatula around the edges to loosen the quickbread, then turn it onto a wire rack, and let cool.

Pear Quickbread

This is an ideal quickbread to make when pears are plentiful—an excellent use for windfalls.

Serves 6–8

INGREDIENTS

scant ¹/₃ cup rolled oats
¹/₃ cup light brown sugar
2 tbsp pear or apple juice
2 tbsp sunflower oil
2 small pears
1 cup self-rising flour
²/₃ cup golden raisins
¹/₂ tsp baking powder
2 tsp pumpkin pie spice
1 egg

small pears

egg

baking powder

sunflower oil

self-rising flour

rolled oats

golden raisins

pumpkin pie spice

light brown sugar

pear juice

1 Preheat the oven to 350°F. Grease and line a 9 x 3¹/₂ in loaf pan with parchment paper. Put the oats in a bowl with the sugar, pear or apple juice and oil, mix well, and let stand for 15 minutes.

2 Quarter, core and grate the pears. Add to the oat mixture with the flour, golden raisins, baking powder, pumpkin pie spice and egg. Stir together until thoroughly combined.

3 Spoon the mixture into the prepared loaf pan, and level the top. Bake for 50–60 minutes, or until a skewer inserted into the center comes out clean.

4 Transfer the quickbread onto a wire rack, and peel off the parchment paper. Let cool completely.

COOK'S TIP
Health food stores sell concentrated pear and apple juice, ready for diluting as required.

Zucchini and Walnut Loaf

Cardamom seeds impart their distinctive aroma to this loaf. Serve spread with ricotta and honey for a delicious snack.

Makes 1 loaf

INGREDIENTS
3 eggs
⅓ cup light brown sugar, firmly
    packed
½ cup sunflower oil
2 cups whole-wheat flour
1 tsp baking powder
1 tsp baking soda
1 tsp ground cinnamon
¾ tsp ground allspice
½ tbsp green cardamoms, seeds
    removed and crushed
5 oz zucchini, coarsely grated
½ cup walnuts, chopped
¼ cup sunflower seeds

zucchini

egg

walnuts

sunflower oil

brown sugar

whole-wheat flour

sunflower seeds

cardamom pods

1 Preheat the oven to 350°F. Line the base and sides of a 2 lb loaf pan with parchment paper.

2 Beat the eggs and sugar together and gradually add the oil.

3 Sift the flour into a bowl together with the baking powder, baking soda, cinnamon and allspice.

4 Mix into the egg mixture with the rest of the ingredients, reserving 1 tbsp of the sunflower seeds for the top.

5 Spoon into the loaf tin, level off the top, and sprinkle with the reserved sunflower seeds.

6 Bake for 1 hour or until a skewer inserted in the center comes out clean. Leave to cool slightly before turning out onto a wire rack to cool completely.

Banana and Cardamom Bread

The combination of banana and cardamom is delicious in this soft, moist loaf. It is a perfect afternoon snack with low fat spread and jam.

Serves 6

INGREDIENTS
²/₃ cup warm water
1 tsp dried yeast
pinch of sugar
10 cardamom pods
3¹/₂ cups white bread flour
1 tsp salt
2 tbsp malt extract
2 ripe bananas, mashed
1 tsp sesame seeds

COOK'S TIP
Make sure the bananas are really ripe, so that they give maximum flavor to the bread.
    If you prefer, place the dough in one piece in a 9 x 3¹/₂ in loaf pan, and bake for an extra 5 minutes.

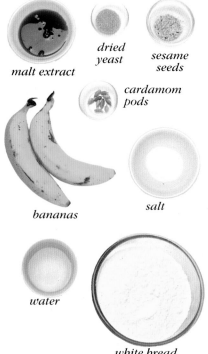

malt extract

dried yeast

sesame seeds

cardamom pods

bananas

salt

water

white bread flour

1 Put the water in a small bowl. Sprinkle the yeast on the top, add the sugar, and mix well. Let stand for 10 minutes.

2 Split the cardamom pods. Remove the seeds, and chop them finely.

3 Sift the flour and salt into a mixing bowl, and make a well in the center. Add the yeast mixture with the malt extract, chopped cardamom seeds and bananas.

4 Gradually incorporate the flour, and mix to make a soft dough, adding a little water, if necessary. Turn the dough onto a floured surface, and knead for about 5 minutes until smooth and elastic. Return to the clean bowl, cover with a damp dish towel, and let rise for about 2 hours until doubled in bulk.

5 Grease a baking sheet. Turn the dough onto a floured surface, knead briefly, then shape into a braid. Place the braid on the baking sheet, and cover loosely with a plastic bag (ballooning it to trap the air). Let stand until well risen. Preheat the oven to 425°F.

6 Brush the braid lightly with water, and sprinkle with the sesame seeds. Bake for 10 minutes, then lower the oven temperature to 400°F. Cook for 15 minutes more, or until the loaf sounds hollow when it is tapped on the bottom. Cool on a wire rack.

Coriander Brioches

The warm flavor of coriander combines particularly well with orange in this recipe.

Makes 12

INGREDIENTS

2 cups white bread flour
2 tsp rapid-rise dried yeast
½ tsp salt
1 tbsp sugar
2 tsp coriander seeds,
    coarsely ground
grated zest of 1 orange, plus extra
    to decorate
2 tbsp hand-hot water
2 eggs, beaten
¼ cup unsalted butter, melted
1 small egg, beaten, to glaze

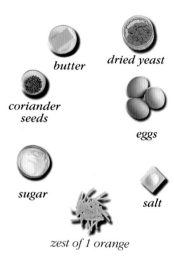

butter   *dried yeast*

*coriander
seeds*

eggs

sugar   *salt*

zest of 1 orange

COOK'S TIP
These individual brioches look particularly attractive if they are made in special brioche pans. However, they can also be made in muffin tins.

1 Sift the flour into a bowl and stir in the yeast, salt, sugar, coriander seeds and orange zest. Add the water, eggs and butter. Beat to make a soft dough. Turn onto a lightly floured surface and knead for 5 minutes, then place in a lightly oiled bowl, cover and leave in a warm place for 1 hour until doubled in bulk.

2 Turn the dough onto a floured surface, knead again briefly and roll into a sausage. Cut into 12 pieces. Break off a quarter of each piece and set aside. Shape the larger pieces of dough into balls and place in 12 greased individual brioche pans.

3 Lightly flour your hands and roll each of the small pieces of dough into small sausages. Lightly flour the handle of a wooden spoon and press into the center of each of the large dough balls to make a small hole. Place the dough sausages into the holes made by the spoon handle.

4 Place the brioche pans on a baking sheet. Cover with lightly oiled clear film and leave in a warm place until the dough rises almost to the top of the pans. Preheat the oven to 425°F. Brush the brioches with beaten egg and bake for 15 minutes until golden brown. Scatter over extra orange zest to decorate, and serve the brioches warm.

Sage Soda Bread

This wonderful loaf, quite unlike bread made with yeast, has a velvety texture and a powerful sage aroma.

Makes 1 loaf

INGREDIENTS
2 cups whole-wheat flour
1 cup flour
½ tsp salt
1 tsp baking soda
2 tbsp shredded fresh sage or 2 tsp
   dried sage, crumbled
1¼–1¾ cups buttermilk

white flour

whole-wheat flour

sage

buttermilk

1 Preheat the oven to 425°F. Sift the dry ingredients into a bowl.

2 Stir in the sage and add enough buttermilk to make a soft dough.

COOK'S TIP
As an alternative to the sage, try using finely chopped rosemary or thyme.

3 Shape the dough into a round loaf and place on a lightly oiled baking sheet.

4 Cut a deep cross in the top. Bake in the oven for 40 minutes until the loaf is well risen and sounds hollow when tapped on the bottom. Leave to cool on a wire rack.

Austrian Three Grain Bread

A mixture of grains gives this close-textured bread a delightful nutty flavor. Make two smaller twists, if preferred.

Serves 8–10

INGREDIENTS
2 cups warm water
2 tsp dried yeast
pinch of sugar
2 cups white bread flour
1½ tsp salt
2 cups malted brown flour
2 cups rye flour
2 tbsp linseed
½ cup medium oatmeal
3 tbsp sunflower seeds
2 tbsp malt extract

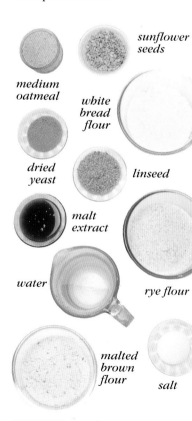

sunflower seeds

medium oatmeal

white bread flour

dried yeast

linseed

malt extract

water

rye flour

malted brown flour

salt

1 Put half the water in a small pitcher. Sprinkle the yeast on top. Add the sugar, mix well, and let stand for 10 minutes.

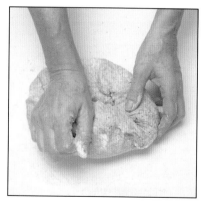

2 Sift the white flour and salt into a mixing bowl, and add the other flours. Set aside 1 tsp of the linseed, and add the rest to the flour mixture with the oatmeal and sunflower seeds. Make a well in the center.

3 Add the yeast mixture to the bowl with the malt extract and the remaining water. Gradually incorporate the flour.

4 Mix to a soft dough, adding water, if necessary. Turn out onto a floured surface, and knead for about 5 minutes until smooth and elastic. Transfer to a clean bowl, cover with a damp dish towel, and let rise for about 2 hours until doubled in bulk.

5 Flour a baking sheet. Turn the dough onto a floured surface, knead for 2 minutes, then divide in half. Roll each half into a 12 in cylinder.

6 Twist the two cylinders together, dampen the ends, and press to seal. Lift the twist onto the prepared baking sheet. Brush it with water, sprinkle with the remaining linseed, and cover loosely with a large plastic bag (ballooning it to trap the air inside). Let stand in a warm place until well risen. Preheat the oven to 425°F.

7 Bake the loaf for 10 minutes, then lower the oven temperature to 400°F, and cook for 20 minutes more, or until the loaf sounds hollow when it is tapped on the bottom. Transfer to a wire rack to cool.

Saffron Focaccia

A dazzling yellow bread that is light in texture and distinctive in flavor.

Makes 1 loaf

INGREDIENTS
pinch of saffron threads
⅔ cup boiling water
2 cups flour
½ tsp salt
1 tsp rapid-rise dried yeast
1 tbsp olive oil

FOR THE TOPPING
2 garlic cloves, sliced
1 red onion, cut into thin wedges
rosemary sprigs
12 black olives, pitted and coarsely
   chopped
1 tbsp olive oil

flour

garlic

rosemary

red onion

olives

saffron

yeast

1 Place the saffron in a heatproof cup and pour on the boiling water. Leave to stand and infuse until lukewarm.

2 Place the flour, salt, yeast and olive oil in a food processor. Turn on and gradually add the saffron and its liquid. Process until the dough forms into a ball.

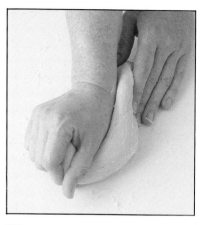

3 Turn onto a floured board and knead for 10–15 minutes. Place in a bowl, cover and leave to rise for 30–40 minutes until doubled in size.

4 Punch down the risen dough on a lightly floured surface and roll out into an oval shape, ½ in thick. Place on a lightly greased baking sheet and leave to rise for 20–30 minutes.

5 Preheat the oven to 400°F. Press small indentations all over the surface of the focaccia with your fingers.

6 Cover with the topping ingredients, brush lightly with olive oil, and bake for 25 minutes or until the loaf sounds hollow when tapped on the bottom. Leave to cool on a wire rack.

Sun-dried Tomato Bread

This savory bread tastes delicious on its own, but it also makes exceptional sandwiches.

Makes 1 loaf

INGREDIENTS
3¼ cups bread flour
1 tsp salt
2 tsp rapid-rise dried yeast
2 oz (drained weight) sun-dried
    tomatoes in oil, chopped
¾ cup lukewarm water
5 tbsp lukewarm olive oil, plus extra
    for brushing
flour for dusting

water

flour

olive oil

rapid-rise yeast

sun-dried tomatoes

salt

1 Sift the flour and salt into a large mixing bowl.

2 Stir in the yeast and sun-dried tomatoes.

3 Make a well in the center of the dry ingredients. Pour in the water and oil, and mix until the ingredients come together and form a soft dough.

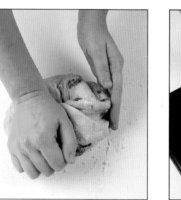

4 Turn the dough on to a lightly floured surface and knead for about 10 minutes.

5 Shape into an oblong loaf, without making the top too smooth, and place on a greased baking sheet. Brush the top with oil, cover with plastic wrap, then let rise in a warm place for about 1 hour.

6 Meanwhile, preheat the oven to 425°F. Remove the plastic wrap, then sprinkle the top of the loaf lightly with flour. Bake for 30–40 minutes until the loaf sounds hollow when tapped on the bottom. Serve warm.

Rosemary and Sea Salt Focaccia

Focaccia is an Italian flat bread made with olive oil. Here it is given added flavor with rosemary and coarse sea salt.

Makes 1 loaf

INGREDIENTS

3 cups unbleached all-purpose flour
½ tsp salt
2 tsp rapid-rise dried yeast
1 cup lukewarm water
3 tbsp olive oil
1 small red onion
leaves from 1 large rosemary sprig
1 tsp coarse sea salt

coarse sea salt

water

olive oil

flour

rapid-rise yeast

red onion

rosemary

1 Sift the flour and salt into a large mixing bowl. Stir in the yeast, then make a well in the center of the dry ingredients. Pour in the water and 2 tbsp of the oil. Mix well, adding a little more water if the mixture seems dry.

2 Turn the dough on to a lightly floured surface and knead for about 10 minutes until smooth and elastic.

3 Place the dough in a greased bowl, cover and let rise in a warm place for about 1 hour until doubled in size. Punch down and knead the dough for 2–3 minutes.

4 Meanwhile, preheat the oven to 425°F. Roll out the dough to a large circle, about ½ in thick, and transfer to a greased baking sheet. Brush with the remaining oil.

5 Halve the onion and slice into thin wedges. Sprinkle over the dough with the rosemary and sea salt, pressing in lightly.

6 Using a finger make deep indentations in the dough. Cover the surface with greased plastic wrap, then let rise in a warm place for 30 minutes. Remove the plastic wrap and bake for 25–30 minutes until golden. Serve warm.

Olive and Oregano Bread

This is an excellent accompaniment to all salads, and it is particularly good served warm.

Serves 8–10

INGREDIENTS

1¼ cups warm water
1 tsp dried yeast
pinch of sugar
1 tbsp olive oil
1 onion, chopped
4 cups white bread flour
1 tsp salt
¼ tsp freshly ground black pepper
⅓ cup pitted black olives,
    coarsely chopped
1 tbsp black olive paste
1 tbsp chopped fresh oregano
1 tbsp chopped fresh parsley

fresh oregano

fresh parsley

black olives

black pepper

white bread flour

olive oil

black olive paste

water

dried yeast

salt

onion

1 Put half the warm water in a small pitcher. Sprinkle the yeast over the top. Add the sugar, mix well, and let stand for 10 minutes.

2 Heat the olive oil in a frying pan, and fry the onion until golden brown.

3 Sift the flour into a mixing bowl with the salt and pepper. Make a well in the center. Add the yeast mixture, the fried onion (with the oil), the olives, olive paste, herbs and remaining water. Gradually incorporate the flour, and mix to make a soft dough, adding a little more water, if necessary.

4 Turn the dough onto a floured surface, and knead for 5 minutes until smooth and elastic. Place in a clean bowl, cover with a damp dish towel, and let rise in a warm place for about 2 hours, or until doubled in bulk. Lightly grease a baking sheet.

5 Turn the dough onto a floured surface, and knead again for a few minutes. Shape into an 8 in round, and place on the prepared baking sheet. Using a sharp knife, make crisscross cuts over the top, cover, and let stand in a warm place for 30 minutes until well risen. Preheat the oven to 425°F.

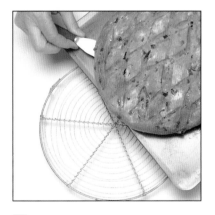

6 Dust the loaf with a little flour, and bake for 10 minutes. Lower the oven temperature to 400°F. Bake the loaf for 20 minutes more, or until it sounds hollow when it is tapped on the bottom. Transfer to a wire rack to cool slightly before serving.

Cheese and Onion Herb Sticks

A delicious bread that is very good with soup or salads. Use an extra-strong cheese to get plenty of flavor without piling on the fat.

Makes 2 sticks, each serving 4–6

INGREDIENTS

1¼ cups warm water
1 tsp dried yeast
pinch of sugar
1 tbsp sunflower oil
1 red onion, chopped
4 cups white bread flour
1 tsp salt
1 tsp dry mustard
3 tbsp chopped fresh herbs, such as thyme, parsley, marjoram or sage
¾ cup grated fat-reduced Cheddar cheese

fresh herbs

sunflower oil

fat-reduced Cheddar cheese

salt   *mustard*   *white bread flour*

water   *dried yeast*   *red onion*

1 Put the water in a small pitcher. Sprinkle the yeast over the top. Add the sugar, mix well, and let stand for 10 minutes.

2 Heat the oil in a frying pan, and fry the onion until golden brown.

3 Sift the flour, salt and mustard into a mixing bowl. Add the herbs. Reserve 2 tbsp of the cheese. Stir the rest into the flour mixture, and make a well in the center. Add the yeast mixture with the fried onions and oil, then gradually incorporate the flour and mix to make a soft dough, adding water, if necessary.

4 Turn the dough onto a floured surface, and knead for 5 minutes until smooth and elastic. Return to the clean bowl, cover with a damp dish towel, and let rise in a warm place for about 2 hours, or until doubled in bulk. Lightly grease two baking sheets.

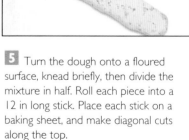

5 Turn the dough onto a floured surface, knead briefly, then divide the mixture in half. Roll each piece into a 12 in long stick. Place each stick on a baking sheet, and make diagonal cuts along the top.

6 Sprinkle the sticks with the reserved cheese. Cover and let stand for about 30 minutes until well risen. Preheat the oven to 425°F. Bake the sticks for 25 minutes, or until they sound hollow when they are tapped on the bottom. Cool on a wire rack.

VARIATION
To make Onion and Coriander Sticks, omit the cheese, herbs and mustard. Add 1 tbsp ground coriander and 3 tbsp chopped, fresh cilantro instead.

Sun-dried Tomato Braid

This is a marvelous Mediterranean-flavored bread to serve at a summer buffet or barbecue.

Serves 8–10

INGREDIENTS

1¼ cups warm water
1 tsp dried yeast
pinch of sugar
2 cups whole-wheat flour
2 cups white bread flour
1 tsp salt
¼ tsp freshly ground black pepper
⅔ cup drained, oil packed sun-dried
  tomatoes chopped, plus 1 tbsp oil
  from the jar
¼ cup freshly grated Parmesan
  cheese
2 tbsp red pesto
1 tsp coarse sea salt

Parmesan cheese
red pesto
black pepper
whole-wheat flour
dried yeast
sun-dried tomatoes
salt
water
white bread flour
coarse sea salt
tomato oil

COOK'S TIP
If you are unable to locate red pesto, use 2 tbsp chopped, fresh basil combined with 1 tbsp sun-dried tomato paste.

1 Put half the warm water in a small pitcher. Sprinkle the yeast over the top. Add the sugar, mix well, and let stand for 10 minutes.

2 Put the whole-wheat flour in a mixing bowl. Sift in the white flour, salt and pepper. Make a well in the center, and add the yeast mixture, sun-dried tomatoes, oil, Parmesan, pesto and the remaining water. Gradually incorporate the flour, and mix to make a soft dough, adding a little water, if necessary.

3 Turn the dough onto a floured surface, and knead for 5 minutes until smooth and elastic. Return to the clean bowl, cover with a damp dish towel, and let rise in a warm place for about 2 hours, or until doubled in bulk. Lightly grease a baking sheet.

4 Turn the dough onto a lightly floured surface, and knead for a few minutes. Divide the dough into three equal pieces, and shape each one into a 13 in long cylinder.

5 Dampen the ends of the three cylinders. Press them together at one end, braid them loosely, then press them together at the other end. Place on the baking sheet, cover, and let stand in a warm place for 30 minutes until well risen. Preheat the oven to 425°F.

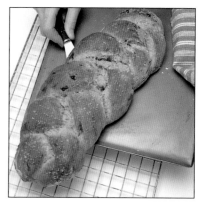

6 Sprinkle the braid with the coarse sea salt. Bake for 10 minutes, then lower the oven temperature to 400°F, and bake for 15–20 minutes more, or until the loaf sounds hollow when tapped on the bottom. Cool on a wire rack.

Caraway Bread Sticks

Ideal to nibble with drinks, these can be made with all sorts of other seeds – try cumin seeds, poppy seeds or celery seeds.

Makes about 20

INGREDIENTS
²⁄₃ cup warm water
½ tsp dried yeast
pinch of sugar
2 cups all-purpose flour
½ tsp salt
2 tsp caraway seeds

caraway seeds

dried yeast

flour

water

salt

1 Grease two baking sheets. Put the warm water in a small pitcher. Sprinkle the yeast on the top. Add the sugar, mix well, and let stand for 10 minutes.

2 Sift the flour and salt into a mixing bowl, stir in the caraway seeds, and make a well in the center. Add the yeast mixture, and gradually incorporate the flour to make a soft dough, adding a little water if necessary.

VARIATION

To make Coriander and Sesame Sticks, replace the caraway seeds with 15 ml/1 tbsp crushed coriander seeds. Dampen the bread sticks lightly and sprinkle them with sesame seeds before baking.

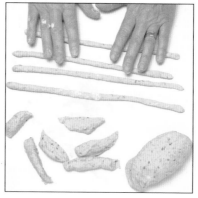

3 Turn onto a lightly floured surface, and knead for 5 minutes until smooth. Divide the mixture into twenty pieces, and roll each one into a 12 in stick. Arrange on the baking sheets, leaving room for rising, then let stand for 30 minutes until well risen. Meanwhile, preheat the oven to 425°F.

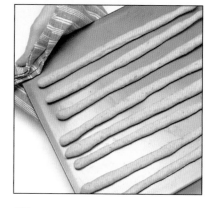

4 Bake the bread sticks for about 10–12 minutes until golden brown. Cool on the baking sheets.

Tomato Bread Sticks

Once you've tried this simple recipe you'll never buy manufactured bread sticks again. Serve with aperitifs, with a dip or with cheese to end a meal.

Makes 16

INGREDIENTS
2 cups flour
½ tsp salt
½ tbsp rapid-rise dried yeast
1 tsp honey
1 tsp olive oil
⅔ cup warm water
6 halves sun-dried tomatoes in olive
   oil, drained and chopped
1 tbsp skim milk
2 tsp poppy seeds

flour

sun-dried tomatoes

honey

yeast

poppy seeds

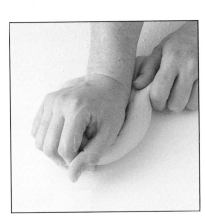

1 Place the flour, salt and yeast in a food processor. Add the honey and olive oil and, with the machine running, gradually pour in the water (you may not need it all). Stop adding water as soon as the dough starts to cling together. Process for 1 minute more.

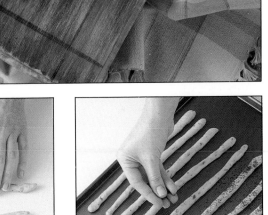

2 Turn out the dough onto a floured board and knead for 3–4 minutes until springy and smooth. Knead in the chopped sun-dried tomatoes. Form into a ball and place in a lightly oiled bowl. Leave to rise for 5 minutes.

3 Preheat the oven to 300°F. Divide the dough into 16 equal pieces and roll each piece into a 11 in × ½ in long stick. Place on a lightly oiled baking sheet and leave to rise in a warm place for 15 minutes.

4 Brush the sticks with milk and sprinkle with poppy seeds. Bake for 30 minutes. Leave to cool on a wire rack.

INDEX